ISSUES IN REGIONAL PLANNING

A selection of seminar papers

edited by

DAVID M. DUNHAM

and

JOS G. M. HILHORST

1971

MOUTON

THE HAGUE · PARIS

LIBRARY OF CONGRESS CATALOG CARD NUMBER : 76-169994

Printed by Geuze, Dordrecht

ISSUES IN REGIONAL PLANNING

PUBLICATIONS OF THE
INSTITUTE OF SOCIAL STUDIES

PAPERBACK SERIES

IV

PROCUL CERNENS

CLARIUS OBSERVAT

INTERNATIONAAL INSTITUUT
VOOR SOCIALE STUDIËN - 'S-GRAVENHAGE
1971

ACKNOWLEDGEMENTS

The organisation of seminars is frequently constrained by the availability of financial means. The Ministry of Foreign Affairs by its understanding of this problem contributed no small part in furnishing an amount equal to the deficit that appeared on our account. Needless to say its contribution came close to the sum total of the budget. The Institute of Social Studies which organised the Seminar is extremely grateful for this help.

It is also grateful to the United Nations Secretariat for making available two of its members and for sponsoring three other participants who are working on projects in which the United Nations is directly involved.

Being closely connected with the organisation of the Seminar, the editors wish to express their appreciation for the pleasing personal contacts they maintained with representatives of these institutions. They are also grateful for the essential help they received from John Rodrigues and Jean Sanders, the former in organisation of the Seminar, the latter in preparing the present selection of papers. Last, but not least, they want to acknowledge the considerable and efficient work performed by Suzanne Brissaud and Lia Jonker in typing the seminar papers and in preparing the manuscript for the Printer.

David M. Dunham
Jos G. M. Hilhorst

CONTENTS

INTRODUCTION

This volume represents a selection of the papers presented at a Seminar held at the Institute of Social Studies, The Hague, in March 1970. This seminar was organised on a rather generalised theme, 'The Regionalisation of National Policies', which as the papers themselves show allowed for a suitable degree of flexibility in interpretation and offered sufficient scope for the authors to raise the particular topics that concerned them as professionals. However, there was a more specific theme by which the papers were more closely related. The seminar was called in connection with the research and training programme that the I.S.S. conducts in the field of Regional Development Planning. Contrary to the research-oriented Workshop on Regional Development Planning which was undertaken in 1967,[1] this seminar was concerned with problems of education in the sense, firstly, that it aimed to identify a number of problems of an educational nature and, secondly, that it was intended to serve itself as an educational device by confronting the ideas of university staff with the problems of regional development as experienced by government officials in the field, and *vice versa*.

Despite the growing interest that it has received the problem of education in regional planning is still by and large an unsolved one. This is partly due to a lack of understanding as to the nature of the regional development process and partly also to the fact that even now the methods of interdisciplinary teaching and research that are generally deemed to be so necessary in this field are virtually non-existent. Not only the practitioner but also the academics who claim to train him are at many points moving in largely uncharted territory and with relatively little experience. There are, to use

[1] See papers of the Proceedings of the Workshop on Regional Development Planning, The Hague 1967.

Perloff's phrase, "practically no firm, well-established parameters".

The first papers in this volume, those by Perloff and Kuklinski, are given, therefore, in order to establish a framework within which the ensuing discussion could find a common focus in terms of their relevance from an educational point of view. They do so, firstly, by briefly sketching the nature of the regional planning problem and by indicating a series of issues that can only be expected to be solved when civil servants with appropriate training become incorporated into government machineries in large numbers. Secondly, as a systematic approach to meeting this need, they turn to the type of institutional network that should be established in order to train these people, and to the levels of training and types of regional planners that are required.

But can we really assess the substantive content of this education and more particularly its effectiveness in solving the kinds of issues that these authors pose? Do we actually know the 'types of regional planner' that are really wanted in the various planning offices? Much rests upon the interpretation of planning problems and upon the establishment of a meaningful dialogue between practitioner and educationalist. In this sense the more general theme of the seminar was to prove useful in that the various authors posed problems that interested and concerned them rather than discussing issues that were carefully prescribed in advance. The results are both revealing and instructive in that they present on the one hand, a considerable diversity in their approach and, on the other, provide certain insights as to what a number of professionals in regional planning and/or regional planning education see to be the 'real' problems at the present time.

The second section which has been entitled 'Regional Development and Planning' opens this discussion and is intended to present a view as to the nature of the more important processes of regional development and planning. These papers pose an interesting contrast to one another. The first, that of Hilhorst, is largely theoretical. It attempts to develop a hypothesis about some of the political processes that play a role in regional development and to come to a typology of regional spatial structures. The second paper, by Haddad, is in contrast based very firmly in the Brazilian experience and discusses the various strategies and basic methodology of regional planning in Brazil.

The third section contains papers of a very different line of thinking. Primarily these papers pose the problem of establishing recognition of the need for regional planning and with it that of gaining recognition for the profession. Shibli in particular, but also Bannerman, does so by showing the extent to which an economic policy that does not adequately take account of spatial aspects can create problems of economic imbalance and urban population explosion which, to their minds, can only be solved by regional planners, even in countries that are as different as Pakistan and Ghana.

Bannerman also raises the problem of participation and his paper therefore provides an introduction to that of Morsink who chooses to focus more specifically on this theme and whose paper in turn opens the fourth section which has been entitled 'Participation in Decision-making'. Morsink presents as it were a statement of principle, examining the need for and barriers to increased popular participation and the question of an organisational structure to facilitate it. His discussion is followed by an account of Dutch experience in this field by van Loon who comes to the conclusion that although popular participation in the development of the backward areas of The Netherlands was instrumental in the relative success of the policy, the forms that it took have since become amorphous and outdated and are in strong need of overhaul, particularly with regard to participation by youth. Datta Chaudhuri's paper which is concerned with the Indian situation complicates the question of participation by pointing to some of the special problems that are posed in the context of a federal state. He maintains moreover that little is available in terms of appropriate decision-making techniques. A partial answer to this problem is, however, offered by Paelinck who provides some models for interregional decision-making.

But Datta Chaudhuri is not only worried by the problems of participation and by the shortcomings of our available decision making techniques; in addition he raises a particularly important issue that is also touched upon by Shibli, Bannerman and Morsink, namely the need for an institutional framework that would facilitate a more effective and more efficient form of regional development planning. This seems to be a point of somewhat general concern. Some of the answers to his questions are provided in the papers of the fifth section on 'The Administration of Regional Development'. The difficulty is, however, that both the frameworks and the methods discussed by Porwit and Viot for Poland and France work in strongly centralised government machineries and may not, therefore, be relevant for a federal country like India. Moreover, even though the administrative structure for planning may look well on paper for a unitary country it may not operate efficiently in terms of the objectives of spatial planning. Dunham, in the last paper of the volume, clearly shows this to be the case for the Netherlands.

Finally in the last section, an attempt has been made to summarise some of the main points that emerged during the seminar discussions and, in turn, some of the conclusions that can be drawn from them. As a whole, the papers go at least part-way to showing why the problem of education in regional planning is so difficult.

Before letting the reader free to explore these papers himself we have chosen to include comment upon the decision to prepare such a seminar and upon the way in which it was organised. As we have already mentioned, it was intended from the outset as an educational device, and involved thirty invited participants from regional planning bodies, universities and international agencies. Because of the type of participants, therefore, it was limited in duration to four weeks. This period was arranged in two stages. In the first week papers were presented by high level regional planning experts and subjected to fairly intensive discussion by the group as a whole. The ISS-library facilities were made available and participants were given as much opportunity as possible for further personal contact on matters of common interest.

During the remainder of the seminar a somewhat reduced group continued the same procedure, in which papers were presented on more specific projects and experiences. In retrospect we would conclude that the particular value of such a seminar lies in the fact that it confronts participants who would not otherwise be free to involve themselves in more extensive study with the opportunity to meet people with very different backgrounds, but often very similar problems and experiences. It can be seen in fact as providing not only intellectual but also emotional support for the regional planner who is often rather isolated in his day-to-day work.

I

EDUCATION FOR REGIONAL PLANNING

1

HARVEY S. PERLOFF

EDUCATION FOR REGIONAL PLANNING
IN LESS DEVELOPED COUNTRIES

Regional planning in the less developed countries today, with only few exceptions, is much more promise than reality. A good many hopes – at least on the part of some dedicated professionals and a small number of politicians – are associated with the possibilities of regional planning. These hopes are related to speeding economic development, decentralizing the national development effort, incorporating in development decisions more effectively than before some key social elements, such as migration and education, overcoming the backwardness of the most extremely depressed parts of the nation and, in general, achieving a more comprehensive, effective and humane development effort.

The reality at the present time, however, is something else again. While there are a number of noteworthy regional programmes in a few countries actually under way, if we look at the world picture as a whole, we must come to the conclusion that regional planning has a very long way to go to be truly meaningful. The problems are formidable. Centralizing traditions in most parts of the world are hard to overcome. The national development effort in most countries is itself not overly strong, and, under such circumstances, the regional aspects tend to be filtered-down and weakened versions of the national programmes. In addition, there is a tendency to use regional projects as a means for political pay-off, and this engenders deep suspicion when broad-scale regional development programmes are proposed. National leaders and the general public are frequently not convinced about the value of trying to develop the depressed parts of the country and generally assume that the more promising areas are already being developed and do not require special attention. Even in circumstances where a government group launches a serious regional effort, it is often the case that the effort is permitted to atrophy when a new government group comes into office (a situation, incidently, that makes employment in regional development programmes rather precarious). And, finally, there is the problem that is of particular concern to us in this conference: Trained personnel is scarce and there is a strong desire generally to conserve its use for critical national tasks. Still, oddly enough, given the in-and-out nature of many regional efforts, it is quite possible for regional planners in a less developed country to be extremely limited in numbers and yet not employed at regional tasks.

Against this background, in reviewing the problem of training regional planners, one can emphasize the great hopes for regional planning and the few significant regional projects already under way – both of which have generated a not insignificant demand for regional planners – *or* emphasize the formidable barriers to the near-term expansion of substantial regional planning efforts. Either view alone is clearly partial and can be misleading as a base for designing training programmes. Both must be seen as part of a bigger picture. A 'systems' view is called for – distinguishing between actual and latent demand for regional planners and seeing the training problem as part of a large and closely interrelated whole. The latter must include a full-bodied view of both the hopes and the fears of the different groups in the various nations, the conditions needed for an expansion of meaningful regional efforts, and the conditions necessary to meet a fluctuating demand for trained personnel.

What we do *not* have in regard to the professional group of concern to us is a situation where (1) the tasks that the professional group is to perform are broadly understood (in contrast to, say, doctors, lawyers and national development economists), (2) the activities to which the professional group is normally attached are firmly established (in contrast to, say, the activities of highway engineers), and (3) the future demand for the professionals can be estimated within reasonable and understandable ranges on the basis of expansions recorded over a number of years in the past. The situation with which we are dealing in the present context is quite different on each score. There are practically no firm, well-established parameters. Everything is open and fluid – and uncertain. Under the circumstances, a plan of action of the training of regional planners must realistically fit the wide-open 'system' with which we are dealing.

The training of regional planners should be directly related to the processes or operations of regional developmental planning; specifically, as they relate to the interconnections and flows among the national, regional and local government activities, as well as between the public and private activities.[1] This view is useful not only in devising the *content* of regional training programmes but also in designing an appropriate institutional and operational setting for such training. Anton Kuklinski has been concerned with a similar set of considerations. He has stressed particularly that the success of regional training programmes will be dependent in no small part on the extent to which key decision-makers in the less developed countries become interested in and knowledgeable about the possibilities of regional planning.[2]

It is useful to try to perceive the full scope and main features of the highly interrelated – and open – system with which we have to deal when we enter the realm of education for regional planning. The following features deserve particular attention.

(1) The demand for regional planners, the purposes for which they are employed, and the nature of their employment will for some time to come be very closely related to the views held by public officials and the general public concerning the possibilities and uses of regional planning in the general development picture. Just as there is no one established view of regional planning so there is no established 'market' for regional planners. Therefore, there is no way to remove the question of supply and demand of regional planners from the broader question of the extent to which, and the ways in which, regional planning will be used in the 1970s and beyond.

(2) The nature of regional planning activities in years to come in developing countries will, to an important extent, be a product of the kinds of relationships that are worked out between such activities and other kinds of planning and development processes. Particularly significant are the ties of regional planning to national economic planning and development. The extent to which there is regionalization of national planning in the less developed countries will

---

1 This is the framework employed by John Friedmann in his "Education for Regional Planning in Developing Countries", *Regional Studies*, Vol. 2, 1967, pp. 131-38, as well as by the author in his volume *Education for Planning: City, and Regional*, Part II (Baltimore: John Hopkins Press, 1957).
2 United Nations Research Institute for Social Development, Programme IV – Regional Development, *Training in Comprehensive Regional Development and Planning* (Material for Discussion) Geneva, January 1969, UNRISD/69/c. 3, GE. 69-2524, pp. 30-31.

obviously have a great deal to do with the activities of regional planners in the future and the demand for their services. The nature of the tie of regional planning to national sectoral planning and programming is similar and equally important. It will be determinant of the extent to which regional planning is of concern to the major ministries and whether or not regional planners become part of the key bureaucratic structure at the centre or remain largely outside this structure.

(3) The breadth and scope of territorially-oriented regional activities in the field will also play a major role. The use of regional planning and of regional planners will be one thing if it is mainly concerned in a traditional manner with large-scale resource-oriented activities (of the river-basin-development variety). It will be quite another thing if it is, as well, broadly concerned with

...social planning, including the development of human resources and a concern for migration and social change;

...urbanization, and, in general, the question of changes in patterns of human settlement and in the spatial organization of human activities;

...institutional innovation, and in general, the creation or encouragement of new organizations capable of dealing with the above kinds of changes and of marshalling major resources for the key regional tasks.

The know-how that may be called for in regional planning tasks can thus extend over a wide range – from quite narrow physical development to an extremely broad set of factors.

A truly effective scheme of education for regional planning would have to cope with each of these three major features in one way or another. Without this, the training programme might only touch a small part of the problem and leave trainees in a highly vulnerable and uncertain situation. There are a number of conclusions for education that would seem to follow from each of the considerations touched on above.

The first item mentioned – concerning the importance of the view of regional planning held by top public officials and the general public – suggests that the educational scheme should be extended to (a) public education about the problems and possibilities of regional planning, and (b) education of policy leaders on the same score. Periodic international seminars on regional planning for policy leaders would help in meeting the latter need. Programmes for training political leaders (as well as technicians) could readily be attached to research-and-evaluation programmes established to examine regional development efforts already under way in various underdeveloped countries. This was one of the objectives of the scheme adopted by the Economic and Social Council of the United Nations, now under the general guidance of the United Nations Research Institute for Social Development in Geneva. Implementation of this scheme has lagged seriously and there may be built-in difficulties which prevent it from functioning properly. An examination of these difficulties would undoubtedly be revealing for the design of future training programmes.

If political leaders could come to understand better than they do now what kinds of regional efforts do or do not work well within their own countries, their sponsorship of regional development programmes in the future would be on a much sturdier basis than in the past.[3] Seminars or other kinds of training programmes for policy leaders could be carried out on a much larger scale (and cheaper) nationally than internationally, although the latter form has certain advantages. Materials now being prepared by the United Nations Research Institute for Social Development could readily be adapted for both international and national seminars for policy leaders. It is also conceivable that the World Bank's well-regarded training institute could broaden its present programme (which focuses largely on national development) to encompass training seminars on regional planning for highly placed government officials from the less developed countries.

Clearly there are many alternative modes for achieving the key objective. The main point at this stage is to establish the importance of training policy leaders in the regional field as a direct complement to the training of regional technicians.

A deeper popular appreciation of the problems and possibilities of regional planning is also an essential part of the broader educational picture. The role that greater popular understanding has played in the development of the public health field in the poorer countries and in the field of national economic development is suggestive of what is called for. The expertise that can be acquired by regional planners through educational programmes can be readily dissipated unless there is enough understanding of the regional tasks to permit regional planners to carry out the func-

---

[3] The U.N. research-and-training programme, based on a proposal that I had developed in 1966 and first introduced in the Social Commission, is described in Appendix A as part of the report on the Israeli regional training programme.

tions for which they have been trained. Again, as in the case of policy leaders, the U.N. sponsored study of regional development programmes around the world – if it could be implemented – would be helpful in the task of popular education. Many other approaches to popular education in the regional realm can, of course, be conceived. To put the need in the most general terms, the importance of the objective is such that probably every regional centre already in existence and others to be established in the future should accept popular education as one of its fundamental training tasks.

The second feature highlighted above – the anticipated ever-closer relationship of regional planning to national economic planning – suggests the value of closely integrating education for regional planning with education for national planning and attaching a strong research component to the two. It seems evident that over time there will be an increasing interest in the regionalization of national plans. This will call for the development of a new kind of planner who will work at the centre on national planning problems but whose expertise lies in the regionalization process. Such a person will have to know a great deal about means for achieving coherence of the various national planning elements at the subnational level. Since the latter are as yet part of a very young and imperfect art, training for such tasks should be carried out within a research setting where new and better techniques are developed and tried out. Also, since a key objective of the regionalization process is to evolve plans that are politically more realistic than in the past, as well as to achieve greater coordination of national planning elements, the education of this new kind of planner will have to be closely related to plan implementation. Thus, training of such planners will have to be as much concerned with political power and public administration as with plan content. Here, too, a good bit of innovation in education will be necessary since, in the past, training for economic development has been largely content-oriented and not closely related to problems of implementation. The integration of knowledge on *both* content and process is clearly the key to the training of planners who will be concerned with the regionalization of national plans.

One of the major difficulties with national planning in the less developed countries has been that the longer range central plans have been little concerned with the shorter term (and administratively much more significant) sectoral or ministry plans. Ministries tend to go their own way, establishing plans, programmes and policies for their own activities with little concern for, or knowledge of, the longer range central plans. The two often live in quite separate worlds, and of course, both suffer as a result. The central planning tends to be mostly concerned with balance of payments problems and problems of national finance, with the investment proportion of the plan being almost hypothetical in nature if compared to the investments actually made during the life-time of the national plan. At the same time, the ministry plans tend to be concerned largely with short term and often transitory issues, little related to the major objectives of the national development effort.

Regionalization of national plans can be meaningful only if it serves to integrate sectoral or ministry plans into the national effort. Thus, the 'regionalizers' (if I may use this awkward term) will not only have to be knowledgeable about the national development issues and plan implementation but also about sectoral planning. This is probably too much of a load for any but the rare breed of true generalists; more 'regionalizers' will probably have to concentrate on either the central planning tasks or the sectoral tasks. And for the latter, there will be a need for persons with special expertise in the regional aspects of given sectoral planning, as in the case of education, health, transportation and communications, and natural resources development. For such persons, training for regional planning might well be closely related to education in the arts of sector planning.

Thus, the second feature highlighted here suggests that, seen in a systems context, a large component of the regional training task will have to be the incorporation of regional planning know-how into education for national planning or, if you wish, 'regionalization' of education for national developmental planning.

The third feature which has been stressed – the extension of territorially-oriented planning beyond the traditional natural resources focus – also suggests a broadening of the scope of education for regional planning. The extent of the broadening processes can be comprehended when one examines the great range of concerns of the larger and better established regional development efforts within various of the less developed countries, as in the development programme in Northeast Brazil, in Guayana, Venezuela, the Aswan project in Egypt and the Lakisch project in Israel (if the latter country can be included among the less developed nations). Important among these concerns, as suggested earlier, are social planning aspects (education, health, welfare, migration), problems of urbanization, the encouragement of industrialization, institutional innovation, and a much more extensive view of natural resources development than in the past.

This suggests that training for regional planning must be much broader and deeper than conceived in earlier periods. But it also suggests that the training of the generalist regional planner is becoming not only more difficult but also more unrealistic. There will be need for an increasing number of regional specialists, individuals who can deal expertly with social problems, urbanization problems, problems of industrialization, problems of regional organization and administration, or problems of regional resources development. Such planners should be able to make a contribution not only to specialist aspects of regional planning in the field but equally well to sectoral planning at the national level.

Again, this would seem to call for the 'regionalization' of education within a number of established fields (that is, the training of regional specialists in various fields) – as for sociologists, social workers, city planners and housing experts for regional social planning tasks; geologists, ecologists, soil and water engineers, geographers, agronomists, economists and other natural resources experts for broadened natural resources planning tasks; city planners, geographers, sociologists, economists and others for regionally-oriented urbanization tasks (or, more accurately described, human settlement tasks); public administrators, business administrators, systems analysts, and others for the institutional development tasks; and economists, engineers, business administrators, area-development experts, and others for the industrialization tasks. These categories are of course for purposes of illustration only and are not meant to be either definitive or comprehensive. Some of this joint training process is already apparent in some places, as in the case of joint programmes in city *and* regional planning, joint programmes in urban *and* regional economics, programmes in *regional* resources development in engineering schools, and the like.

Because of the in-and-out, up-and-down character of the regional planning in many of the less developed countries, such joint training is not only a matter of educational logic but of career necessity as well. Thus, for example, the regional social planning expert should not only be able to get a job in any one of several of the national ministries when a regional effort with which he has been associated is dissolved, but he should be able to get a job with any number of social and community agencies or in teaching at a school in his own discipline or in city planning if that is where his initial training lay. Similar considerations would hold for the other fields of regional expertise referred to above.

To generalize, the evolving situation in regional planning in the poorer countries calls for a *variable* response in looking for more and better education for regional planning. This response should encompass different kinds and different intensities of training, rather than seek a uniform educational pattern, such as the establishment of a very small number of new training centres specifically for the education of generalist regional planners (although the latter could conceivably be part of a larger and more variable training network). The major training needs suggested by the above analysis can usefully be summarized within the framework of the different *levels* of education as normally organized.

1. TRAINING AT THE PH. D. LEVEL

There are a large number of fields in which a student could prepare himself for work in regional planning through study at the Ph.D. level. These include not only study in regional planning as such but also in (a) developmental economics with a regional specialization, (b) regional science, (c) urban and regional economics, and (d) a wide variety of disciplines and fields of study, such as natural resources engineering and business administration, with specialization in regional development. Courses of study in these various categories are available at universities around the world, in the less developed as well as the economically more advanced countries. Training at such universities would be of only limited value unless it is closely related to a substantial research programme concerned with evolving improved approaches to regional planning and development, so that the student is prepared for a lifetime of search for improved concepts and methods. There are two important needs here. One is for information about such Ph.D. training programmes to be made available to students in the less developed countries, with special concern for the amount of attention devoted within each university to education and research on regional problems in the poorer countries. The other is for fellowships for Ph.D. study to students in the less developed nations, a wellknown need that does not require elaboration here.

2. PROGRAMMES LEADING TO A MASTER'S DEGREE OR ITS EQUIVALENT, EXTENDING OVER A ONE OR TWO-YEAR PERIOD.

Here, too, the possibilities are very extensive, including direct training in regional planning and development or involving a regional concentration in such fields as economics, agronomy, city planning, geography, sociology, public administration, and other fields. There are a number of education centres where focused training in regional planning and development is available, including the Institute of Social Studies at The Hague, as well as in Venezuela (CENDES), Chile (CIDU), Poland, Ireland, France, Israel and Japan.

In the case of Israel and Japan, the training is associated with the United Nations "programme of research and training on regional development based on current regional development activities in different parts of the world".

Because the U.N. programme is just getting under way and has important potentialities for the future, a description of the Israeli programme, carried out by the Settlement Study Centre at Rehovot, is to be found in the appendices of this volume.

Master degree programmes or their equivalent in various fields with a regional concentration are commonplace at universities in the more advanced countries, but are also available in a number of the less developed countries. As in the case with Ph. D. programmes, there is need for information as to the pertinence of the training for students from the poorer countries as well as need for fellowships. If there were possibilities for a more ambitious and costly programme of education for regional planning, then arrangements could be made for students who went through such regionally oriented training programmes to continue to receive materials about regional planning and development after graduation to keep them posted on new intellectual and practical developments in the field. Such an informational programme could conceivably be provided by the United Nations Research Institute for Social Development if funds were made available for this important purpose.

3. SHORTER TERM CERTIFICATE PROGRAMMES, EXTENDING OVER A PERIOD OF TWO TO NINE MONTHS

Courses in subjects of relevance to regional planning in the less developed countries have been organized by the United Nations, the World Bank, the Organization of American States, and other international agencies, as well as by universities in various countries. This is a useful and remarkably flexible form of training regional specialists, and particularly in providing in-service training. This form of training could readily be expanded to fit evolving needs in the regional field, if two conditions were met; namely, if information on the need for training was provided on a regular basis to the international agencies equipped to organize such certificate programmes and if funds could be mobilized to help finance such programmes.

4. CERTIFICATE COURSES OF SHORT DURATION, RANGING FROM TWO TO EIGHT WEEKS.

These can, and do, cover a very broad spectrum of training from highly specialized, intensive training in subjects of relevance to regional planning (e.g., project evaluation, or information systems), to more general 'refresher' courses, and on to 'executive' training programmes. The latter could readily be extended to cover regional-development 'orientation' seminars for political leaders, as discussed earlier, a critical requirement for the future of regional planning and development. Here, too, the problem is one of information and money for fellowships. There are university facilities and study centres in most parts of the world which can be utilized to provide such short-term training. If they are to be rapidly expanded in the near future, this could be done under the auspices of the various United Nations regional commissions.

SUMMARY AND CONCLUSIONS

The main points stressed in this paper can be summarized as follows: (a) Given the broad range of tasks carried out within the scope of regional planning, and variable conditions existing in the less developed countries, the training problem should be approached by thinking in terms of a *network* of regional training facilities; (b) Existing university and national study-centre facilities should be employed for the training tasks, to the extent possible, in both the more and less developed countries, with an emphasis on strengthening the facilities in the latter countries; (c) The training facilities of the various international organizations, including the various U.N.-sponsored centres, the World Bank training institute, and the institutes functioning under the auspices of the U.N. regional commissions, should be mobilized for the task at hand; (d) Concern for regional training should extend to Ph. D. programmes, Master degree programmes, and both longer-range and short-range certificate programmes; (e) Special attention should be devoted to the mobilization of resources for the establishment of a world-wide system of information on regional training, for the provision of a substantial number of fellowships for students from the developing countries, and for the vitalization of the U.N. programme established some years ago for training associated with in-depth studies of ongoing regional development projects.

The question of the appropriate content for education in regional planning has not been touched on here for several reasons. First, because content must be adjusted to the level of training, the length of the training programme, the location of the programme (e.g., whether it has to satisfy the need of students from the more developed as well as the less developed countries, or can concentrate on the latter alone), the special capabilities of the staff, and other considerations. It would be a formidable task to attempt to discuss content covering all the possible variations. Secondly, there are materials on course content already available which can be drawn on by any faculty which is given the task of designing training programmes in regional planning.[4] However, it would be extremely

---

[4] Discussion of course content is to be found in the following (among other sources): Harvey S. Perloff, *Education for Planning: City, State and Regional*, Part II (Baltimore: Johns Hopkins Press, 1957). John Friedmann, "Regional Planning as a Field of Study", *Journal of the American Institute of Planners*, Vol. 29, 1963. W. Isard and T. Reiner, "Regional Science: Retrospect and Prospect", *Regional Science Association Papers* (European Congress, Cracow), Vol. 16, 1966.

Resources for the Future: Harvey S. Perloff et al., *Design for a Worldwide Study of Regional Development: A Report to the United Nations on a Proposed Research – Training Program*, Washington, D.C., 1966. John Friedmann, "Education for Regional Planning in Developing Countries", *Regional Studies*, Vol. 2, 1967. United Nations Research Institute for Social Development, Programme IV – Regional Development, *Training in Comprehensive Regional Development and Planning* (Material for Discussion), Geneva, January 1969, UNRISD/69/G. 3, GE 69-2524, various commentaries. Harvey S. Perloff, "Regional Planning in Less-Developed Countries", in *Regional Planning: Challenge and Prospects*, edited by Maynard M. Hufschmidt, (New York: Frederick A. Praeger, 1969) as well as papers by Hufschmidt, Barclay G. Jones, I. S. Lowry, Lyle E. Craine, and Edward Ullman in the same volume.

helpful if provision could be made for the exchange of course materials among faculties involved in training tasks. The major problem at the present time in promoting education in regional planning is not study content but rather the question of mobilization of resources and appropriately organizing a world-wide effort to encourage such education. It is to these matters that this paper has addressed itself.

2

A. R. KUKLINSKI

EDUCATION FOR REGIONAL PLANNING

1. REGIONAL PLANNING IN THE OVERALL SYSTEM OF PLANNING[1]

It would be very difficult to discuss education in regional planning without first attempting to define the scope of this activity. Over the past twenty-five years or so, we have observed in most countries a clear trend to widen the scope of regional planning. Regional planning was started as an activity to plan the development of specific regions which had to solve important economic and social problems (underdevelopment, depression, over-congestion).

The experience of socialist countries was instrumental in demonstrating the necessity to establish a system of interregional planning at the national level. In recent years, this approach has been accepted in a growing number of developing countries and also in many of the so-called Western countries.

We have also seen a trend to integrate the traditionally different and sometimes antagonistic approaches to regional planning and sectoral planning. In the framework of sectoral planning, a special activity has been established which deals with the problems of how to design and implement optimal patterns of location for a given

[1] Compare: P. Sen Gupta and G. Sdasyuk, *Economic Regionalization of India – Problems and Approaches*, Registrar General and Ex-Officio Census Commissioner for India (New Delhi, 1968); J. Hilhorst, *Regional Development Theory – An Attempt to Synthesize*, (Mouton, 1967); J. Kruczala, *Problemy Teoretyczne Planowania Regionalnego*, Vol. XXVII (Warsaw, 1968); A. Kuklinski, *Regional Development, Regional Policies and Regional Planning – Problems and Issues*, UNRISD/69/C.50 (Geneva, May 1969); N. Nekrasov, *Soviet System of Regional Studies* (Soviet Association of Regional Science, Moscow, 1967); Sovet po Izuchenyu Priozvoditelnych Sil pri Gosplanye SSR, *Obshchaya metodika razrobotki generalnoj schemy razmeshchenya priozvoditelnych sil SSR na 1971-1980 gg* (Moskva, 1966); H. Perloff, "Key Features of Regional Planning", *Journal of the American Institute of Planners*, May, 1968.

sector (industry, agriculture, transportation, social services and amenities, etc.).[2]

Therefore, regional planning, *senso largo*, now incorporates three types of interrelated activities: 1) interregional planning within a nation; 2) interlocal planning within a region; and 3) locational planning within a sector. For the sake of clarity, the following is a simple scheme of planning activities:

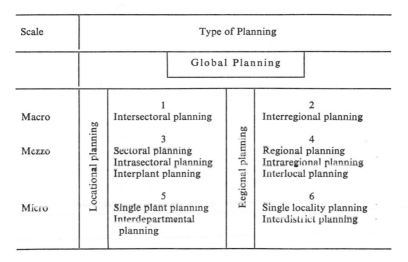

Scale	Type of Planning			
		Global Planning		
Macro	Locational planning	1 Intersectoral planning	Regional planning	2 Interregional planning
Mezzo		3 Sectoral planning Intrasectoral planning Interplant planning		4 Regional planning Intraregional planning Interlocal planning
Micro		5 Single plant planning Interdepartmental planning		6 Single locality planning Interdistrict planning

Fig. 1.   A Simplified Scheme of Planning Actitivities

The scheme would be helpful perhaps in a discussion of the *senso largo* definition presented above. In summarizing, it can be said that over the past twenty-five years, an important change in the approach to regional planning has taken place. It is no longer recognized as a more or less autonomous activity dealing only with specific regions but it is incorporated into the general planning system of a country. It can even be said that at the present time regional planning is first of all a method of imaginative and rational thinking about the regional dimension in the development of a given country. Therefore, perhaps a *senso largissimo* definition of regional planning should involve a fourth type of activity – regional

[2] Compare: L. H. Klaassen, *Social Amenities in Area Economic Growth – An Analysis of Methods of Defining Needs* (Organisation for Economic Cooperation and Development, Paris, 1968); *Criteria for Location of Industrial Plants* (*Changes and Problems*) (United Nations, New York, 1967), pp. 68-74.

futurology or prognosis – as a testing ground for different hypotheses which can be applied by long-term interregional planning.[3] Here, an aspect which is important for the development of regional planning activities should be mentioned, i.e., the problem of broadly defined information and statistics. The system of regional information is one of the most important inputs in the effective performance of all regional planning activities and a channel for incorporating them into the general system of planning.[4]

2. THE DEMAND FOR REGIONAL PLANNERS[5]

The remarks presented above clearly indicate that the demand for regional planners is not homogeneous. It is really misleading to

[3] Compare: G. Weill, "Ver un Schéma Général d'Aménagement de la France", *2000 Avenir Aménagement du Territoire*, No. 12, Mars, 1969.

[4] Compare: S. Boisier, *An Information System for Regional Planning, Chile: Experience and Prospects*, UNRISD/69/C.24 (September 1969); T. Hermansen, *Requirements and Provision of Information for Regional Development Planning in Sweden*, UNRISD/69/C.56 (August 1969); W. Kawalec, *Perspective Development of Regional Statistics in the Polish Experience* (paper prepared for Seminar on Information Systems for Regional Development, 13-18 October, 1969, Lund, Sweden).

[5] Compare the following statement by A. Kuklinski: "The solution of regional problems in the developing countries will be one of the more important issues to be dealt with within the framework of the Second Development Decade (1970-1980). The success of all regional development activities will depend on many factors but it can be agreed that one of the most important will be the supply of qualified personnel. The Institute of Social Studies in The Hague has presented a tentative evaluation of the size of the deficit of regional planners in the developing countries and has indicated that this deficit has the scale of about 2,000 persons. The first impression suggests that this is an exaggeration, but if we take into account that in a country like Poland, the regional planning offices employ about 300 professional regional planners, then the deficit of 2,000 persons for the developing countries of Latin America, Asia and Africa could be regarded rather as an underestimate. It can be added that the evaluation of the Institute of Social Studies is dealing with the present situation of the late 1960s. If we take into account the prospective of the middle 1970s, when the size and scope of regional planning in the developing countries will be much larger than it is now, then the evaluation of the prospective deficit must be revised upward, perhaps to a number in the range of 5,000. Therefore, if the UN would like to generate a big push in its activity in the field of training of regional planners for the developing countries, this big push must be adapted to the size of the problem. All discussions on how to train a few tens or even a few hundred planners for the developing countries have to be regarded as marginal since such discussions would only result in concealing the real problem rather than trying to solve it. The real problem can be formulated as follows: How to train, under the auspices of the UN programme, a few thousand regional planners as a contribution to the achievement of the goals of the Second Development Decade". *Training in Comprehensive Regional Development and Planning (Material for discussion)*, UNRISD/69/C.3 (January, 1969).

discuss the problem of how to educate and train regional planners *en bloc* without taking into account that the aims and scope of the activities of the various types of regional planners can be quite different. In the next paragraphs of this paper, the education of the following five different types of regional planners will be discussed:

(i)   Regional futurologists
(ii) Interregional planners
(iii) Interlocal planners
(iv) Locational planners
(v)   Regional statisticians

3. THE EDUCATION OF REGIONAL FUTUROLOGISTS

It would be a mistake to discuss the goals of regional policies and the objectives of regional planning as topics that are not integrated into the general stream of thinking about the future of a given society. The answer to the question, how to define the goals of regional policy depends on the answers to questions of a much more general nature, such as: What type of society would we like to have in the future? What values will be accepted and promoted in this society? Which pattern of consumption and leisure will be chosen as optimal? How will the basic problems of technological and institutional progress be solved? This model of the society of the future will reflect three types of expectations: (a) forecastings (the extrapolation of past trends); (b) projections (forecastings based on the assumption of a change in past trends, and the promotion of new trends via the implementation of consistent sets of economic and social policies); and (c) predictions (expectations based on intuition and imagination). We know that in futurology, the role of intuition and imagination is quite important. In different fields, the time horizon of rational and scientific thinking about the future is limited in different ways. For example, in field A, with our present knowledge, the time horizon of rational forecasting and projections may be twenty years, in field B twenty-five, in field C ten, and so on. Beyond these limitations, strictly rational thinking is replaced by intuition and imagination. Therefore, in outlining a model of a society in the year 1985 or 2000, it has to be acknowledged that in the different elements of the model, different proportions between forecasting, projections and predictions are reflected.

Regional planners should participate very actively in futurologic discussions. This would be an excellent opportunity to see the broad framework in which ideas concerning economic, social and cultural policies are generated and, at the same time, would provide the opportunity to integrate regional preferences into the general model of the society of the future. In this way, regional preferences would be incorporated into the basic system of the values accepted in the model. A different situation can be envisaged when the model is designed without taking into account regional preferences. In this case, regional problems are introduced not in the designing stage of the model but in the stage of its implementation, assuming only secondary importance as means in the implementation of non-regional goals.

It can be safely said that within the next few years in the general field of futurologic activities, a specialized group of questions, problems and hypotheses will emerge that will try to present several sets of answers and approaches discussing the regional dimension of the society of the future. In an increasing number of countries, discussions on the year 2000 are becoming more and more popular by both planning and academic groups, and some regional planners are already participating in the discussions. Nevertheless, I feel that a systematic and comprehensive effort should be made to improve the knowledge and general qualifications of interested and gifted regional planners in order to develop regional futurology as a new field which would discuss new horizons, present new hypotheses and help to diminish the influence of past experience on our thinking about the future.[6] Therefore, I would like to raise the question –

6 We need substantial efforts in this field to avoid in the future statements of the following type: "If one takes the configuration of Ecumenopolis shown in Fig. 1, which represents one of its more probable models, these primary centres are seven in number, according to some simple geometrical considerations concerning regular polyhedrons inscribed in or circumscribed around the earth, as well as other considerations on the economy in the hierarchical layout of settlements (but entirely unrelated to present political conditions). In the northern hemisphere they form a sort of belt in middle latitudes with the main centre among the four larger ones being the one of Western Europe (London, Paris, Randstadt). Next in importance come the two centres on the eastern edges of the two main continents, i.e. a centre close to the present eastern megalopolis of the U.S.A. and another close to the East coast of China around Shanghai, with Tokyo as a twin one. A fourth in the northern hemisphere is in California. In the southern hemisphere, again in middle latitudes, we find three main centres: one in South America, around Buenos Aires, one in South Africa, and one in South-East Australia, in the Melbourne-Sydney area. These seven centres, with a probable eighth in the Antarctica at a still more remote future time (when Antarctica will have been more fully conquered in its habitabiliʌy) constitute the

which to my mind is a vital one – how should regional futurologists be educated and trained?

4. THE EDUCATION OF INTERREGIONAL PLANNERS

In an increasing number of developing and developed countries, different types of central planning authorities and institutions are being established, and I believe that even more will be set up in the future. The central planning authorities are involved in three types of activities: global planning, intersectoral planning, and interregional planning.[7] At the present time there are very few interregional planners who are well prepared to perform functions of this type. I think that the education of modern, well-qualified interregional planners is a matter which deserves special attention and a special type of comprehensive training. An interregional planner must be well versed in the broad field of macro policies and plans at the national level. His knowledge should not be restricted to economic policies, plans and models but he should also be able to integrate the economic and social approaches in his planning activities,[8] and he should understand perfectly the mechanisms of global and intersectoral planning. Only under these conditions would he be a valid member of a central planning team promoting interregional planning, and be able to demonstrate that the central

---

main focal points on which urban development around the earth will depend. A system of secondary and then tertiary, quaternary, etc. centres can be developed around these primary ones, all of them interconnected by urbanization axes of a corresponding hierarchical level, the highest order axes being those connecting with highest order centres and so on." Paragraph 11 of a paper on *Future Urbanization Patterns in Europe* by John G. Papaicannou, which was presented at a very interesting international colloquim on "The Mastery of Urban Growth", Brussels, 1969. For a positive example of regional futurology, see the following articles: 1) W. Steigenga, "Recent Planning Problems of the Netherlands", *Regional Studies*, Vol. 2, pp. 105-113; 2) Maryse Ferhat-Delessert, "Méditerranée 2000 – Eden ou Cloaque", *Analyse & Prévision*, IX (1970), pp. 3-14.

7 Compare: *Regional Disaggregation of Nations Plans*, UNRISD/69/C.76 (November, 1969); P. Viot, *La Régionalisation du Plan en France* (manuscript, Paris, 1970).

8 Compare: J. Drewnowski, *Social and Economic Factors in Development*, UNRISD (Report No. 3, Geneva, February 1966); A. Stinchcombe, "Social Attitudes and Planning in the Guayana", *Planning Urban Growth and Regional Development*, Cambridge, Mass.: The MIT Press, 1969; J. Szczepanski, "Some Remarks on Macrosociology", *Information sur les Sciences Sociales*, VII-6, December 1968; J. Ziólkowski, *Methodological Problems in the Sociology of Regional Development*, UNRISD/69/C.2 (January 1969).

plan is not complete until the interregional problems are solved, as far as this may be possible under the actual conditions in a given country.

5. THE EDUCATION OF INTERLOCAL PLANNERS

Interlocal planning within a region has been in the past and will be in the future the type of regional planning which will absorb the greatest number of specialists. It can be added that the experience in the training of interlocal planners is relatively the best developed. There are three streams of this tradition which seem to converge now. The first is the old tradition of physical planning, which tried to interpret interlocal planning as an extension of the problems involved and the methods applied in classical land-use planning. The second is the tradition of community development, which is oriented toward solving social problems, in most cases at the micro level. The third is the tradition of national economic planning, which tries to impose its methods and approaches on interlocal planning at the regional level. I think that it is extremely difficult to develop a proper approach to interlocal planning. This is probably the weakest point in the planning methodology – the mezzo level standing on its own feet and not being a mixture of models, methods and approaches applied at the macro and micro levels.

6. EDUCATION OF LOCATIONAL PLANNERS

One of the basic weaknesses of regional planning, *senso stricto*, is the fact that this type of activity has only an advisory capacity in the decision-making process which is solving crucial problems of investment (what to invest, how to invest and where to invest). In most cases, these questions are answered within the different frameworks of sectoral planning or programming. It is therefore impossible to determine the regional dimension of the future of a given society without the participation of the sectoral planners responsible for the locational decisions involved in the development of the given sector.[9] It is sometimes said that a dialogue between

[9] Compare the following statement by S. M. Zawadzki: "The next problem is of a different character. In my opinion it might be of interest to examine the influence of the 14-year tradition of Polish regional planning on our present way of thinking.

sectors and regions is a decisive factor in the design and implementation of long-term plans and programmes. However, a dialogue is impossible if interregional and interlocal planners do not find their counterparts in the sectoral planning institutions. Thus, there is an urgent necessity to train locational planners who are specialized in the location of different economic and social sectors (industry, agriculture, transport, health, culture, tourism, etc.). These planners must have a deep and comprehensive knowledge of a given sector. They should be able to present a locational interpretation and prognosis of technological, economic and social changes that are shaping the future of the given sector. If possible, they should also absorb the ecumenical qualifications of listening and understanding the arguments of the *altera pars* of the planning process of the interregional and interlocal planners. Figure No. 2 indicates the place of locational decisions in the process of industrial programming.

7. EDUCATION OF REGIONAL STATISTICIANS

In traditional regional planning, vast amounts of effort and time of the professionals involved were taken up by the so-called collection

---

Fully appreciating our regional planning achievements, I believe, however, that its further development cannot consist of a simple evolution on actual basis. If our requirements become actual we shall have to revalue the effects of our experiences, to actualize our tradition and to get rid of traditional thinking. In that I see the only chance for a successful development of regional planning, of teaching the planners and assessing the demand for planning staff on real basis. In our discussions the branch system of national economy is often opposed to the spatial one. It is a vicious circle, difficult to get out of. The deep conviction of the inherent inability of spatial planning to maintain its stand when faced with the privilege of priority accorded to the branch system not only affects our own mode of thinking but also that of our actual or eventual 'customers'.

..."The system of branch planning will elaborate the analysis and solutions. I believe it is the branch system that will become the 'nursery' of regional planning. I think we shall have to do with regional or spatial planning, not only in connexion with planning a service centre of a new industrial complex, but also when planning a simple self-service shop. The changes in the planning and managing system, as well as in the socio-economic development of the country, will generate the demand for so-called regional analyses.

"As I remarked before, planners should not undertake tasks and obligations they are unable to carry out satisfactorily. Planners, however, must try to assure the highly trained staff not only at the disposal of institutions of regional planning but also of the branch planning system, in order to impart to them more 'regional character'." *Gospodarka i Administracja Terenowa* (Warsaw, 1969).

and transformation of data. This was due to the fact that regional statistics and other types of regional information were scattered, disintegrated and, generally, not adapted to the needs of regional planning. Now the situation has changed. There are quantitative and qualitative changes in the field of regional information and statistics which emerge as a new type of specialized activity supplying well-processed and adapted data inputs into the process of regional planning. We are inclined to think now that in each region there is a need for a regional data bank as well as a regional planning office. The education process must take into account this new situation and devote special attention to training regional statisticians or, more generally, persons specialized in the design and operation of regional information systems.[10]

8. VERTICAL INTEGRATION VERSUS HORIZONTAL SPECIALIZATION IN THE EDUCATION OF REGIONAL PLANNERS

The arguments put forward above could easily raise objections and criticisms along the following lines. It is perfectly true that it is possible to distinguish the above-mentioned five types of regional planners and statisticians. However, the divisions are slightly artificial if we discuss in a comprehensive way the whole set of problems involved in the development of an economy and society. Therefore, if the above typology is recognized as valid, we have to accept very often the principle of vertical integration in the education of regional planners. This principle means that the training curriculum of a regional planner would include items which would give him some elements of techniques and qualifications to perform and practise any of the five types of regional planning activities mentioned above. Such an approach to training would enable the graduate to accept and perform different duties within the regional planning machinery. This approach is, perhaps, the best one at present for developing countries, where the basic problem is to educate the regional planner so that his activities become well-

---

[10] Compare the following statement in the *Conclusions of the United Nations European Seminar on Regional Statistics* (Warsaw, 30 September – 8 October 1969): "The view was expressed that it is necessary to set up an international institute for regional statistics which would be a centre of studies and information in the field of regional statistics and planning."

integrated in the given society,[11] and particularly in countries where the need for a differentiated and highly developed planning machinery is not of top priority. In this context, stressing the case of developing countries, it can be said also that in many developed countries the vertical approach may be perfectly valid.

At the international level, the advantages of horizontal specialization are much more evident. If we think about a comprehensive scheme of international cooperation in the field of education and training of regional planners, then it is easy to justify the following proposals. Let us establish a network of ten to twenty international centres or institutes which would specialize along the above lines.[12] In this way, each country would be able to send some regional planners to one of the centres or institutes in order to acquire the skills and knowledge missing in the regional planning machinery of the country involved. The vertical and horizontal centres would supply on a world-wide scale complementary approaches to the education and training in regional planning. There is no need to add that the centres and institutes would have to be carefully selected and planned in order to create a balanced coverage of the experience of countries representing all continents and the most important types of economic and social systems. It would be particularly important to establish centres and institutes not only for, but also in, the developing countries. This does not mean that the developed countries should not set up and develop institutes specializing in the education of regional planners for the developing countries.

9. TYPES OF EDUCATION AND TRAINING ACTIVITIES

The deficit[13] of well-qualified regional planners in both developing

---

11 Compare: J. Coussy, "Adjusting Economics Curricula to African Needs", *International Social Science Journal*, Vol. XXI, N. 3, 1969; G. Myrdal, "Cleansing the Approach from Biases in the Study of Underdeveloped Countries", *Social Science Information*, VIII-3, June 1969.

12 This is a modification of a proposal incorporated in the RFF study, *Design for a Worldwide Study of Regional Development* (Baltimore: The Johns Hopkins Press, March 1966).

13 Compare the following statement by B. Gruchman: "There are a number of reasons why we should attach more importance to regional planning in developing countries than we do in advanced economies. The developing countries usually have a strongly differentiated spatial structure with marked disproportions in the level of development between the competent parts of the system. If nothing else, there is

and developed countries is so acute that we need a very flexible approach to promote different types of training in this field. In this connection, I would like to mention five types of such activities:

1. The first would be a well-organized international exchange programme which would give on-the-job training. A multilateral exchange programme of this kind could give the opportunity for a regional planner of country A to spend a year working in a regional planning institute in country B. This type of approach is used now in the form of so-called study tours; however, these study tours include too much lip service and too many ceremonies which belong to the sacred ritual of international visits. An international exchange programme as proposed above, would mean that participants would work as members of a regional planning team in a country which would give the best experience to the visiting regional planner.

2. The second type of training would be seminars of different character and duration. Seminars of this type would be successful if organized for a well-defined type of participant and devoted to a well-selected set of problems.

---

almost always the contrast between the central city and the rest of the country. In developing countries, the planning of infrastructural facilities which are prerequisites for a take-off and sustained growth also calls for a regional approach owing to the very nature of such basic facilities. Development planning in these countries puts a strong emphasis on individual projects and consequently exposes the locational aspects at an early stage of the planning process. Last but not least, there are numerous political factors which explain the growing attractiveness of regional planning to the developing countries.

"Therefore, the demand for regional planners in such countries is going to be a sizeable one. It will be oriented toward two categories of people:

(a) To 'full-time' regional planners working both on the national and regional levels;

(b) To 'part-time' regional planners working in sectors with particularly strong regional aspects of development (for instance, agriculture, transportation, housing).

"We have to be oriented toward both groups of planners because each of them will contribute to the overall spatial growth of the economies in developing countries. In particular, the second group should not be left out of our focus as regional planning evolves from formulating long-term plans for individual regions to action programmes on a national level embracing all parts of the country.

"In a country like Libya with its relatively small population and yet with a vast territory, a preliminary estimate of a ten years' demand for the first category of planners sums up to about 120 persons. The need for the second category would add another 120 to 150 persons to the overall demand. It follows that the general world deficit for regional planners in the Second Development Decade is likely to be closer to 5,000 persons (if not an even higher figure) than to the conservative estimate of 2,000 persons." *Training in Comprehensive Regional Development and Planning (Material for discussion), op.cit.*

3. Here I would suggest post-graduate courses at a high level for persons having had some experience in regional planning and interested in extending their knowledge and qualifications. At the present time, post-graduate courses would probably be the best way to quickly increase the number of relatively well-qualified regional planners. I used the term 'relatively well-qualified' as it is clear that post-graduate courses of six months to two years have limited possibilities, especially from the point of view of achieving some excellence in the horizontal specialization mentioned earlier. As far as I am aware, in the post-graduate courses given in the past, the vertical approach was applied more than the horizontal. The experience and achievements of the courses are outstanding and are an inducement to preparing a large-scale international programme in the education of regional planners. There are several examples of training of this type. Two post-graduate courses in regional planning best known to me are those held at the Institute of Social Studies in The Hague[14] and at the Central School of Planning and Statistics in Warsaw.[15]

4. M.A. studies. Throughout the world, universities are being criticized for not changing quickly enough to cope with the needs of society. One such criticism has indicated that the universities have frozen systems of division into traditional disciplines which are not able to grasp separately the valid problems and issues. A new approach to new fields is necessary which would be of an inter-disciplinary or, better still, a meta-disciplinary character.[16] It is necessary to create modern M.A. studies in regional planning which should be problem oriented. The amount of knowledge and the scope of techniques should be designed in such a way that the graduate would be qualified to take his place in a regional planning

---

[14] See *Calendar of the Regional Development Planning Course*, October 7, 1968 – July 4, 1969 (Institute of Social Studies, The Hague).

[15] See *Gospodarka i Administracja Terenowa* (Warsaw, 1969).

[16] Compare the following statement by W. Alonso: "My point, in brief, is that especially in the hard social sciences but also in the soft ones, there has begun to develop a meta-disciplinary competence that rests in particular individuals, and that this provides a better model for the incorporation of the social sciences into the planning process than does the idea of an inter-disciplinary team. The key difference is that members of a meta-disciplinary team share a common ground, while members of an inter-disciplinary team are brought together because of their diversity. If my basic point is granted, the urgent need is to develop means of producing greater numbers of individuals with such competence to meet the demands of the work that must be done, and to do everything possible to advance these meta-disciplines." *Beyond the Inter-Disciplinary Approach to Planning*, Working Paper No. 90 (Center for Planning and Development Research, University of California, Berkeley).

team. There are two schools of thought on this topic – one stressing that regional planning can only be a specialization within a traditional university discipline, such as economics, geography, sociology, architecture; the other that the curriculum of M.A. studies in regional planning can be designed as a new meta-disciplinary field. Meta-disciplinary in the sense that it is beyond the existing academic disciplines.

5. Ph.D. studies. So far, we have discussed the pressing problems of the education of regional planners in the '70s, but we have to think also about the more distant future. One solution to this problem would be to train now a sufficient number of persons at the Ph.D. level. They, in turn, should be candidates for posts as heads of new departments and institutions (in the developing countries) that would promote regional research and training activities which would create new types of regional planning, not only responding but anticipating the needs of development planning in Asia, Africa and Latin America. I would disagree with those who feel that Ph.D. studies can be located only in the developed countries – they should be started as soon as possible in the most advanced centres in the developing countries.[17]

10. EDUCATION IN REGIONAL PLANNING – A META-PROFESSIONAL PERSPECTIVE

This paper has maintained a rather narrow approach, trying to outline problems involved in the education of professional regional

[17] Compare the following comments by J. Friedmann and A. Kuklinski: J. Friedmann: "*The highest level* would include doctoral programmes in regional economics and regional science. At the present time, such studies can be pursued only in the U.S. at such centres as the University of Pennsylvania, Pittsburgh University or Washington University at Saint Louis.

A. Kuklinski: "I would like to disagree entirely with your statement that at the present time the Ph. D. programmes can be pursued only in the United States. I agree that in the U.S. centres there are some elements of technical excellence and sophistication which are perhaps the best in the world, but even in this field, I would not be quite sure. I feel that in a Ph. D. programme, technical excellence and sophistication are not the only important factors. I am convinced that centres can be found in Europe, Asia and Latin America that are able to create Ph. D. programmes in regional development and planning which could compete effectively with the U.S. centres, particularly in stressing the experience in planning and programming of regional development activities at the national level where the U.S. experience is at least limited." *Training in Comprehensive Regional Development and Planning (Material for discussion)*, *op.cit.*

planners. But the success or failure of regional planning in a given country not only depends upon the perfection or imperfection of the planning institute and its staff. Regional planning should be recognized as a political, social and cultural phenomenon.[18] The question is therefore not only how to educate the regional planner, but how to improve the understanding of the basic issues of regional planning in society, especially in the younger generation. There is so much talk about popular participation in regional planning, but so little or nothing done to prepare the average citizen for this participation. Do the press, radio and television in our countries devote enough attention to regional planning problems? Do high school programmes include sufficient information about regional planning? Is the young generation informed about the issues and problems

---

[18] Compare the following statement by J. Friedmann: "In a *new nation* that has risen only recently from colonial status and has started on its long trek towards modernity, we are likely to find an overriding preoccupation with the *political* impact of regional investment distribution. This will be specially true for federal states where the prices of national union may be a measure of financial autonomy for the member states. But a federal structure only emphasizes a tendency that will operate in any event, for the government of a new state must establish a presence in all parts of its territory, seeking in this way to replace local with more comprehensive loyalties and to create what is, in effect, a common political space. Apart from the extension of an institutional structure into the provinces in representation of the national idea, one of the most effective means for establishing a presence is through the construction of roads, bridges, schools, power stations, and the like in all of the more densely populated parts. The political criterion of *national presence* thus tends to link investments to population and will lead to a more or less equal per capita distribution across the effectively settled space of the nation." *The Politics of Regional Development Planning* (The Ford Foundation Urban and Regional Advisory Program in Chile, October, 1967).
Compare the following statement by B. de Jouvenel: "A better understanding of human beings, this seems the essential condition for a better future. We need such understanding in order to move intellectually from goals stated in broad terms toward better specifications; we need such understanding also in order to move in fact, since such moving depends upon human conducts; and for that we must be able to make estimates of how people shall react to this or that warning, vision, facility, or incentive.
"It is clear enough from the allocation of research funds that the understanding of human beings is not presently regarded as a main subject of interest. It is even clearer from public discourse and indeed from public decisions, that, whatever progress may have been achieved in such understanding in scientific circles, no trace thereof has come through upon the public scene. Any schoolboy has a more complex image of the atom than the highest scientists of the nineteenth century, but hardly any public statement reveals any but the most naive standard image of man. This may indeed be due to the heavy sententiousness which is a professional obligation of politicians.
"Progress in our mastery of nature has come from a progress in understanding it; similarly our progress in the service of men requires a progress in our understanding of them." "On Attending to the Future", William R. Ewald, Jr., (ed.) *Environment and Change – The Next Fifty Years* (Bloomington: Indiana University Press), 1968.

involved in regional planning, which is an activity that will guide the creation of the new environment for the society of the future? I feel that this type of social education in regional planning is a *conditio sine qua non* for the long-run success of professional planning in a given country.

11. EDUCATION IN REGIONAL PLANNING IN THE UNITED NATIONS PERSPECTIVE

On 30 July, 1965, the Economic and Social Council adopted resolution 1086 C which requested the Secretary-General "to prepare a draft programme of research and training in connection with regional development projects presently under way in selected Member States as a means of developing suggestions as to methods and techniques that could assist countries in promoting development and achieving optimum patterns of rural and urban human settlement and production activities...".[19]

The assumptions and objectives of the programme are expressed in the following paragraphs of the resolution:[20]

Noting the common aspiration of developing countries to modernize their economies through industrialization and agricultural improvement programmes as a basis for raising levels of living of their population, and recognizing that regional development and an appropriate distribution of population within a country are essential factors in achieving such modernization and social development;

Noting with concern that, as a by-product of population growth and economic development, many social and economic problems of both developing and industrialized countries arise from the vast migration to the cities often far beyond the capacity of the cities, particularly the capital cities, to absorb the total labour force in productive employment;

Convinced that the effectiveness of measures to deal with these problems can be greatly enhanced by study in depth of the practical experience of existing regional development projects within countries, and the training of manpower in the new methods and techniques resulting from such research;

Considers that there is an urgent need for carefully organized and co-ordinated research and training effort by the United Nations to promote modernization in the cities and the countryside and to minimize the undesirable effects of overcentralization of population and of industries through the development of improved patterns of human settlement and programmes of planned social and economic adjustment.

---

[19] Economic and Social Council, Document No. E/CN.5/403, 28 February 1966.
[20] *Ibid.*

The basic ideas of resolution 1086 C were further elaborated by Resources for the Future, Inc., which presented a "Design for a Worldwide Study of Regional Development".[21]

In implementing the above resolution, some success has been achieved in the promotion of the research component of the programme.[22] Achievements in the field of training regional planners under the auspices of the United Nations have not come up to expectations. Training activities have started in the UN Centre in Japan and in the Economic Commission for Latin America, Santiago. Nevertheless, it is clear that efforts in this direction should be accelerated. A new strategy for UN activity in the field of training of regional planners should be worked out. The Polish Government has suggested that a UN seminar on the training of regional planners and statisticians be held in Warsaw in 1971. I think that the present seminar will confirm the necessity to convene such a seminar in order to continue the discussions which we have started so successfully here.

[21] *Design for a Worldwide Study of Regional Development, op.cit.*
[22] *Research Notes,* No. 2, UNRISD (Geneva, July 1969), pp. 56-65.

II

REGIONAL DEVELOPMENT AND PLANNING

3

JOS. G. M. HILHORST

SPATIAL STRUCTURE AND DECISION MAKING*

INTRODUCTION

Perloff recently implied that the regional planner has hardly a leg to stand on when advising on matters of regional development planning:[1] discussions as to what the region is have not yet ended and there is very little consensus regarding the forces that underlie regional development. The disappointments encountered so far in theory construction have been caused not so much by any confusion in the mind of the regional planner, but rather by the extreme variety of problems that he is required to solve. The use of the Weberian tool of the 'ideal type' in an attempt to establish order out of chaos therefore seems justifiable.

Various authors have felt the need for typologies, notably Klaassen and Friedmann, whose types will be briefly sketched here. Klaassen mentions four types as shown in Table 1, where Y stands for a country's gross product per capita, and Y_r for an area's gross product per capita; G indicates the growth rate of Y and G_r that of Y_r. Klaassen defines Y_r and Y as referring to the present and G_r and G as expected for the near future, adding that G_r and G will be based upon past performance.[2]

Klaassen's typology is of purely economic nature; a political factor is mentioned only with regard to the extent of an area, which is determined by:

(i) the size of the market (for labour, goods and services);

(ii) the economic structure (an area should be homogenous and not include parts of neighbouring areas of different structure);

* First published in *Development and Change*, Vol. I No. 1, 1969-70.
[1] Harvey S. Perloff, 'Key Features of Regional Planning', *The Journal of the American Institute of Planners*, May 1968, p. 153.
[2] L. H. Klaassen, 'Programmes for Area Economic and Social Development', OECD (Paris, 1964), p. 20 ff.

TABLE 1 *Klaassen's Typology of Areas*

G_r/G ╲ Y_r/Y	$\geqslant 1$	< 1
$\geqslant 1$	Prosperity Area	Developing Distressed Area
< 1	Potential Distressed Area	Distressed Area

(iii) the degree of local understanding (an area is too large if there is insufficient understanding and willingness to cooperate).

Criteria (i) and (iii) are difficult to utilize. Given the openness of subnational areas, proper delineation seems possible only if a systematic enumeration of activities of regional or 'areal' importance is added; moreover, the sources of information as to who is co-operative and who is not will scarcely be impartial.

Although perhaps not well-defined, the introduction of the political criterion gives Klaassen's typology an advantage over others that have been proposed such as, for instance, that of Friedmann. Friedmann's typology seems more interesting, however, containing as it does a broader set of criteria, especially with regard to space. In addition, it can be easily introduced into a system in which power is an explicit variable. Friedmann mentions the following types.[3]

1. *Core regions* "consist of one or more clustered cities, to-gether with an encompassing area, that may be conveniently delimited by the extent of daily commuting or, alternatively, by the distribution of agricultural activities that furnish sustenance to central urban populations". Their main characteristics include a high potential for economic growth and a high immigration rate.

2. *Upward-transitional areas* have a favourable location in relation to core regions which, together with their natural resource endow-ment, suggests the possibility of greatly intensified use of resources. This kind of region normally encompasses several cities and receives a net inflow of population. It "will show a strong admixture of forestry, agricultural and cattle-raising activities" and therefore have a lower population density than core regions. *Development*

3 J. F. Friedmann, *Regional Development Policy* (Cambridge, Mass., 1966), p. 41 ff.

corridors connecting two core regions represent a special type of upward-transitional area.

3. "*Resource frontier regions* are zones of new settlement in which virgin territory is occupied and made productive." Resource frontiers are normally related to agricultural activities and may or may not be contiguous with settled regions.

4. "*Downward-transitional areas* are old, established settlement regions whose essentially rural economies are stagnant or in decline, and whose peculiar resource combinations suggest as optimal a less intensive development than in the past." Such an area may also have an aging industrial structure or may have exhausted its natural resources. The three cases are also characterized by a net outflow of population.

5. *Special problem regions* form a category of areas which, because of their location or the peculiarity of their resources, require a specialized development approach. They frequently include regions along national borders, water resource development regions, military zones, tourism development areas etc.

A remarkable fact in Friedmann's typology, although not of overriding importance, is that it does not refer to regions in the sense that he defines them, but rather to parts of regions.[4] In fact, two of his types (1 and 4) refer to the regional centre and two (2 and 3, the case of contiguity) to the region's periphery. Type 4 might also refer to the periphery, inasfar as density remains low. The non-contiguity mentioned under 3 could be conceived as a special case, inasmuch as Friedmann considers water development 'regions' to be special cases.

If we recognize Friedmann's four criteria,[5] these can be used to identify his types which, excluding the special problem regions, are in fact six in number (see Table 2). Although 24 possibilities can be determined on the basis of combinations of two values for four criteria, the six mentioned by Friedmann are those that can be observed in reality.

It should be emphasized that it is possible and even more meaningful to characterize six types of *regions* (in Friedmann's own sense of the word) that present useful combinations of the six types of *areas* mentioned by him. These are: (1-2); (1-3a); (1-4b); (4a-4b);

---

[4] See for example, his definition as implied in the centre-periphery model, *Ibid.*, pp. 8-16.
[5] Friedmann also mentions migration, but this seems to be directly related to growth potential.

TABLE 2 *Friedmann's Typology of Areas*

	Types	Population density		Natural resource endowment		Growth potential		Location with respect to regional centre	
		High	Low	Rich	Poor	High	Low	Close	Far
Centre	1. Core regions	x				x		x	
	4a. Downward Transitional Area	x					x	x	
Periphery	2. Upward Transitional Area		x	x		x		x	
	3a. Resource frontier (contiguous)		x	x		x			x
	4b. Downward Transitional Area		x		x		x		x
	3b. Resource frontier (non-contiguous)	x			x	x			x

(1-2-3a) and (1-2-4b). In fact, Friedmann's typology of areas concerns homogeneous parts of polarized regions, the present and future functioning of which can only be understood by their interrelations.

While Klaassen's typology is rather too abstract to permit predictions as to the kind of growth process through which an area may be expected to pass, Friedmann's is more explicit in this respect and is therefore also more elucidating for the policy-oriented observer. However, the omission of any indication as to the kind of decision-making machinery by which the region is governed, makes his typology less useful than one would like it to be. Nevertheless, it should be considered as an important step forwards.

In attempting to bring some order into the problems encountered in regional development and planning, this article proposes a typology which gives specific attention to some of the organizational aspects of the decision-making process, based on an elaboration of Perroux's domination model.[6] It is realized that the conclusions

---

[6]   François Perroux, *L'Economie du XXe siècle* (Paris, 1964), p. 25 ff.

reached will be liable to change as cognition increases of the basic problems of regional development.

The paper has been organized in four sections. In section 1, the factors underlying a nation's spatial structure are discussed, after which some of the resultant features of this structure will be mentioned. In section 3, we shall move from the national to the regional level, in an attempt to show how the decision-making process affects a region's spatial structure, given a number of locational factors. Finally, in section 4, a typology of regions is proposed.

1. NATIONAL SPATIAL STRUCTURE

Traditional economic geography considers transport costs, economies of scale and of agglomeration to be the major factors underlying the emergence of regions as sub-systems of the nation. This does not satisfy the regional planner whose major concern is with developing countries, however, since such factors do not explain many of the phenomena observable in reality and apparently crucial to the process of regional development.

One such phenomenon of major importance, for example, is the occurrence of primate distribution of cities by size; that is to say, distribution in which one or a few very large cities dominate numerous smaller towns and villages, while no intermediate-sized cities are represented. These so-called primate distributions are not explained by theory which, however, does to some extent explain the so-called lognormal distributions that seem to obey the law

$$P_r^\alpha = P_1/r$$

where P_1 = size of the highest ranked city

P_2 = size of city of rank r

and α = a constant characteristic for the sample of cities.

Various attempts have been made to explain the different types of distribution. Among the most recent is that by Berry who tested the hypothesis that the type of distribution is a function of the relative degree of economic development.[7] He made this test using data for 37 countries. Berry concludes that no such relation is apparent in his sample. He therefore points to factors of a politico-administrative and/or economic nature to account for the different types of city size distribution. Thus he says:

[7] Brian Berry, "City Size Distributions and Economic Development", *Economic Development and Cultural Change*, July 1961, p. 573 ff.

Countries which have until recently been politically and/or economically dependent on some outside country tend to have primate cities, which are the national capitals, cultural and economic centres, often the chief port, and the focus of national consciousness and feeling. Small countries which once had extensive empires also have primate cities which are on the one hand "empire capitals" (Vienna, Madrid, Lisbon etc.) and on the other hand centres in which such economies of scale may be achieved that cities of intermediate size are not called for.[8]

Berry restates his argument in more general terms when he suggests that lognormal distributions are the result of a 'stochastic' growth process, in other words, a process in which many forces act randomly. In other types of distribution, however, fewer but stronger forces act and the resulting distributions show a tendency towards primacy.

It seems possible to argue that the forces mentioned by Berry are decision-based, the underlying aim of the decisions being improvement of the welfare of the persons making the decisions or of those for whom they are made. If these decisions are many and random, they do not reflect a general scheme of action that governs them. The evidence then points to a high degree of freedom in decision making, that is to say, it implies that decisions are made in a system of complete decentralization. It also implies that the decisions carry little weight, bind few people, and consequently have a relatively small area of influence. In other words, a system of complete decentralization, if maintained over a relatively long period, will tend to result in a city-size distribution that is oddly shaped: all centres will be of approximately the same (small) size.

On the other hand, if all decisions are made in one centre, other places will have executive tasks only. This one centre will be the focus of all information and the greater part of the decision-making apparatus will be located there. The result will be an extreme example of primate distribution: a main centre will be surrounded by a great number of similarly-sized satellites.

In reality, such 'ideal types' naturally do not occur. However, over a relatively long period of time, some countries have shown a stronger tendency towards centralization than towards decentralization. For other countries the reverse is true. Whatever the case, the way in which the decision-making process is organized must reflect the set of values and attitudes characteristic of the system – especially those with regard to the use of power and the nature of

---

[8]   *Ibid.*, p. 582.

authority – as well as the use which has been made of communication technology. The more widespread the access to information, the more likely it will be that decision making has a relatively high degree of independence. Decisions that are essential to the behaviour of a system have economic and social implications, apart from political; institutions and organizations that have to some degree specialized in performing functions in either of these fields, will therefore tend to cluster in places where decisions are made, bringing with them the greater part of their own decision-making apparatus. The implication of this reasoning appears to be that if a system's organizing value system has led to a trend to centralization, decision makers will tend to cluster in a few relatively large cities; if the reverse holds, the city size distribution will tend to have lognormal shape.

Some support for this hypothesis is found when we arrange Berry's data for the 37 countries under study according to the type of politico-administrative principles that were applied in organizing the decision-making process for a relatively long period of time (see Table 3). As the available data show, 25 of the 37 follow our hypothesis. Of the twelve remaining countries, two (Japan and Sweden) would probably have been in the proper box had their ecologically favourable areas been larger.[9] Canada, Australia and New Zealand, and Yugoslavia, which have not really had the time to establish themselves as countries, should perhaps not have been included in the selection.

Although our hypothesis has not been subjected to strong testing, the evidence provided by the data allows the assumption of a strong relationship between the organization of a country's decision-making process and its distribution of cities by size. It is to be noted that differences in the decision-making process refer to differences in power exercized at the various levels of the city hierarchy.

The evidence thus seems to justify an attempt to add to the analysis provided by economic geographers and to follow Perroux in his discussion of the relationships between sub-systems at the international and national levels in terms of domination, a concept which relates to the urge for power.[10] This concept presupposes the existence of centre-periphery relations which are reflected in the phenomenon of polarization, that is, the tendency for a number of

---

9   See also the argument put forward in section 3.
10   François Perroux, *op. cit.*, p. 25 ff.

TABLE 3 *City Size Distribution and Government Organization: 37 countries* *

Types of City Size Distribution	Type of Government Organization			
	Historically Decentralized		Historically Centralized	
Rank-size	Belgium Brazil China Finland W. Germany India	Italy Poland Switzerland Union of South Africa U.S.A.		
Intermediate	Australia Canada Yugoslavia	England & Wales New Zealand Norway	Ecuador Nicaragua	Malaya Pakistan
Primate	Japan Sweden		Austria Ceylon Denmark Dominican Republic Greece Guatamala	Mexico Netherlands Peru Portugal Spain Thailand

activities in one or more areas to be geared to and led by, decisions made in another area, called the pole or centre. In other words, the centre dominates the periphery. Writings of authors such as Friedmann[11] show that in a national system the centre should, in the majority of cases, be identified with the sub-system in which the nation's capital city is located. It is there that, within the limits set by the international system, decisions of direct or indirect allocative nature are made, which influence the entire system.

Perroux has made it clear that domination of sub-system B by sub-system A occurs when the former's reactions are insufficient to offset the actions of A with regard to B. This insufficiency is explained by one or a combination of the following factors: (i) A may be considerably bigger than B; (ii) A may have a superior structure, or (iii) A may have a greater bargaining power. The significance of each of these factors will be discussed at some length, starting with the last.

---

* Data concerning the type of government organization were kindly provided by Mr. M. Faltas, Institute of Social Studies.

[11] *Regional Development Policy*, Chapters I and II, and the cited literature.

A basic conclusion of bargaining theory is that a party's bargaining power increases with its ability to alter the opponent's preferences and/or to control the alternatives open to the opponent.[12] It would seem useful to apply this conclusion to a centre-periphery situation in order that some characteristics of centre-periphery relationships may be better indicated.

In any deal between A (the centre) and B, A will have the advantage, being better able to know B's preferences and alternatives than *vice versa*, simply because its isolocation with the system's communication centre gives it better access to more information. This advantage is particularly clear regarding data about alternatives. Whereas A has access to information from sub-system B as well as from the international system with which it is connected, B's knowledge of its own alternatives is most likely restricted to the preferences of neighbouring sub-systems that also form part of the periphery. B's information concerning A's alternatives will be practically nil.

Being better informed than B with regard to alternatives as well as preferences, A has a better position to start with. But in the bargaining process, A also holds the winning cards; while it is well-situated to alter B's preferences, whether through the use (or abuse) of the national communication network or through the arguments which it knows are sufficient to make B change its mind, B will normally fail to alter A's preferences since the latter's access to superior information can be used to better advantage.

Also to A's advantage is the circumstance that national decision makers have a tendency to overestimate interests close at hand and to underestimate those more distant; A will make facile use of this psychological effect of distance in its attempt to enforce control on B. The significance of this factor will diminish at a later phase of the development process when politicians from B participate more fully in the decision-making process.

The two other factors that may underlie domination (differences in size and structure) are often interrelated in the sense that a superior structure is often the consequence of larger size.[13] Size is understood here in terms of population rather than in terms of area. If a sub-system has a larger population than any of the others in the national system it will be able to produce under conditions not

---

12   See, for example, A Kuhn, *The Study of Society* (Homewood, 1963), p. 245 ff.
13   This applies particularly to the components of a relatively small system.

available to the others; that is, it will reap the fruits of economies of scale and of agglomeration as well as of a degree of specialization that cannot be attained in the other sub-systems. The larger sub-system will normally have a higher income per capita and, in turn, a different demand structure. This different demand structure will tend to cause a production structure as well as a level of technology in advance of developments in the other sub-systems. Hence, the dominant sub-system finds itself in a monopoloid situation with regard to technology. This is also the case with respect to information: its central position allows it access to more information concerning the whole system, while its position as the link with the international communications network enables it to take first choice of innovations transmitted through this network.

Thus, it is argued that differences in size among sub-systems may lead to differences in their structures, in the sense that the larger will have a superior structure, that is to say, will perform more functions. However, sheer size differences may also cause a situation of domination, even if the dominating sub-system performs fewer functions and has an inferior socio-economic structure. This case is especially relevant when domination is established through warfare between two equally well-equipped sub-systems. The larger of the two opponents – who might even be slightly less equipped than the smaller – will be able to acquire a dominating role.

In sum, a country's spatial system is defined by the existence of a number of interrelated sub-systems, one of which acts as the dominant sub-system,[14] the others being the periphery. The emergence of these sub-systems is explained by factors such as transport costs and economies of scale and of agglomeration, whereas the emergence of centre-periphery relations that mould the sub-systems into one system is explained by differences in power among the sub-systems. The latter factor is principally based on differences in access to information, but also on differences in levels of technology. The use that is made of available technology, especially of communication networks as well as the prevailing sets of values and attitudes, determine the degree to which decision making is centralized and the part of the population that is engaged in functions mainly characterized by their executive aspect. It thus seems that the sub-systems can be organized into a hierarchic structure of three-

[14] This is the general case. There are a number of countries, however, where competition exists between two such sub-systems.

dimensional nature; the decision-making space in which the first two dimensions refer to area and occur on a country's territory, while the third dimension is decision-making power. This three-dimensional space has a maximum over the system's centre and relative maxima at the centres of the sub-systems, the minima occurring between them and at the country's frontiers.

2. DOMINATION AND INTEGRATION

Domination appears to have two complementing components: extraction and regulation. It is extractive inasfar as it enables the centre to gain a net profit from its relations with the periphery. It is regulative inasfar as the periphery is enabled to make use of the existing field of forces to promote its own development. The two components are complements in the geometric sense of the word: if the one increases, the other decreases and *vice versa*. The hypothesis can be advanced that the extractive complement in domination is the more important when the periphery is relatively under-developed; in such a situation, the centre can more easily forge structures that allow centre-periphery relationships to operate to its advantage.

Among the structures by which extractive relations between centre and periphery are imposed, the centre will be especially interested in those that enable the execution of centrally-made decisions and control over their execution. In this connection, three sets of processes designed to bring about such structures seem to be of particular importance: (i) the formation of cadres at the peripheral sub-system level responsible for executing decisions made at the centre; (ii) the formation of institutions and organizations that enable control of these cadres as well as of essential aspects of the periphery; and (iii) the formation of transport and communication networks that enable control over flows of goods and information.

On the understanding that these structures never entirely respond to the centre's objectives even in the earlier phases of domination, the first set of processes, if and when the extractive component is of major importance, will lead to the establishment of economic and political administrations that are manned by agents of the dominating sub-system. Their role is initially made possible by investment in economic ventures on the one hand, and in a transport and communication network that allows goods and information to be channelled to the centre, on the other hand. Basic to their success is the superior technology by which the actions of the cadres are supported, although the agents may also require the cooperation of the local population. Whether or not this cooperation is based upon the use of force, it is essential for the spreading of the centre's technology.

The integrative process thus set in motion will lead to increased exchange of commodities between central and peripheral sub-systems. Increased trade, however, will tend to be in the centre's extractive interest, it being the centre's technology that makes the exchange possible; the system of commodity distribution will therefore tend to fall under direct control of the centre. Decisions concerning the direction in which goods will move through the distribution system will be made known through the communication system.

Price being a major signal in the allocation of commodities, and the price to be paid depending basically upon the credit obtainable by the prospective buyer, establishment of complete control over distribution systems requires control over credit-facilitating institutions. Thus the second set of processes is essential, not only inasfar as they enable control over the periphery, but also in that they serve to control the centre's agents who might wish to take independent action on the basis of credit or control over distribution systems.

While the third set of processes is instrumental in enabling the formation of cadres, it also reinforces the second set. Obviously, the creation of centripetal transport (both road and rail) and communication networks strongly influences the spatial structure of a system as a whole, not only in the third dimension but also in the first and second mentioned above. The significance of the transport network is shown by the fact that while a sub-system is of little importance for the centre's extractive purposes, or its relative isolation does not endanger the system, the centre will not devote any of its resources to changing the situation. Development of natural resources in such sub-systems will therefore tend to stagnate, and is more likely to occur in those in which the centre has already taken an interest and which have been more fully integrated into the system.

An essential element in the present attempt to elaborate Perroux's domination model is that its outline of the extractive component of the process contains factors that will cause this component to shrink while the regulative component expands. These factors are principally the formation of cadres and transport and communication networks.

Although cadres are formed for the purpose of executing decisions made at the centre, they introduce new technology and information into the sub-system, which is then put to uses other than that envisaged by the centre. The need to employ people from the periphery induces the centre to establish educational facilities by which the periphery can better adapt itself to the new technology. The information and technology – although introduced in support of the centre's agents – will eventually be integrated in the periphery and used to its advantage.

While central influence over the periphery grows as extractive activities increase, the extractive nature of the relationship will be recognized more and more by future agents of the centre who, as time progresses, will be inclined to identify themselves more with interests of the periphery.

It should be recognized that the regulative component in the centre-periphery relationship is present from the beginning. This is based on the fact that all societal systems include groups which consider it meritorious to be responsible for improving the welfare of others. It is characteristic of such groups that their members accompany the cadres when they settle in the periphery. Such people soon recognize the extractive character of the centre's activities in the periphery and will report accordingly to the centre, hoping for its intervention. They also tend to bring about changes by direct action in the periphery itself.

Although the centre may change some aspects of extraction in response to such actions, it will basically attempt to maintain the extractive component at a maximum level by manipulating the distribution system and credit institutions. It will not be able, however, to prevent use of the transport and communication networks in favour of the periphery, which will be promoted by the following:

(i) conflicting interest groups at the centre make use of relevant information from the periphery;
(ii) the gradual involvement of persons from the periphery in the national decision-making process;
(iii) the emergence of local banking institutions and commercial centres in the periphery.

The extractive component in centre-periphery relations will continue to be stronger than the regulative component until the periphery creates regional elites (usually educated in the centre) with sufficient power to replace the alien agents. Contact between the two groups will lead to this replacement, eventually covering administrative as well as economic and political functions. Participation in such functions, especially when they concern international and national activities (as opposed to regional and local) by persons from the periphery will decrease the extractive component of the domination because these people will be concerned more with the periphery's welfare than with the centre. Access by regional elites to the centre's technology and information systems, and their participation in the relevant decision-making processes, will cause the values and attitudes of periphery and centre to gradually overlap.

This in turn will facilitate the political integration of centre and periphery, essential to the latter's attempts to establish a new spatial pattern of government expenditure that will be favourable to the periphery's further development. Once this objective has been attained, further social integration based on a better spread of educational facilities also becomes possible, giving the periphery wider access to superior technology. Use of this technology by the periphery will eventually also enable economic integration to acquire a horizontal character.

3. REGIONAL SPATIAL STRUCTURE

In the discussion of issues relevant to the formation of a system's decision-making space, a number of factors have been omitted that are significant to a study of spatial structure at the level of the sub-system or region. These factors are: (i) the spatial distribution of exploited mineral resources; (ii) the relative size of the ecologically most favourable area in exploitation within the region; and (iii) the number of resource-based functions the region performs within the national system. A fourth factor is the degree of centralization in the region's decision-making process, which has been discussed at some length in the preceding section. It may therefore suffice to concentrate on the first three factors, especially insofar as these affect decision-making space in the first and second dimensions. Each factor will be discussed in relative isolation, that is to say, that while discussing variations of one factor, other factors will be held constant.

The natural resources mentioned under (i) refer especially to those that may lead to mining and quarrying, although exploitation of hydro-electric potential may also significantly influence an existing structure. The distribution of mineral resources (especially when under exploitation) over the region's area will strongly influence the distribution of population. If resources are concentrated, people engaged in their exploitation will tend to live in one large mining town or a cluster of mining towns. If resources are dispersed, mining towns will also be dispersed, although probably linked by some central place whose primary or secondary function is the provision of services. If the scale of exploitation is determined by outside demand and all resources are in demand outside the region, it is obviously more advantageous if resources are dispersed as the transport networks required to ship the deposits out will basically influence the region's potential to start other activities along these networks. In this connection, the function efforts described by Perroux[15] (positive effects of crossroads on the emergence of economic activity) also play an important role. It should be added, however, that similar though less strong effects will occur even if the scale of operations is not based on external demand.

Whereas there will be a tendency for a primate city size distribution to emerge if natural resources are concentrated, the tendency will be towards development of a lognormal distribution if they are fairly dispersed. More important, however, a concentration of natural resources will tend to create a relatively large regional periphery, while a dispersed distribution will cause the periphery to be relatively small.

With regard to the second factor, the ecologically most favourable area may be defined as that area of a region's surface where natural conditions result in a higher productivity per hectare than elsewhere, assuming that the same amount of inputs per hectare are everywhere used. Although in principle the extent of this area is subject to variation because of technological change, it may justifiably be assumed that such changes do not occur during the first phases of a region's development process: they occur either before a region becomes settled or in a rather advanced phase of its settled history. Whatever the case, it is obvious that settlers will tend to concentrate in the ecologically most favourable area, and that there will be greater opportunity for a strong urban centre to emerge if

15 "La notion de pôle de croissance", *Economie appliquée (1955)*, Nos. 1 & 2.

this favourable area is large. In addition, however, the larger the area the more chance there will be for equality of such magnitudes as productivity per man and per hectare, as well as of variables strongly correlated with these indicators. If the extent of this area in relation to that of the region is large, and since differences between centre and periphery can be directly measured in terms of the indicators already mentioned, it may be concluded that the region's periphery will then be relatively small.

The third factor mentioned was the number of resource-based functions which the region performs in the national system. If the region has only one such function, e.g., the production of sugar or wheat or iron ore, development will tend to be concentrated in the area most suitable for that activity. Due to the influence of the national centre, little attention will be devoted to other activities; in other words, the national centre will attend only to the development of that function which serves the rest of the country. Inversely, if more than one such function is performed, there will be various foci or poles of development in the region; the process described in section 2 will then occur more rapidly. In such a case, the positive internal effects on the national transport networks mentioned above will necessarily be felt. It follows, therefore, that performance of a single 'national' resource-based function will tend to result in the emergence of a primate city size distribution, in this case implying a system in which the periphery covers a relatively large part of the region's area. The performance of various such functions, however, will tend to result in lognormal distribution of cities by size, and the region's periphery will remain relatively small.

The fourth factor (degree of centralization in the decision-making process) is taken to have two effects. First, it is assumed that a high degree of centralization finds physical expression in a city size distribution of the primate type, and that a low degree of centralization leads to a lognormal distribution of cities by size. An argument in support of this hypothesis (not mentioned in the previous section) is that fewer centres of government administration are established in systems with a high degree of centralization; in other words, the average territorial size of a country's second order administrative units is larger, given an equal distribution of population at the time their boundaries were established. In a decentralized system, the average extent of such units will be smaller, under the same assumption with regard to population density. With some exceptions, however, both systems tend to have almost equal populations contained in a second-order administrative unit. A centralized system will have fewer administrative centres and therefore less need for establishing networks of transport and communication between such centres, whereas the reverse holds true for the decentralized system. The latter will therefore show clear physical evidence of a relatively small periphery, whereas the former will tend to be related to a relatively large periphery.

4. A TYPOLOGY OF REGIONAL SPATIAL STRUCTURES

The typology presented below is based on recognition of a three-level hierarchy of forces: (i) those that act within the centre-periphery model as outlined in section 2; (ii) those that are of economic nature and concern transport cost minimization as well as the effects of economies of scale and agglomeration; and (iii) those that emanate from data of a physical nature, by which is understood the relative location of resources in the broadest sense of the word. Thus, whereas the first level is understood as of prime importance for the functioning of a spatial socio-economic system, it is recognized that these forces act within the constraints of those working on the second and third levels. It is assumed that the four factors discussed previously are the most important by which to show the relationship between the first and third levels of forces, while simultaneously enabling an examination of the role of economic forces.

The four factors can be grouped according to their effects upon the relative territorial size of the periphery on the one hand and, on the other, the type of city size distribution. It is understood that the four factors affect both and that both are to a large extent inter-related; it is therefore felt that a factor may more effectively be identified by its strongest effect rather than by its effect on both. An exception to this principle is made for the third factor, concerning the number of resource-based functions of national importance performed by the region. For the other three factors, it is assumed that distribution of natural resources as well as the relative size of the ecologically most favourable area mainly affect the relative territorial size of the periphery, while the degree of government centralization is presumed to particularly influence the type of city size distribution.

The typology based upon the effects of the four factors is presented in Table 4. It will be observed that each of the four factors is considered by attaching alternatively extreme values as 'high' or 'low', 'various' or 'one' etc. The effects of each factor upon the two classifying criteria are entered in the column headed 'score' in the order of the foregoing columns. The scores can be:

'L', meaning that the effect of the value attached to the factor is a tendency towards a relatively large territorial extent of the periphery;

'S', meaning that the effect of the value attached to the factor is a tendency towards a relatively small territorial extent of the periphery;

'R', meaning that the effect of the value attached to the factor is a tendency towards the formation of a rank size distribution of cities;

'P', meaning that the effect of the value attached to the factor is a tendency towards the formation of a primate distribution of city sizes or, for the factor concerning the number of national functions, a combination of two of these scores.

As two criteria for classifying types of regions are used, that is to say, two scores can be made with respect to the extent of the periphery and two concerning the type of city-size distribution, there are four possible types: Type I which is defined as RS; type II which is defined as PS; type III which is defined as RL and type IV as PL, these letters having the meanings given above.

For a combination of scores acceptable as fitting either of these four types, each letter should be scored at least twice. Thus, combination 2 in Table 4 cannot be identified as a type, because although the score 'S' has been made 3 times, 'P' and 'R' are scored only once. Similar arguments hold for combinations 4, 5, 7, 10, 12, 13 and 15, indicated in the table by the word 'unclear'.

Combination 1 is taken as the clearest case of type I, as it contains two scores for 'R' and three for 'S'. The tendency towards rank-size distribution is equally strong in combinations 3 and 9, but less so in the direction of the relatively small periphery, 'L' showing up in the score column for both of them. Types II and III occur only once, while type IV is found again three times: combinations 8, 14 and 16. Combination 16 is obviously the strongest representative of this type.

Of the four types, II and III should be interpreted als intermediate types, I and IV being the two extremes on our scale.

Type II could be interpreted as the type of a relatively 'young' region, which has not yet been fully integrated in the national

TABLE 4 *A Typology of Regions*

No.	Ecologically most favourable area under exploitation		Spatial distribution of exploited natural resources		No. of national resource-based functions performed		Degree of centralization in government		Score	City size distribution		Relative extent of periphery		Type No.
	L	S	D	C	V	O	S	L		R	P	S	L	
1	x		x		x		x		S, S, SR, R	x		x		I
2	x		x		x			x	S, S, SR, P		unclear		x	I
3	x			x	x		x		S, L, SR, R	x		unclear		
4	x			x	x			x	S, L, SR, P		unclear	unclear		II
5	x		x			x	x		S, S, LP, R			x		
6	x		x			x		x	S, S, LP, P		x	unclear		
7	x			x		x	x		S, L, LP, R		x	x		IV
8	x			x		x		x	S, L, LP, P		unclear	unclear		I
9		x	x		x		x		L, S, SR, R	x		x		
10		x	x		x			x	L, S, SR, P	x			x	III
11		x		x	x		x		L, L, SR, R	x		unclear		
12		x		x	x			x	L, L, SR, P		unclear		x	
13		x	x			x	x		L, S, LP, R		x	unclear		IV
14		x	x			x		x	L, S, LP, P		unclear		x	
15		x		x		x	x		L, L, LP, R		x	unclear		IV
16		x		x		x		x	L, L, LP, P		x		x	IV

L = large; S = small; D = dispersed; C = concentrated; V = various; O = one; R = rank size; P = primate.

system. Type III appears as an 'old' region, which has become fairly well-integrated in the national system. Contrary to type II, it is not likely to undergo much political change. Its major problem would seem to be to stimulate more activity in its periphery. It cannot justifiably be said that types II and III should be interpreted as stages in the process that a region would go through, say, in the direction from IV to I. This cannot be so, primarily because the amount and distribution of natural resources in both cases is quite different.

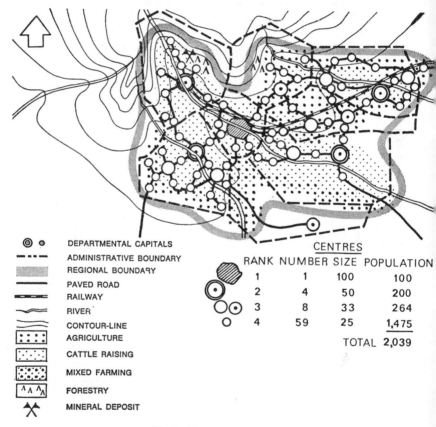

| | | CENTRES | | |
RANK	NUMBER	SIZE	POPULATION
1	1	100	100
2	4	50	200
3	8	33	264
4	59	25	1,475
		TOTAL	2,039

Legend:
- ◎ ○ DEPARTMENTAL CAPITALS
- ADMINISTRATIVE BOUNDARY
- REGIONAL BOUNDARY
- PAVED ROAD
- RAILWAY
- RIVER
- CONTOUR-LINE
- AGRICULTURE
- CATTLE RAISING
- MIXED FARMING
- FORESTRY
- MINERAL DEPOSIT

Fig. 1. Type I (Combination 1)

An example of each type is given, each example based upon the same starting point in order to facilitate comparison of the types.

It will be noticed that numerous examples can be given of each type.

The most favourable of the four types has been depicted in figure 1, most favourable from the point of view of the level of development it has reached. Type I is the case in which the ecologically most favourable area is relatively large, the region performs various interregional resource-based functions, the location of natural resources is dispersed and the system of government is decentralized. Ecological conditions are most favourable in the valleys of the three rivers, but especially along the central river. As in the other three examples to be discussed, the region's centre is located at the intersection of this river with the NE-SW road along which three of the seven department capitals belonging to the regional system are located, the road being part of the interregional transport system. Two more such capitals are located along the main river valley, the upstream town being also the region's mining centre. The two other administrative centres are located between the northern river valley and the main valley, and also perform central place functions for their surrounding cattle-raising areas.

The region's export activities are concerned with minerals, which explains the presence of the railroad so far upstream, as well as cattle raising and/or meat products and processed agricultural products. Industries of this nature have developed especially in four of the five major towns, the fifth being the mining centre.

The spatial structure resulting from the various activities is very tightly knit. All centres – even the fourth rank ones – are well-served by infrastructure and at a short distance from major centres. The region has reached a stage in its development in which certain sub-systems become discernible. One such sub-system contains the northeastern department plus parts of adjacent departments. Another has developed in the southwestern department and is moving into the eighth department, the capital of which is as yet in the influence of another regional centre. A third sub-system has come into being in the department east of the region's centre. As it is, the region's spatial structure has become 'shock-resistant', even to the disappearance, for whatever reason, of demand for one of its export products such as minerals. If this were the case, both the western part of the system and its centre would face difficulties, especially the former. However, the degree of dynamism in the rest of the area would seem to guarantee the possibility of expansion

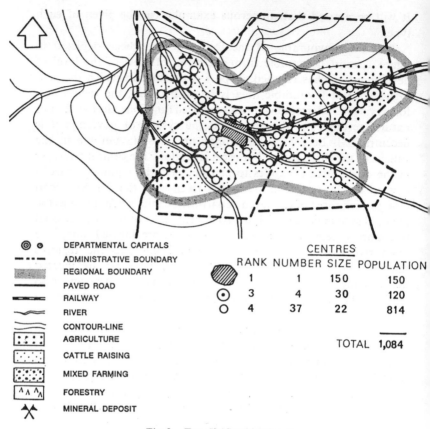

	RANK	NUMBER	SIZE	POPULATION
DEPARTMENTAL CAPITALS			CENTRES	
ADMINISTRATIVE BOUNDARY	1	1	150	150
REGIONAL BOUNDARY	3	4	30	120
PAVED ROAD	4	37	22	814
RAILWAY				
RIVER			TOTAL	1,084
CONTOUR-LINE				
AGRICULTURE				
CATTLE RAISING				
MIXED FARMING				
FORESTRY				
MINERAL DEPOSIT				

Fig. 2. Type II (Combination 6)

in various directions, while more industrial development can also be expected in the cattle raising plain between the northern and central valleys, especially in the city along the railroad.

A comparison of figures 1 and 2 shows quite some difference between the two types. Far less activity is carried on in type II than in type I, although ecological conditions are supposedly identical. The region's centre has never seen fit to stimulate more than intra-regional demand for its cattle raising and mining products, the only export items deriving from agriculture and processing industries. In addition, far less decision making is done outside the region's centre: only three other administrative centres have emerged. Thus, cattle-raising activity did not develop to such an extent as in type I, where it was largely made possible by roads connecting the administrative centres. The low scale of mining operations explains why the west remained underdeveloped.

The region's spatial structure is therefore not very firm, partly because its population density is low as compared to type I. In type I, a tapering-off of extra-regional demand could to some extent be absorbed by internal demand, and other bad effects somehow offset by using existing infrastructure for upward-transitional and resource frontier types of development. In the case of type II, however, a fall in demand for the region's export product(s) will hurt the heart of the region to a far greater extent.

On the other hand, if prospects are basically good, there is a danger that the region will not be able to respond quickly to increased demand because the information will be late in arriving; it is equally probable that the region's infrastructure would not permit the potential growth of output due to sheer lack of overcapacity.

Thus, the region is vulnerable because of its single interregional function and also because of its rigid spatial structure, the main characteristics thereof being the smallness of the towns at the regional boundary and the fact that all roads except one radiate, as it were, from the centre.

In type III we have to do with a decentralized government organization (equal to that of type I), with a relatively small ecologically favourable area under exploitation. Mineral deposits are found near the region's centre and form the basis for one of the region's interregional functions.

The four administrative cities which are not situated along the NE-SW road serve little else than this administrative function. Cattle-raising activities carried on in the vicinity of the two nearest administrative towns north of the centre are of no more than regional significance. This also holds for the two other cattle-raising areas. The valley's agricultural produce is partly consumed in the region and partly exported, accounting for the development southeast of the capital.

The spatial structure of the region is more developed than that of type II, but the poor ecological conditions have prevented the region from fully profiting from this situation. Given funds for investment, therefore, it seems that some dynamism could be introduced in the system, especially along its transport network. The region's capital would be badly affected if its main non-administrative activity (mining) should be brought to a standstill

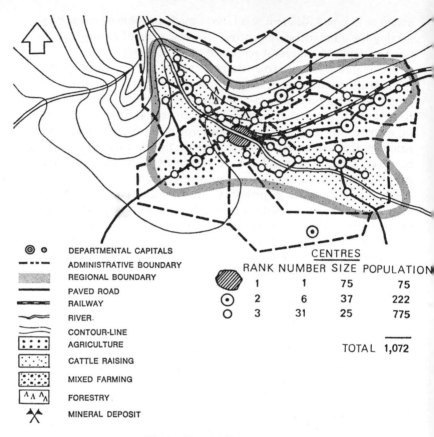

	RANK	NUMBER	SIZE	POPULATION
(hatched)	1	1	75	75
⊙	2	6	37	222
O	3	31	25	775
			TOTAL	1,072

Legend:

⊚ ⊙ DEPARTMENTAL CAPITALS
▪-▪-▪ ADMINISTRATIVE BOUNDARY
(shaded) REGIONAL BOUNDARY
━━━ PAVED ROAD
▬▬▬ RAILWAY
〜〜 RIVER
≈≈ CONTOUR-LINE
AGRICULTURE
CATTLE RAISING
MIXED FARMING
ᴧ ᴧ ᴧ FORESTRY
⋏ MINERAL DEPOSIT

CENTRES

Fig. 3.   Type III (Combination 11)

due to lack of demand. The system as a whole, however, would not be very much affected as it must be moving at a rather low level of development.

Type IV (see figure 4) differs from type III in that its governmental system is more centralized and in that it performs only one inter-regional function. This is assumed to be mining, and occurs near the region's centre. There we also find a strong concentration of infrastructure. The region's other activities are of regional interest only, largely because of unfavourable ecological conditions.

The road network shows almost only centripetal forces. Thus, if extra-regional demand disappears, the shock will be felt throughout

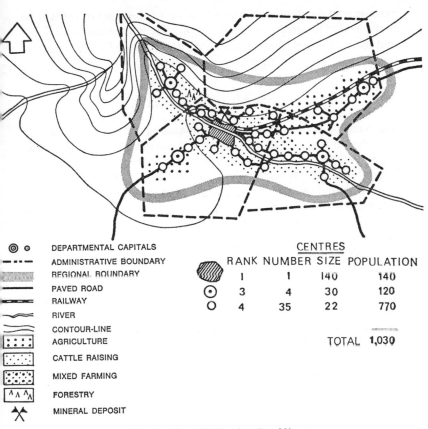

	CENTRES			
	RANK	NUMBER	SIZE	POPULATION
	1	1	140	140
	3	4	30	120
	4	35	22	770
			TOTAL	1,030

Legend:
- ◎ ○ DEPARTMENTAL CAPITALS
- — · — · ADMINISTRATIVE BOUNDARY
- REGIONAL BOUNDARY
- —— PAVED ROAD
- RAILWAY
- RIVER
- CONTOUR-LINE
- AGRICULTURE
- CATTLE RAISING
- MIXED FARMING
- FORESTRY
- MINERAL DEPOSIT

Fig. 4. Type IV (Combination 16)

the system, probably most of all in the upstream department and in the cattle-raising area.

The most important conclusion to be drawn from the discussion of the four types seems to be that a region's economic shock resistance is much greater when its spatial structure is more closely knit. Many regional functions must have then emerged, forming a substantial part of the region's total activities. As communications are then better than in a looser spatial structure, much more information pertinent to what is going to happen reaches the lower echelons of the decision-making hierarchy; and as the degree of freedom at the various levels is greater, there is more freedom to start countervailing measures if the region should be threatened by extra-regional activities. Although some of these measures will be in the field of interregional functions, most will be related to regional and local activities, these being tightly intertwined by the input and output relations existing between them.

5. CONCLUDING REMARKS

The basic objective of interregional planning can be identified with concern on the part of the national government for further integration of the country's spatial system. This concern will become less urgent once all sub-systems have achieved full participation in the socio-economic activities carried on within the system. The regional planner whose advice is asked by a national government may break the problem down into three questions: (a) in terms of the system as a whole, what significance should be ascribed to each of the sub-systems? (b) by what criteria does the government determine the priorities regarding the further integration of sub-systems? and (c) how should the chosen sub-system(s) be integrated into the system?

The present paper has devoted little or no attention to problems (a) and (b). Instead, it has focused on ways of putting the third problem in such a manner that it is consistent with the forces underlying the regional development process. It has been suggested that this problem may present itself in four basically distinct ways, called types I, II, III, and IV respectively; we have suggested that it is meaningful to ask: how do you plan the further integration of a region characterized by type I, type II etc.? In other words, we imply that it is relevant to analyze the organization of the decision-making process as rigorously as possible before any attempts are made at proposing development strategies.

We have not tried to imply that a classification of problems is identical with a classification of solutions. This will largely depend on the problem cluster mentioned under (b) above, as well as on the factual content of the factors employed in classifying our types.

A final remark emphasizing the relative nature of the present paper would seem to be called for. The sense or nonsense of the proposed typology will have to be tested, firstly by a rigorous formulation of the development process characteristic for each type, and secondly against evidence available in reality. As the four types occur within the same theoretical framework, whence there can only be a difference of parametric nature, these tests will not easily be executed.

4

PAULO ROBERTO HADDAD

PROBLEMS AND POLICIES OF REGIONAL PLANNING IN BRAZIL

The main problems of regional planning in Brazil arose in the late 1950s when a climax was reached in the process of import substitution. The country was tied to the great concentration of industrial activities in one region, and by the intensified migratory process between its several regions, resulting from differences in the spatial distribution of economic opportunities. How Brazil dealt with these problems will be discussed in the first part of this paper. Later we shall examine in more detail two other problems of regional planning policies in Brazil: i) choice of the regions for planning, with particular emphasis on some methodological problems of regionalization; ii) the development of the Brazilian Northeast and some observations on a possible economic evaluation of experiences regarding fiscal incentives in that region.

1. REGIONAL INEQUALITY AND PLANNING

The 1946 Constitution anticipated the problems of regional development in Brazil by reserving 3 percent of federal gross revenue for development of the Amazon region and an equal amount for investments in the Northeast. Nevertheless, the planning agencies only began considering a better regional distribution of economic development as a goal of economic policy in the late 1950s. The process of import substitution, intensified in the second half of the 1950s, resulted in the geographic concentration of propulsive activities in the Southern Centre, where complementary industries, directly or indirectly related to the former through forward and backward linkages, were also located. In this same period, the volume of internal immigration greatly expanded, affecting the country's pattern of regional development.

1.1. *Industrial Activity and Geographic Concentration*

The locational patterns observed in the industrialization process were analysed with the aid of the methodology proposed in a study by Perloff and Wingo on natural resource endowment and regional economic growth in the United States.[1] We consider three industrial groups: (a) resource industries (agriculture, mining); (b) first stage resource users: those sectors in the Brazilian input-output table for 1959 that received more than 10 percent of their inputs (in value terms) from resource sectors; (c) second stage resource users: those sectors that received little directly from resource sectors but more than 10 percent of their inputs from the first stage resource users. Later, a series of rank correlations was drawn up, based on the relative position of the Brazilian States regarding population and production value in the three industrial groups in 1959.

Similar to those for the United States, the results show that proximity to markets (intermediate and final) tends to be the dominant locational factor; even in the first stage manufacturing industries (food products, beverages and tobacco, textiles, leather and hides, non-metallic minerals, etc.) production has a high degree of geographic association with population, but a relatively limited association with resource production. The correlation results are merely indicative.

Although no quantitative analysis had been made in research into locational patterns and processes of regional growth in the past, industrial concentration in the Southern Centre was based on the arguments of the export-base theory[2] in its original explanation.[3]

At the beginning of the 20th century, the coffee economy had given rise to a structure of income distribution favourable to the creation of an internal market, relatively large and geographically concentrated in the Southern Centre, which stimulated the expansion of residentiary secondary and tertiary activities. While regional income increased, the country's capacity to import under-

[1] H. Perloff and L. Wingo, Jr., "Natural Resources Endowment and Regional Economic Growth", J. Friedmann and W. Alonso, *Regional Development and Planning* (Cambridge: M.I.T. Press, 1964).

[2] Douglass C. North, "Location Theory and Regional Economy Growth", *Ibid.* In this Reader, Charles M. Tiebout's article "Exports and Regional Economic Growth" is also found; this emphasizes the relationship between the export-base concept and the determination of income theory.

[3] Celso Furtado, *The Economic Growth of Brazil* (Berkeley: University of California Press, 1963). Werner Baer, *Industrialization and Economic Development in Brazil*, (Irwin, 1965).

TABLE 1 *Rank correlations of selected resource-using manufacturing groups with resource production and population, by States, 1959*

Correlated Sectors	Coefficient
(1) Production in the 1st stage resource-using manufacturers with resource production	0.572
(2) Production in the 2nd stage resource-using manufacturers with resource production	0.532
(3) Population with resource production	0.769
(4) Production in 1st stage resource-using manufacturers with population	0.841
(5) Production in 2nd stage resource-using manufacturers with population	0.841

went difficulties due to crises on the international coffee market. The coffee-producing sector consequently shifted savings for its application to new activities, at first to meet local demands and later on to diversify the export base of the region through producing consumer goods which were previously imported. The financial and commercial organizations, the social and economic infrastructure, the labour market, and urban facilities created in the Southern Centre for the coffee economy and later to meet the needs of new industries, resulted in cumulative advantages for this region, such that its locational conditions became obviously superior when compared with those of other regions. When, at a later stage of the industrialization process, Brazil began intensifying the import substitution of intermediate products and capital goods, these new industries settled near their potential clients in the existing industrial centre.

1.2. *Internal Population Migration*

The postwar development period was also characterized by very uneven demographic growth rates in several regions. In recent research on divergence and convergence patterns of regional economic growth of Brazil, D. G. Graham points out the impossibility due to lack of data of estimating internal migration by satisfactory techniques. Graham reckons that the whole population shift is the absolute result of the difference between the demographic growth rates of the country and of the States from 1950 to 1960.

The Brazilian States have been classified according to two criteria of homogeneous area determination:

(1) the development level measured by the ratio

$$X_{ia} = \frac{X_i \cdot 100}{\overline{X}}$$

where Xi is the capita income of State i, and $\overline{X}$ is the per capita income of Brazil, in 1955;

(2) the development rate measured by the ratio

$$Y_{ia} = \frac{Y_i \cdot 100}{\overline{Y}}$$

where Y_i is the geometric rate of annual growth of State i's real product between 1950 and 1960, and $\overline{Y}$ is the growth rate of the country in the same period. This is shown in Table 2. (Unfortunately, it has not been possible to obtain information about the growth rates of some States.) In three categories on each of the two criteria, we have tabulated the values that, in each State, express the total of the displacements (positive and negative) as the average population percentage, 1950 to 1960.[4]

TABLE 2 *Migration total displacements by Brazilian States as the average population percentage 1950 to 1960*

X_{ia} / Y_{ia}	Level of Development					
	High $X_{ia} \geqslant 100$		Intermediate $50 \leqslant X_{ia} < 100$		Low $X_{ia} < 50$	
Rate of Development: High $Y_{ia} \geqslant 100$	* S. Paulo	+ 4.5	* S.Catarina	+ 27.5	* Amazonas	+ 5.7
	* Paraná	+ 43.4	* Goiás	+ 26.4	Maranhão	+ 16.2
	* M. Grosso	+ 27.5			Pará	+ 2.4
Inter $50 \leqslant Yia < 100$	Guanabara	+ 2.1	* M. Gerais	— 8.5	R. G. Norte	— 15.5
	R. Janeiro	+ 9.3			Sergipe	— 17.2
	* R. G. Sul	— 5.0			Bahia	— 11.4
Low $Yia < 50$			E. Santo	+ 1.1	Piaui	— 14.3
					Ceará	— 11.4
					Paraíba	— 17.3
					Pernambuco	— 13.3
					Alagoas	— 9.4

[4] Values estimated in D. H. Graham, "Convergence and Divergence Patterns in the Regional Economic Growth and Migrations in Brazil – 1940/1960", *Revista Brasileira de Economia*, July/September 1969.

* Data on growth rates available.

Unfortunately, the available data do not permit analysis of the orientation of migratory movements between the different classes of States[5]. The summary scores of Table 2 suggest that migratory flows are associated with the economic opportunity distribution among States as shown through the growth rates of the 1950s. The different intensities of the migratory flows also seem to depend upon an equally relevant variable, the composition of the productive structure of the States: expansion of the agricultural frontier (Parana, Mato Grosso, Goiás, Maranhão) through labour-intensive activities resulted in an increasing demand for rural labour force in those States. The Northeastern drought and the construction of Brasilia also had great influence as causal factors in migratory movements.

1.3. *Regional Development Policy in Brazilian Development Plans*

As a result of different growth rates of income and population in various regions, Brazil ended the 1950s with a series of problems which should interest national planners:

1) the problem of developing the resource region of Amazon, whose basic characteristics are as follows: it covers about 60 percent of the total national area, with a population of about 7 million irregularly distributed over a territory with very poor transportation and communication with all other regions of the country;

2) the problem of the old regions of the Northeast: making up 32 percent of the Brazilian population and contributing only 16 percent of the national income;

3) the problem of the national metropolitan areas: unemployment, insufficient public facilities and high costs of social overheads being some problems of national importance that appear in the metropolitan areas of Rio and Sao Paulo, where 5.9 percent and 6.2 percent of the total population are concentrated.

Regional growth problems only became subject to economic policy analysis in the national development plans elaborated in the 1960s. Economic planning in Brazil, although intermittently implemented since World War II, when it was started in order to solve problems of bottlenecks in key sectors, has recently made

5 See B. Okun and H. W. Richardson's highly suggestive article, "Regional Income Inequality and Internal Population Migration", *Economic Development and Cultural Change*, January 1961.

PAULO R. HADDAD

TABLE 3 *Aspects of Regional Development*

	1 – Plan Salte and Joint Commission Brazil – USA (1949/1953)	2 – Programme of Goals (1956/60)
A) Strategies on Regional Development	Emphasis given to the development of the Centre-South through elimination of bottle-neck points in that region (electric power and transport).	Consolidation and integrat of the development of Centre-Southern region; at end of the period, spe emphasis to the North-east problems.
B) Importance assigned to the goals of the spatial policy.	Inadequate: Emphasis given to sectoral policies.	Adequate for relieving so political tensions.
C) Types of policies proposed for the regional development.	Investments in socio-economic infrastructure (L).	Investments in the so economic infrastructure (H
D) National problems of Regional Development more emphatically approached.	Shortage of infrastructure services in the national metropolitan region (H).	Problems of the old regior Northeast: organization SUDENE in 1959 (L).
Average value of V_w	0.731	0.655

L = Low emphasis
H = High emphasis

various national plans in Brazil – 1949-1968

3 – Triennial Plan (1963/65)	4 – Programme of Action (1964/66)	5 – Strategic Programme (1968/70)
~elopment expansion for less developed areas with ersion of efforts in spite of ial emphasis to the North-	Development expansion for the less developed areas with concentration of efforts in problem areas.	Development expansion for the less developed areas with concentration of efforts in problem areas.
quate for relieving socio- ical tensions.	Adequate for relieving socio-political tensions.	Critical for the National Development.
stments in socio-economic structure (H). Fiscal in- ves (L).	Investments in socio-economic infrastructure (H). Fiscal in-centives (H).	Investments in socio-economic infrastructure (H). Fiscal in-centives (H).
lems of the old region of Northeast (L).	Problems of the old region of the Northeast (H). Develop-ment of the resource region of Amazon (L).	Problems of the old region of Northeast (H). Development of the resource region of Amazon (H). Problems of the metropolitan areas (H).
0.611	0.592	Not available

great progress. [6] Official tasks of the planning agency increased to cover monetary, fiscal and exchange policies; the goals and number of sectors involved in the plans were expanded; methods employed in the planning process became more sophisticated, etc. Roberto Campos presents as chief hindrances to Brazilian progress in the experience of planning:[7] (1) technical factors: statistical deficiencies of fundamental data, scarcity of experienced planners, the immensity of the agricultural sector, the importance of the foreign sector; (2) institutional problems: the existence of autonomous political subdivisions, the inadequacy of the implementation machinery, lack of consensus-building political machinery, political instability.

Table 3 illustrates the approach to regional development policies in the various attempts at national planning in Brazil in the postwar period. This table is based on an analysis of official documents and on the consensual opinion of some technicians whom we consulted. The last indicator of the table shows the tendency observed in various years with regard to the regional imbalances measured by the V_w index proposed by J. G. Williamson. [8]

This index is given by the formula:

$$V_w = \frac{\Sigma \, (Y_i - \overline{Y}) \frac{2 f_i}{n}}{\overline{Y}} \text{ where,}$$

f_i = population of State i;
n = national population;
Y_i = income per capita of the State i;
$\overline{Y}$ = national income per capita.

The nearer the value V_w is to 1, the greater the degree of regional imbalance in the national income distribution.

In spite of the progress shown in more recent plans, the problems of regional development policy in Brazil have so far not been

6 This progress can be checked by collating the various stages of economic planning in Brazil with the criteria proposed by Tinbergen for establishing an international comparison of planning processes. See J. Tinbergen, *Central Planning* (New Haven: Yale University Press, 1964).

7 Roberto de Oliveira Campos, "A Retrospect over Brazilian Development Plans", *The Economy of Brazil*, Howard S. Ellis (ed.) (Berkeley: University of California Press, 1969). Equally important for a picture of the Brazilian experience is Robert T. Dalland's book *Brazilian Planning* (Chapel Hill: University of North Carolina Press, 1967). In this book the political and administration aspects of planning are emphasized.

8 J. G. Williamson, "Regional Inequalities and the Process of National Development: A Description of Patterns", *Economic Development and Cultural Change*, Vol. 13 (1965), pp. 3-45.

satisfactorily dealt with. We have not yet reached a planning stage in which regionalization of a national plan is looked upon consistently, in which national coordination of regional planning is established in a continuous form; or in which institutionalizing of interregional cooperation is possible among the State planning agencies which have proliferated in late years with the basic purpose of framing projects within technical rules in order to secure resources from national and international financial organizations. Furthermore, the solution of specific regional problems is not considered an integral part of an overall development policy for all regions, or in terms of national goals for the spatial organization of the economy.[9]

Lastly, we should consider the role played in the planning process by the development councils and banks that have been organized in almost all Brazilian States during the last decade. They have improved the rationality of the decision-making process in allocating financial resources coming from federal and international funds to be invested in the different sectors of the State economies. Through different sectoral studies they have also improved and elaborated the statistical data needed for planning. With some few exceptions, however, these institutions have given too much emphasis in their work to project evaluation and implementation without organizing a system of planning for the region as a whole. Reasons for this lack of a systematic approach to the problems of the State economies include the scarcity of experts in regional planning theory. This problem becomes more crucial in the case of the river basin development commissions, which need experts acquainted with the techniques of multiple-purpose project evaluation. Owing also to problems of non-defined administrative autonomy, these commissions have never taken an outstanding part in Brazil's planning process.

2. REGIONALIZATION IN BRAZIL: SOME METHODOLOGICAL PROBLEMS[10]

The goals of the Federal Government Strategic Programme for

9 See John Friedmann's study, *Regional Development Policy* (Cambridge: M.I.T. Press, 1966) as an example of this type of approach applied in Venezuela.
10 Prepared with the cooperation of Professor Carlos Mauricio de Carvalho Ferreira of CEDEPLAR.

1968/70 set by the National Policy for Regional Development, are: 1) to establish in each problem area of the country the basis for a self-sustained development process; 2) to form an integrated national market. Among the problem areas priority is given to Northeastern Region because of the need to relieve social tensions which can have national repercussions, and the Amazon, because of the need for demographic and economic occupation of its territory.

The effects orginating in more dynamic regions were considered to benefit the other regions by enlarging the natural economic boundaries of the polarized centres. The strategy of the Public Sector is to concentrate its activities on planning and research, and on expansion of the economic and social infrastructure of the regions, reserving the profitable activities to private investors preferentially.[11]

As the Northeast and the Amazon areas cover more than two-thirds of Brazilian territory, the Federal Government needed to specify the basic goals of its regional development policy. Political and social pressure will be exercized by States within those areas for simultaneous and harmonic development, or at least for the levelling of the growth rates of those States. Owing to locational criteria, the fiscal incentive policy for the Northeast resulted in the concentration of industrial investments from 1960 to 1966 in two States: 37.3 percent in Pernambuco and 43.0 percent in Bahia. Industries aiming at the Northeastern market had mainly been located in Pernambuco, and Bahia holds in that area privileged locational advantages for supplying the national market. Based on the assertion that spatial concentration of investment in the Northeast is harmful to long-term development of the region, a system of points to classify the projects to be financed by the Government has been established. This influences determination of priorities in financing plans aimed at stimulating the location of new industries in less-developed States. In the Amazon, where there is disharmony of development between western and eastern regions, compensation for the imbalance has been sought by creating a set of special fiscal incentives in Manaus's free zone.

In 1969 experts of the Ministry of Planning, concerned about the obstacle to national development formed by lack of markets, proposed that CEDEPLAR organize research into the national

---

11   *Strategic Development Programme 1968/70*, Chapter 18.

poles of development, the growth of which would be able to stimulate expansion of the Brazilian internal market.

The intention was to implement a policy of decentralized concentration in peripheral areas of the country. There are evidently strong arguments in favour of concentrating development efforts in some regions besides those pertaining to the integration and expansion of the internal market:[12]

i) the fact that the simultaneous overall development of an entirely new spatial system for the country will have little capacity for adaptation to a changing environment;

ii) the scarcity of skilled personnel to elaborate and properly implement regional plans;

iii) the scarcity of capital resources to finance an overall programme that would be characterized by a large dose of infrastructural investments; and

iv) the inability of an existing administrative structure to adapt rapidly to the entirely new situation required for such a programme.

The main objective of a policy of concentration is to achieve the maximum rate of economic growth, and investments aiming at accelerating the development of economic growth in selected centres are the best means to achieve this goal. The assumption that spatially concentrated investments sustain themselves reciprocally and bring forth agglomeration and dispersion effects is basic to a concentration strategy. Such a strategy may be accomplished in various ways in several possible combinations, the three principal being:

i) concentration in existing or potential subregional centres

ii) concentration in existing or potential zonal centres

iii) concentration in any other area with sufficient potential.

The option for a decentralized concentration policy made by the experts of the Ministry of Planning involved identification of poles[13] which might be chosen, and among which there would be a final choice to determine those to be activated in the field of an overall development policy. This selection would depend on research involving information on candidate poles, covering such topics as: social-economic infrastructures, studies of potentiality

[12] J. G. M. Hilhorst, "The Case for Regional Planning", CEDEPLAR (mimeographed paper).

[13] L. Rodwin, "Choosing Regions for Development", Friedman and Alonso, op. cit.

A survey of regionalization methods is given by Chauncy D. Harris, "Methods of Research in Economic Regionalization" in Methods of Economic Regionalization (Geographia Polonica, n. 4, Warsawa, 1964), p. 59-86.

and performance, locational condition analysis for the implantation of national or international activities, interdependence analysis between activities of the poles, etc.

The results of these researches would be considered in terms of the relative importance of each indicator for the other goals established by the central plan: equilibrium of the balance of payments; growth rate; employment policy, etc.

Although all aspects of the methodology of this research are of interest, we shall discuss only the surveys already accomplished in Brazil and that proposed by CEDEPLAR.[14]

2.1. *The Choice of Regions*

In the 1940s, the Instituto Brasileiro de Geografia (Brazilian Geographic Institute, IBG) established a regional division of Brazil in a four-levelled hierarchy: the Great Region, Region, Sub-Region, and Zone. "The Great Regions corresponded to the vast and complex territorial units differentiated by their position, degree of development, historical evolution, natural conditions, etc. The Regions and Sub-Regions corresponded to natural units and the zones were units differentiated by economic activities included in the Sub-Regions."[15] This regional division, which led to a purely formal hierarchy, has not become a planning problem since socio-economic statistics were revealed at a local district level which permitted some flexibility in the regional regrouping of information. In 1959, for example, when the Superintendency of the Northeastern Development (SUDENE) was established, the regional division was not taken into account. Still more important is the evidence that there was no preoccupation with regional planning in that period, so that the regionalization presented by IBG was not collated according to the planner's needs.

The studies of economic regionalization were taken over again in 1966 by the Instituto de Pesquisas Econômicas Applicadas (Institute of Applied Economic Researches, IPEA) with the co-operation of the IBG, the principal goal being to establish a basis for the formulation of a policy of development poles, and for the organization of an integrated local planning system.

[14] CEDEPLAR'S working group included Professor J. G. M. Hilhorst working for UNTA's programme, in the preparation of the research design to be presented to IPEA.
[15] Instituto Brasileiro de Geografia, *Regionalization and Regional Division of Brazil*, 1967.

2.2. *A Study of the Polarized Regions in Brazil*

The methodology used in this study was based on studies employed in France by Rochefort and Hautreux, founded on Christaller's central place theory "which defines the hierarchy of a city at least theoretically, by its functional equipment, which indicates the polarization capacity of this city in a given space".[16] The research has been carried out in two parts: firstly, the functional equipment of the cities was calculated, and secondly, their area of influence was verified.

In determining the functional equipment of 550 urban centres (originally those with 10,000 or more inhabitants in 1964), the distribution of goods and services was considered the basic function of a city and the following was verified: 1) the distribution equipment of 25 industrial products, empirically selected, through a chain of branches and representatives of manufacturers who were established in Rio de Janeiro and Sao Paulo, the most important centres in the country; 2) the service distribution equipment, analyzed through 16 indicators corresponding to five large categories of services able, by their nature, to perform central functions: services concerning capital, management and administration, education, health and communications. Next, grades were assigned to each in such a way that, in the total estimate of each city's grades, an identical value was given to the distribution of services. The distribution of services has been internally weighted, but there has been no weighting in the case of distribution of industrial products. The area of influence of the city has been verified through municipal questionnaires, applied to the whole country, in which the local people were asked where they sought a given industrial product or service if that product or service did not exist in the city. Finally, after being identified, the polarized centres were classified in different levels according to their position in the urban hierarchy. This is, briefly, the methodology utilized in the determination of polarized regions in Brazil.

The final results show: a) that there is a great amplitude of grades and a lack of an increasing sequence of cities with progressively minor grades; b) that cities of similar regional importance do not have the same functional equipment; c) that there are different

---

[16] *IBG Contributions to Regionalisation*, 1969. The description of the methodology utilized by IBG was based on this publication.

degrees of organization in regional urban networks, due to the existence or non-existence of centres considered as pertaining to the 3rd order and finally due to the spatial distribution of central localities.

A national meeting on development poles was held by IPEA in November 1967 at which the results of IBG's research were examined alongside the results of similar studies accomplished by the States, although the latter were carried out under different methodologies. As a result of this meeting, 242 priority centres were selected which might possibly, by their own economic potential, serve as supporters of the spatial policy objectives to be adopted by federal agencies. No systematic or continuous governmental action at the federal level has followed that selection aiming at establishing a national policy for development poles.

2.3. *Division into Homogeneous Micro-Regions*

In July 1968, the IBG published a division of Brazil into homogeneous micro-regions set up by matching physical, social and economic factors: "First, areas which are identified through a combination of geographic elements, were individualized under a given level of generalization; whenever there was any substantial change of one of the elements, the combination changed and we shifted to other units."[17] Later on, the preliminary results obtained were further studied by Regional Divisions of the organization (IBG) and also compared with parallel studies made by several regional organizations for economic planning.

This regional division has different functions for the activities of public agencies; the delimited micro-region network will become "the table of minor units of statistical data aggregation as a substitute for the old physiographic zones". Nevertheless, from the point of view of economic planning, this regionalization has been useful only for local integrated planning goals.

2.4. *Choosing Regions for Planning*

IBG is continuing with its studies on the delimitation of regions

---

[17] IBG, *Homogeneous Micro-Region Division of Brazil* (4 vols., 1968). This publication of IBG is not sufficiently clear concerning how the IBG's experts dealt with a series of theoretical problems which arise in the delimitation of homogeneous areas, such as: classification and relative relevance of variables, problems of index combinations, etc.

which are adequate for a policy of development poles. These studies are recognized as necessary since regionalization made from the cities' functional equipment is not appropriate for the choice of core regions.

In Christaller's theory[18] regionalization is more compatible with the explanation of the spatial distribution of tertiary activities and the polarization effects of cities of higher degree in regions within which industrial and mining activities are insignificant in forming the regional product. Thus, IBG's study had to include the hypothesis that "tertiary structure directly reflects the importance of industrial activity: tertiary structure as observed in the main through trade activities and data on services is directly reflected in the structure and diversification of industrial activities."

The identification of development poles to be activated by the federal government requires an initial survey of the present polarization structure of Brazilian geographic space. Also, it should take into account a regionalization according to areas of influence of dominant centres at several levels of domination: regional, subregional, zonal, sub-zonal and local. Understanding of the polarization structure has its support in the centre-periphery concept. Therefore, the spatial economic development theory must explain the dynamic process whereby economic and social development is generated from poles to periphery, their results, their possibilities and the hindrances to the integration process of the periphery in economic and social development.

The objective of identifying centres as poles is to establish what is the present city system of the country, to facilitate the determination of relationships of interdependence between these cities, and to obtain a list of those centres which polarize the others. The area of influence of these centres will be the first criterion for establishing a hierarchy among them.

Regional planning must limit the areas of influence of the various centres of the system within which it is inserted, so that several consistent socio-economic and spatial strategies may be formulated which aim at the preliminary understanding, qualification and/or quantification of the interactions which are brought forth in each group of cities, making it possible to obtain a better knowledge of the region, and for more appropriate tools to be designed for carrying-out economic policies.

[18] E Von Böventer, "Towards a Unifying Theory of Spatial Economic Structure", *Regional Science Association, Papers and Proceedings* (Vol 10, 1963)

The following pole categories have been considered in the research which CEDEPLAR has proposed to the Ministry of Planning:

a) attraction poles or natural poles;
b) present and potential development poles;
c) final choice of poles.

Attraction poles are centres where economic, social and political factors are developed which make other centres in their areas of influence contingent on them. An interdependence relationship of various degrees is thus brought about, so that a given action, affecting the principal centre, directly and indirectly affects the area of influence of that centre, as well as its own relative position in the system within which it is inserted.

Various systems of centres within one country may present different growth rates. Generally these differences are explained by the nature of the centres' activities and the growth rate differential of these activities in each system. Thus, while principal centres are attraction poles, they are also characterized by factors which make the systems increase at different rates. Those which present a greater increasing rate of socio-economic activities are the most important.

The poles which show these characteristics are known as development poles. Although they are not ranked significantly among present development poles, the potential development poles are centres which present feasible conditions for securing an important socio-economic performance in the near future if appropriately activated.

The first step in the identification of development poles must be the determination of the existing polarization structure. No matter what the choice of the development poles, it is imperative to consider the future consequences arising from the spatial-structural changes of the country, and also the limitations to the objectives imposed by the present structure.

Developing countries do not usually have a system of well-integrated centres. There will be important centres but without a strict hierarchy between them; the situation may also be characterized by competition between the principal centres for attaining a decisive influence on a given area of the country. A policy oriented by principles which support the development pole theory will have to choose amongst these centres, and to choose others which, in spite of being located in areas of influence of more powerful centres, may possibly surpass the poles of greater influence in the region. In deciding about centres which might be candidate poles for activation, the policy-makers are in fact deciding about the future spatial structure of the area. The spatial development of a socio-economic system cannot be separated from the development of its socio-economic sectors. The locational optima for each activity of these sectors must be kept in mind when deciding about the future spatial structure. On the other hand, the development strategy must try to attain a better integration of the system of centres, that is, of the spatial structure of the area; this aims simultaneously at a greater and more efficient utilization of the available natural resources of the region, improvement of the income distribution, and expansion of the regional and national markets.

2.5. Identification of the Attraction Pole

Only cities with a population of over 40,000 inhabitants were to be considered in the first step of our research.[19] As the strategy is one of concentrated dispersion, or simply, of concentration on core regions holding a minimum of social and economic infrastructure, only regional and sub-regional centres are considered. These have both a greater area of influence and the infrastructural and functional equipment necessary to attract heavy investments. The justification for considering centres with over 40,000 inhabitants is based on the hypothesis that a certain correlation exists between the importance of a centre and its number of inhabitants.

According to this hypothesis, more populated cities present more developed infrastructural and functional equipment, more powerful social, political and economic attraction factors, and a higher rate of development. In fact this statement should be carefully considered, particularly when identifying potential development poles, and verified by means of special studies to which candidate poles should be submitted.

In most countries five city ranks below that of the national centre can be observed, according to the area of influence and provided that systems are relatively integrated. These are as follows: regional,

---

[19]   This criterion will be adopted in less developed areas. In the other areas it will stand at cities having over 80,000 inhabitants.

sub-regional, zonal, sub-zonal and local centres. Their populations are regularly found within the following limits respectively: from 300,000 inhabitants to 1,500,000 and over; from 50,000 inhabitants to 500,000; from 20,000 inhabitants to 200,000; from 5,000 to 50,000 inhabitants; and finally, from 1,000 to 10,000 inhabitants.[20]

Classes overlap because population sizes are related to the development stage and also to the nature of the on-going activity of the city and to the population density in the system of centres. As a whole, the first strata of centres dominate in the sense that activities of sub-zonal and local centres are forced to follow the patterns established by the regional, sub-regional and zonal centres.

Moreover, the role of sub-regional and local centres is of minor importance in the region's development process, their decision power being limited and contingent on decisions by centres of greater importance. These cities may be eliminated, at least in the initial part of the study.

Data about the flows to be utilized in identifying attraction poles may be classified as follows:

1 – Flows indicating economic polarization:
   a) Highway cargo transportation,
   b) Wholesale trade area of influence.

2 – Flows indicating the area of influence of social services:
   c) University education area of influence,
   d) Secondary education area of influence,
   e) Area of influence of hospital services.

3 – Other flows by origin and destination:
   f) Bus transportation,
   g) Telephone calls,
   h) Telegram flows (mail),
   i) Air transportation.

Flows included in this classification are particularly recommended; the experience acquired in determining development poles in the State of Minas Gerais, which became a partial analysis of the Brazilian spatial structure, verified the immediate possibility of attaining reasonable data on these flows.

'The area of sub-zonal influence' of each centre has been considered as a unit of observation in the study for the State of Minas Gerais. Sixty-four centres have been studied and the interaction

[20] J. G. M. Hilhorst, "A Methodology for a Study of Polarization and the Selection of Development Poles in Minas Gerais" (Preliminary Notes) CEDEPLAR/UNTA (Unpublished monograph, 1969).

between them determined by means of various flows. The area of influence was the first criterion for the selection of 30 out of these 64 centres. Thus, the geographic space of Minas Gerais was 'regionalized', allowing the initial formulation of strategies more consistent with the possibilities, structure and interest of the region. The b, f and g flows mentioned above were utilized in the study and proved relevant for delimitation of the area's spatial structure. Thus, available data may be handled and mapped indicating the flows necessary to determinate the area of influence of each centre of the country.

3. THE BRAZILIAN NORTHEAST: THE PROBLEMS OF INDUSTRIALIZATION OF A DOWNWARD TRANSITIONAL AREA.

In the late 1950s, the Brazilian Northeast presented the basic characteristics of old regions: "They have been inhabited for a relatively long period, their relative gross product per capita is falling, their technology is backward, they are expelling the majority of their best trained young people that come available for the labour force and their leading politicians exert pressure at the national level to do something about the situation."[21]

In 1958, President Kubitschek organized a work group to recommend solutions for social and economic problems which then afflicted the Northeast due to drought. Celso Furtado wrote a report which was to become the first significant step in attempting to change the colonial-like relationship prevailing between the centre and the periphery of the country.[22]

Furtado showed that the inequalities of income levels existing between the Northeast and the Centre-South were greater than those observed between the Centre-Southern economies and between the industrialized countries of Western Europe; income being much more concentrated in the Northeast, the inequalities in terms of standards of living were even greater. Moreover, the rate of economic growth in the Northeast had in the last decades been substantially inferior to that of the Centre-Southern economy. Next,

---

[21] J. G. M. Hilhorst, "Regional Development Strategies", CEDEPLAR (mimeo); see also J. Friedmann, *Regional Development Policy: A Case Study of Venezuela*, Ch. 5.
[22] *A Policy of Economic Development for the Northeast*, Presidência da Republica, 1959.

Furtado analysed relationships between the two regions, making it clear that the exchange and import selection policy created conditions for the transfer of foreign exchange credits resulting from the Northeast economy to the Centre-South, thus helping to eliminate one of the most serious hindrances to the growth of that region: reduced capacity to import. He also showed that the private sector operated as a transfer instrument against the Northeast, while the Federal Government acted in its favour. Transfers through the Federal Government were resources that were either dissolved into consumption transfers during the arid years or applied to non-direct productive investments. The private sector, lacking investment opportunities in the region, transferred investable funds from the Northeast in search of profitable application in other regions.

After analyzing the dynamic elements of the Northeastern economy and the economic aspects of the drought problems, the document made several helpful observations for a possible plan of action to be coordinated by the Superintendência do Desenvolvimento do Nordeste (Superintendency of the Northeastern Development) SUDENE, organized in the same year with Celso Furtado as its first superintendent. SUDENE coordinates the execution of Federal Government policy in the Northeast and, through directive plans, sets up over-all sectoral and spatial goals for the region's development. Several aspects of SUDENE's activities deserve analysis, but we shall confine ourselves to evaluating some features of the use of fiscal incentives as instruments for an industrial development policy.

The Federal Government created stimuli for investments allocated to the SUDENE area, including income tax incentives which produced the greatest results: in 1962 investments related to these incentives represented 0.7 percent of the Northeast internal income, and by 1966 had increased to 4 percent. These investments had to contribute to projects approved by SUDENE, whose value represented 1.7 percent of the Northeast internal income in 1962 and 5.3 percent in 1966.

3.1. *Fiscal Incentives*

Various kinds of fiscal incentives are offered to investors willing to start an enterprise in the Northeast: customs duty exemption on imported equipment (since 1959); income tax total exemption for ten years for new industries approved by SUDENE (1963);

exemption from the various non-federal taxes of State and municipal authorities, etc. The most remarkable incentive, known as article 34/18 and developed into legislation during 1961-63, allows any Brazilian enterprise to deduct up to 50 percent of its income tax, provided that it deposits the corresponding amount in a blocked deposit account at the Banco do Nordeste do Brazil (BNB). With these funds, the taxpayer may buy shares in industrial or agricultural projects approved by SUDENE in new or in expansion industries. The depositor is allowed a three-year term in which to choose the project for application; if the term falls due before an option is made, the funds are turned over to the National Treasury.

SUDENE has set up three priority categories determined through a system of points. The investor may participate for 25 or 50 or 75 percent in the resources offered by article 34/18, according to the sectoral orientation of the investment, the region where the project will be located, its capacity of labour absorption, etc. In addition, the BNB may also grant loans to industrial enterprises up to 50 percent of the capital required to cover all other investment expenditures. Thus, an investment ranked as grade A may have its capital budget financed up to 75 percent out of article 34/18 funds, 12.5 percent by credits granted by the BNB at highly advantageous interest rates, and only 12.5 percent out of own resources.

From the viewpoint of raising funds for development of the Northeast, the results were highly satisfactory. The effect of overall investments approved between 1960 and 1967, if concretized, will be almost three times the industrial capital stock existing in the Northeast in 1962. SUDENE and BNB incentives are also responsible for 65 percent of the increase in value added verified in the Northeastern industrial sector between 1959 and 1965, participation having increased in the last years.

3.2. Observations on the Economic Evaluation of the Mechanism

Criticism has recently been voiced of the fiscal incentive mechanism of article 34/18. For some, the dephasing between deposit collections and investment expenditure represents drainage of funds from the rest of the country, creating shortage of working capital for Centre-Southern enterprises and increasing difficulties in obtaining short-term banking credits as a result of the monetary stabilization policy. Others consider that income tax resource drainage to Northeastern investments might worsen the problems of the National Treasury deficit, making it difficult to control the inflationary process.

When confronted with available data, such criticisms do not show the quantitative relevance assigned to them. Furthermore, some distortions created by the fiscal incentive legislation could be corrected causing greater troubles to national economic growth. There are, however, two points regarding this experiment that deserve special consideration: first, it is necessary to evaluate fiscal incentives as an instrument of regional development policy, and to inquire whether they would not have given rise to an unprincipled allocation of resources favouring social justice purposes in relation to the periphery. Second, it is necessary to examine the extent to which the results of Northeastern development efforts have contributed to solving some of the present problems of Brazilian development.

It is very difficult to establish criteria for evaluating the impact of fiscal incentives as a tool of the Northeast regional growth policy. In the first place, the largest expenditures with regard to organization of industrial projects have become effective only during the last four years. Given the shortage of relevant statistical information, it becomes difficult to organize more sophisticated analytical studies through which the results for national development of the fiscal incentives to the Northeast could be checked. Finally, the choice of pertinent indicators is difficult when it comes to evaluating a perspective plan in which goals such as integration and expansion of the internal market, greater balance in the regional patterns of development, etc., are unfolded through slowly maturing structural changes. However, some isolated observations may be advanced regarding the two points presented for analysis.

Efficient regional distribution of resources is crucial for expanding the long-run capacity of the economic system; it places problems of choice between strategies that involve consolidation of the internal structures of developed regions or the expansion of development to other areas. As the income tax depositors of the BNB do not have costs for the formation of such funds, the fiscal incentive policy might stimulate the implantation of an industrial system in the Northeast without competitive conditions on internal and international markets, unless the Federal Government increases the intensity degree of subsidies and the protection given to new industries. We could also take into consideration the case in which the costs of locational inefficiency could be turned over to the national consumers through monopolistic practices of geographic price discrimination on the internal market; projects being carried into effect in the Northeast are generally under the control of Centre-Southern enterprises, whence most of article 34/18 funds originate. However, some elements in the fiscal incentive mechanism preserve some of the basic principles of efficient allocation of available resources. Once the fund is made up, the depositor may choose between application of his deposit to projects of his own or of someone else. "Consequently, there is an alternative cost objectively determined in the utilization of resources for a private project measured by the return of a financial application to someone else's project.

It is little likely that the enterprise makes use of blocked deposits for one of its own projects, unless it expects to obtain results at least proportional to what would be obtained if it opted for another alternative."[23]

Thus, when the total value of approved and current projects surpasses the available deposits, competition ensues among alternative projects. This enables the determination of a long-run shadow price for capital in the Northeast.

How does the development policy for the Northeast compare with other goals established by the Federal Government Programme? There are no studies of great depth on this subject to show the interrelation between regional development policies and monetary stabilization goals, the equilibrium of the balance of payments, the recovery of the region's economy etc. At most, joint efforts have been made to match sectoral and spatial goals at the level of Federal Government budget programmes. At any rate, it can be seen that the fiscal incentive policy has had unfavourable effects on the industrial labour market.

During the post-war Brazilian industrialization spurt, the capacity of the manufacturing sector to offer new employment opportunities was quite low, for which the following causes have been considered responsible: exchange incentives in the 1950s for importing equipment; artificial rates of interest on long-term loans made by official credit institutions; institutional interference in non-qualified manpower wages; and finally, benefits through social

[23] A. O. Hirschman, "The Brazilian Northeast's industrial development and the fiscal credit mechanism based on article 34/18", *Revista Brasileira de Economia*, December 1967.

legislation irrespective of productivity considerations.[24] Thus, a different basis has been established for an employment policy which aims at absorbing the increasing numbers of unemployed who accumulate in great urban centres.

A recently published study[25] shows that incentives representing a capital price reduction, in relation to labour, to less than 50 percent of its previous level, cause a strong substitution of labour by capital in industrial activities. Available data show that new projects present a capital-labour relation almost four times greater than the average relation observed in 1959. Moreover, the labour-saving nature of the new investments has not been compensated by a more than proportionate production increase, so that, during the period 1959-1965, the total of industrial employment actually dropped to 14 percent. Finally, it is expected that, if the new investments approved by SUDENE up to December 1967 are realized until 1970, they would represent the direct absorption of only 12 percent of the economically-active population increase entering the Northeastern labour market between 1968 and 1970, even without altering the present unemployment levels.

In the period 1959-65 the average salaries of industrial workers increased slightly, although proportionally less than the increase in industrial product per worker, thus lowering the share of labour income in industrial product to around 23 percent.[26] As a consequence, the Northeastern internal market may not expand at a satisfactory rate because substantial parts of the profit and interest will be remitted outside the region, thus widening the gap between income generated and income spent in the region. Unfortunately, satisfactory statistical data on income and employment levels in primary and tertiary activities are not available. Thus, it was not possible to use export base multipliers to evaluate the extent to which this occurred. We are thus prevented from reaching any conclusion as to whether the income distribution and expenditure pattern taking shape in the Northeast will cooperate with the growth of new industries, thus greatly benefiting the expansion of non-basic sectors.

[24] Economic Action Programme, 1964/66 (Programacao de Acao Econômica do Governo – 1964/66).
[25] Otto G. Wasted, "The Industrialization of the Northeast – Some aspects in the long run", APEC, July, 1968. This article puts special emphasis on labour absorption in the Northeastern economy.
[26] *Ibid.*

4. PERSPECTIVES

Creation of an economic infrastructure is only a permissible factor for regional development.[27] The fiscal incentives in the Northeast attracted directly productive investments which could utilize the infrastructural investment made in the region by the Federal Government.

Thus, this innovation has become an adequate complementary measure to the direct expenditures of the public sector in the region, which now show annual growth rates of 7 to 8 percent.

The increasing expansion of the total value and number of projects approved by SUDENE since 1960 demonstrates that some of the investment opportunities in that region might be under-estimated by the centre-southern entrepreneurs. It is not yet possible to evaluate how deeply the financial alternatives brought forth by fiscal incentives would have changed the relative advantages of the various points in the locational surface of the country. Certainly, the operational costs of enterprises will mostly have to be realized independently of the subsidy given to fixed capital; the entrepreneur will therefore tend to invest only in projects for which the Northeast can offer good locational conditions. This tendency will increase, for fiscal incentives have been spread in recent years over other regions (Amazon) and activities (reafforestation, tourism), which will compete in terms of profitability with the preferences of income tax-paying enterprises. As far as the North-east is concerned, better opportunities for heavy investments are expected to be concentrated in sectors devoted to markets outside the region.

The desirability of suppressing fiscal incentives for the North-east has been recently discussed, especially by those Centre-Southern regions which do not enjoy Federal Government fiscal incentives and which, on the other hand, cannot count on cumulative advantages such as those which exist in the Sao Paulo-Rio development axis. National planners recognize that establishment of a fixed term for the duration of the system based on article 34/18 may rationalize the SUDENE and BNB programmes, defining priority sectors for over-all application. On the other hand, it is feared that the Northeast is not yet in a condition to keep its present dynamism if fiscal incentives are suppressed.

27 H. B. Chenery, "Development Policies for Southern Italy", *Quarterly Journal of Economics*, Vol. 76 (1962) pp. 515-47.

5. SUMMARY

The degree of regional inequality in Brazil decreased in the 1960s owing to government policies favouring the Northeast and, more recently, the Amazon. The main instruments used for developing these areas are public investments in economic and social infrastructure and fiscal incentives for the establishment of new industrial and agricultural activities; these incentives consist of the exemption of up to 50 percent of the income tax of enterprises desiring to buy shares of new projects approved by SUDENE. Although elements in the successful legislation of the fiscal credit mechanism based on article 34/18 prevent an unprincipled allocation of resources transferred to the Northeast and Amazon, it is difficult to evaluate the results of SUDENE's experience in the long-run development of the country. Moreover, regional planning in Brazil is very recent and the main problems of choosing regions for development have not been tackled adequately by the Ministry of Planning, although progress has been made in this direction by recent studies in regionalization by IBG leading to the delimitation of homogeneous and polarized areas in the country. Problems of the regionalization of national policies and the organization of a national system to coordinate the actions of the numerous post-war agencies of regional planning are now becoming a crucial problem for policy-makers at the national level, who are also aware of the lack of sufficient experts in regional development planning. These problems are considered to be among the greatest challenges to Brazilian development at the beginning of this new decade.

III

PROBLEMS OF RECOGNITION

5

KHALID SHIBLI

REGIONAL PLANNING AND DEVELOPMENT IN PAKISTAN

I. BACKGROUND

Although historically the areas which constitute Pakistan are very old, politically Pakistan became an independent state in 1947. It is split into two separate geographical parts: West and East. In 1967-68, the estimated population was approximately 122 million. After the Provincial level, each Province is divided into Divisions. West Pakistan has 13 Divisions and East Pakistan four. These are further sub-divided into Districts etc.

Pakistan is a very poor country and its urban areas are crowded with low-income families. The following table gives some idea of urban incomes:

TABLE 1 *National Grouping of Income Groups in Urban Areas of Pakistan*

Group	Classification	Monthly Income Range*	% of total urban households
I.	High Income	Rs. 2,000 & above	
II.	Upper Income	Rs. 1,500 — 1,999	
III.	Middle Income		5.4%
	a) Upper Middle Income	Rs. 900 — 1,499	
	b) Middle Income	Rs. 500 — 899	7%
	c) Lower Middle Income	Rs. 300 — 499	15.6%
IV.	Lower Income	Rs. 100 — 299	53%
V.	Lowest Income	Rs. 0 — 99	19%

Source: Published and Unpublished Data of Central Statistical Office, Pakistan; U.N. Data; Indian and Asian Data; Scattered Pakistani Material; Discussion with Economic Planners, etc.

* The monthly income indicated here is that of the principal earning member of the family.

The following table shows the urban and rural division of Pakistan according to the 1961 census.

TABLE 2 *Urban Areas, Municipalities & Trusts*

	West Pakistan	East Pakistan
Urban Areas	313	78
Villages	37,061	64,729
Municipalities	87	29
Improvement Trusts & Development Authorities	21	3

The future population of Pakistan is estimated as follows:

TABLE 3 *Preliminary Estimates of Population* (in millions)

	1970	1975
Total	Approx. 136	Approx. 158
East	Approx. 74	Approx. 86
West	Approx. 62	Approx. 72

These purely indicative estimates are being revised and corrected in the light of new data, information, research and analysis.

2. PLANNING HISTORY

When Pakistan started its economic career as an independent State, it did so with few assets. National production was largely derived from crops grown on small units of cultivation. It had received no industrial legacy worth the name since all centres of modern industry in the Indo -Pakistan sub-continent happened to be located in areas that became Indian territory. The country was deficient in known mineral resources. The antiquated economy yielded a very low standard of living for the people, the majority of whom lived on the margin of subsistence.

Agricultural methods were for the most part primitive, and average yields were among the lowest in the world. Industry was nearly non-existent. Financial institutions to provide credit and to collect the savings and channel them into productive investment were rudimentary. The social services – education, health, housing, and welfare – were limited in quality as well as quantity. The systems of land ownership, business activity and family relationship had changed little in hundreds of years. The people living in the villages were virtually untouched by the scientific and social advances of the past two centuries.[1]

Pakistan's economic prospects were therefore considered to be bleak. Some people confidently predicted that the initial economic difficulties coupled with the Muslim's known inaptitude for commerce and industry and inexperience in matters of economic and financial management would lead to the country's economic collapse.

Pakistan's ability to endure as a political and economic entity was severely tested by the disruption and upheaval that accompanied the partition of the sub-continent. The country had then to cope with problems created by transfer of population on a tremendous scale. Food and shelter had to be provided for several million refugees who poured across the frontier. An operation of major proportions was launched to relieve the distress of these refugees. This made a great demand on national resources and energies when it came to carrying out plans for their permanent resettlement. The large-scale transfer of population also affected Pakistan in another way. Many non-Muslim migrants had played an important part in the economic life of the country as traders, money lenders, bankers, insurers and as doctors, engineers, lawyers etc. The mass exodus of non-Muslims caused dislocation by creating gaps which could not be readily filled by the incoming Muslims.

Before the leaders of the new country could address themselves to problems of long-term development, they had to deal with these and other effects of Partition. The economic life of the land was in a state of complete chaos. Transport and communications had to be restored and conditions created in which normal business could be resumed and commercial organizations revived. Another vital task was that of setting up a new central Government for the country and of re-organizing the administration in the Pakistani sections of the Punjab and Bengal.

From the outset, industrialization was viewed as the central task in the economic development sphere. Of 921 factories employing 1,137,150 persons in undivided India, only 34 (less than four per cent) employing 26,400 persons had come to Pakistan, many being

1   The *First Five-Year Plan*, p. 7.

small units serving simple needs. The Pakistan Government realized that a deliberate policy of promoting industrial development was needed and that it had to play a commanding role in assisting and directing the growth of manufacturing.

The first attempt at industrial planning was made soon after Independence. The First Industries Conference, called in December 1947 and attended by representatives of Government and business, led to the formulation of a basic Statement of Industrial Policy. This envisaged the promotion of industries using indigenous materials such as jute, cotton, hides and skins and the development of consumer industries which would save on imports. It favoured the granting of free scope to private enterprise, subject to certain conditions; arms and ammunitions factories and plants and facilities for the production of hydro-electric power, atomic energy, railway wagons, telephones etc., were to be owned and operated by the State. The statement also dealt with industrial finance, protective tariffs, fiscal incentives, education facilities, research and training, and outlined the terms on which foreign private capital would be welcomed. It accepted the Government's responsibility for guiding industrial growth and training conditions and facilities conducive to the growth of manufacturing enterprises. The principles embodied in the statement served as the basis of industrial planning. The high rate of growth of industry which the following years witnessed showed that this basic approach was sound and realistic.

In the years that followed Partition the Government set itself to certain vital tasks of reorganization and improvisation so as to permit productive operations to be developed and the economy to move towards diversification. Several organizations were formed in order to fill serious gaps in different branches of national economic life. A Development Board was set up in 1948. The State Bank of Pakistan was established in July 1948, with the object of reorganizing and developing the banking and credit system which had been hopelessly dislocated by the flight of non-Muslim personnel, including key banking officials. Efficient organization of the credit and banking system was absolutely essential for economic progress, and the State Bank made every effort to supply this need. The National Bank of Pakistan was established in 1949, ahead of schedule, in view of the Indo-Pakistan trade deadlock that followed the non-devaluation of the Pakistan rupee in September 1949. This new bank, together with other banking organizations whose headquarters were in Pakistan, played an important part in facilitating the movement of cash crops and in providing short-term credit for new industries.

A number of specialized credit institutions were formed to meet the medium and long-term credit needs of industry and agriculture. In 1949, the Government established the Pakistan Industrial Finance Corporation to provide medium and long-term industrial finance and to underwrite issues of stocks and bonds. (This Corporation was subsequently renamed as the Industrial Development Bank of Pakistan). The Agricultural Development Finance Corporation was formed in 1952 to fill the void which the departure of the Hindu money lender had caused in the field of rural credit. (The ADFC and the Agricultural Bank were merged in 1961 into the Agricultural Development Bank.) The House Building Finance Corporation and the Refugees Rehabilitation Finance Corporation were set up in 1952 to help integrate displaced persons into the country's economic life. All these institutions contributed significantly to the development of the economy.

Several measures were taken to foster the growth of manufacturing and to facilitate industrial planning. The Protective Duties Act of 1950 established a Tariff Commission to recommend protection to nascent home industries which were unable to compete with foreign rivals. In January 1952, the Government established the Pakistan Industrial Development Corporation, later bifurcated into two provincial organizations, in order to promote industries of national importance which were not sponsored by private enterprise because they either required heavy investment or did not offer quick returns. A Directorate of Cottage and Small Industries was also set up in 1952. The Government's powers of import control were used increasingly to support its industrial plans and priorities. In late 1952, the Government began to reduce the importation of consumer goods and instead favoured, subject to the availability of foreign exchange, the purchase of capital equipment and raw materials to foster home production. Import control thus proved an important tool in promoting industrial development.

2.1. *The Planning Machinery*

Events exposed the great weaknesses and vulnerability of Pakistan's economic structure. The political and administrative elite and the commercial community realized from the outset that the national

economy could not be left to take care of itself, and that extra-
ordinary efforts would be needed to break through the stagnation
and to create conditions of rapid and balanced progress. This could
not be achieved without the Government's assumption of heavy
responsibilities in respect of national economic planning and the
implementation of a coordinated programme of development.

The planning machinery and procedures have evolved slowly.
From an imperfect beginning two decades ago when it exercised
very little influence on economic life, the planning organization has
acquired a position where it exerts a great deal of leverage on the
Government and all public and private bodies engaged in economic
activity.

The evolution of the planning machinery can be divided into
three phases. The first covers the periods between 1947 and 1953.
In the immediate post-independence period, before economic and
administrative chaos had been fully overcome, the Government
began to think about economic priorities, programming and co-
ordination. A Development Board, a Planning Advisory Board and
an Economic Committee of the Cabinet were set up in 1948. The
following year saw the formation of the Ministry of Economic
Affairs for the purpose of inter-ministerial economic coordination.
The first formal exercise in planning was carried out by the Development Board, when it produced the Six-year Development Plan
(1951-57) envisaging an outlay of Rs. 2,600 million, of which
Rs. 1,200 million were to be financed externally and the rest raised
internally. This Six-year Plan was framed at the instigation of the
Consultative Committee of the Colombo Plan (for Cooperative
Economic Development of South and South East Asia). It was
incorporated in the Colombo Plan and adopted by the Pakistan
Government in November 1950. The Plan was in fact little more
than an assorted set of projects, each considered essential in its
own right. It was taken to outline a flexible programme, and quite
a few changes were made. This does not detract from the significance
of the portfolio of projects which the Plan embodied. As against the
modest outlay of Rs. 2,600 million envisaged over a period of six
years, actual expenditure in the first five years exceeded Rs. 3,000
million.

The country had no prior experience of planning and those who
framed the Plan were severely handicapped by lack of essential data
regarding human, physical and financial resources. The Government set up an autonomous administrative machinery comprising

an Economic Council, a Planning Commission and a number of Sub-Commissions replacing the Development Board, the Planning Advisory Board and the Economic Committee of the Cabinet. But none of these elements which constituted the planning organization was quite equal to the task. The period covered by the Plan was one of great economic uncertainty, caused by the Korean War boom and the subsequent recession. Thus, what development took place did not follow the course charted by the Plan. Economic decisions were made mostly as appeared relevant to the project in question.

The second phase in the evolution of the planning machinery began with the creation in July 1953 of the National Planning Board, later renamed the Planning Commission, and lasted a little over five years. The terms of reference of the Board included: a review of development since independence; an assessment of the resources which could be made available over the five-year period beginning April 1954 (later changed to April 1955); the preparation of a national development plan; the making of proposals regarding the administrative machinery with a view to assuring the successful implementation of the Plan; and the formulation of any other recommendations deemed essential to the success of the Plan.

The task of the Planning Board was rendered difficult by a serious insufficiency of statistical and staff resources; moreover, its status was very uncertain. Ministerial and other authorities making economic decisions appeared to consider the process initiated by the Board as an encroachment on their rights. These and other factors caused delays in the formulation and finalization of the First Five-year Plan, which was published in draft form in May 1956 to serve as a basis for discussions with the Provincial Governments and Central Ministries. The Board later revised the Plan in the light of these discussions and the comments made, and submitted it for the consideration of the National Economic Council in February 1957. The NEC recorded general approval to its targets and programmes in April 1957, two years after the Plan period (1955-60) began.

The Plan analysed the problems of economic growth, defined the concept of balanced growth for the first time, and gave excellent suggestions for adapting the administrative machinery to the needs of development and for carrying out vital institutional improvements. The Planning Board also continued to offer advice on policy matters to implementing agencies during the Plan period. Unfortunately, the Plan's promise could not be fulfilled because there was no firm governmental commitment to its execution.

The third phase began with the change of political regime in October 1958. The revolutionary Government was keenly aware of the need for changing the planning machinery in particular and the administration in general so as to hasten the process of development.

A series of changes were introduced to raise the status of the planning agency, institutionalise the planning process and to integrate the national Plan's prescriptions and targets into the administration's practice. The President became the Chairman of the Planning Commission and the Deputy Chairman, the operational chief, was given the ex-officio status of a Minister. The Planning Commission was constituted into a Division of the President's Secretariat. As part of the attempt to build the development process into the working of the administration, Planning Departments were organised in the Provinces and Planning Cells set up in Ministries and departments. The Planning Commission is now represented on the National Economic Council, the Executive Committee of the National Economic Council, the Central Development Working Party which scrutinises public sector projects, and the Foreign Exchange Control Committee. The Industrial Investment Schedule for the private sector and the Annual Development Programme which is part of the Budget, are formulated within the framework of the Five-year Plan.

2.2. *The Planning Commission*

The main functions of the Planning Commission are: (a) formulation of the Five-year Plan; (b) formulation of the Annual Development Programme within the framework of the Five-year Plan; (c) planning for the private sector; (d) evaluation of progress; and (e) advice on development policies.

2.3. *Formulation of the Plan.*

The formulation of the Five-year Plan is a fairly elaborate process. The Planning Commission evaluates the past performance of the economy and prescribes tentative targets in overall terms for national income saving, investment, taxes, imports and exports. It also estimates the foreign resources likely to become available in the form of loans, credits etc. This tentative Scheme is modified after discussions with all concerned Government agencies, and then submitted to the NEC for approval. Sectoral programmes are sub-sequently prepared and competing claims of projects sorted out and adjusted. After the Plan is approved, it is implemented mainly through successive Annual Development Programmes, always observing the discipline of the Plan and its schemes of proportions and balances. The Plan can be altered when necessary, although not without the concurrence of the NEC.

2.4. *The Annual Development Programme.*

The Annual Development Programme is a crucial component of the planning process, embracing projects which have been approved by the normal Government machinery after technical, financial and organisational scrutiny. After approval by the NEC, the Annual Development Programme is incorporated into the annual budget. The Finance Ministry has an important say in determining the size of the ADP because of its responsibility for the mobilisation of resources.

The introduction of an Annual Plan from 1968-69 is intended to facilitate the coordination of development activities in public and private sectors and to enable a yearly review of development and of necessary adjustments. The Annual Plan is expected to include an evaluation of past performance, a presentation of the main targets, an assessment of the resource position for the year, an outline of the investment programme in the public and private sectors, and a broad outline of the economic policies that may be necessary to achieve the targets.

With the introduction of the Annual Plan, the process of planning has moved to a new stage in its evolution.

Pakistan is now preparing its Fourth Five-year Plan (1970-75), which is being drawn up within the framework of a perspective plan.

2.5. *The Perspective Plan*

When it came to framing the Third Plan, the planners were convinced that longer-term goals should be spelled out, based on a scientific forecast of resource availability. Planning for successive five-year periods does not provide a sufficiently broad framework for the determination of economic goals and policies. This thinking led to the formulation of the Perspective Plan (1965-85), which will embrace four five-year plans. Although it is subject to modification, it can be legitimately expected to help refine the concept of planning and to ensure a broad continuity of aims, objects and methods over a long period of time.

The Perspective Plan confronts the country with the following goals:

a) quadrupling GNP and increasing the per capita income by 100 percent;

b) full employment by about the middle of the Perspective Plan period;

c) parity in per capita incomes between East and West Pakistan;

d) universal literacy; and

e) the end of dependence on external aid.

The Plan aims at the following changes:

TABLE 4 *Planned Structural Changes in the Gross National Product 1965-85*

	1965 %	1970 %	1985 %
Agriculture	49	45	36
Manufacturing	12	14	21
Other Sectors	39	41	43
Total:	100	100	100

2.6. *The Objectives of the Fourth Plan*

In preparing the Fourth Plan, it is natural that questions relating to the form, speed and priorities of future economic growth and the direction of social development should receive serious attention. These and other relevant questions were studied and analysed by the Planning Commission in the booklet entitled *Socio-Economic Objectives of the Fourth Five-year Plan* published in November 1968.

This document did not intend to present a definitive verdict on fundamental issues that must be sorted out before the Fourth Plan could take shape, but rather to define these issues, to point out the options, and to present the background against which decisions have to be made for the future. Thus, it frames the issues and outlines the conflicts which arise when a choice has to be made between alternative courses of action. Who is to make these choices and determine the fundamental socio-economic postulates of the Plan?

The Government decided some time ago that the people should be associated with the formulation of the Fourth Plan through a National Debate which will help evolve a pragmatic consensus of opinion on the guiding principles of future planning. These principles have to be defined with the help of popular consultation before the experts can specify the Plan's targets and work out the strategic concepts to be applied in the first half of the 1970s. After all, planning can evoke the whole-hearted sympathy and active cooperation of the people only when it is in tune with their sentiments and is manifestly designed to satisfy their aspirations.

The document suggests that the following main objectives should be borne in mind in formulating the Fourth Plan: to maintain the rate of growth; to reduce interregional and intra-regional disparities in per capita income; to aim at increasing self-reliance in essential fields; to move towards a viable synthesis between the claims of economic growth and social justice through the pursuit of pragmatic policies and to direct the forces of economic and social change towards the establishment of a just society. The document recognises that "the conflict between economic dynamism and social justice has become fairly sharp", but cautions against the adoption of superficial solutions and pleas for the pursuit of both objectives simultaneously. According to the document, greater social justice can be advanced considerably within the following framework: (a) greater equality of opportunity; (b) a fair return to farmers and industrial workers for their labour; (c) phased introduction of social security and medical care for a growing segment of the population; and (d) greater use of the fiscal machinery to promote a better distribution of income and wealth.

In spite of the major effort the country has made to reduce poverty and provide a decent living standard, much remains to be done. The income earned by 75 percent of the households is still below Rs. 200 per month. The daily calorie intake is around 2,100 per person as against the minimum international standard of about 2,600 calories. Only about 20 million people out of 125 million are literate. There is one doctor for every 7,000 persons. About 1.2 million families in urban areas live in slums. The document cites these facts in order to convey the magnitude of the task to be performed. Again, it estimates a further increase of about seven million in the labour force during the Fourth Plan period, the absorption of which alone would require the creation of one-and-a-half million jobs a year. The employment potential of the Plan will thus have to be bigger still if the backlog of unemployment is to be reduced.

The document underlines the need to rely increasingly upon the country's own resources and energies and to reduce dependence on external assistance. By the end of the Fourth Plan, the country will be required to finance 80 percent of the development effort out of its own sources. This will call for a massive effort to increase domestic savings and to augment export earnings. A move towards greater self-reliance will also make it necessary to attain self-sufficiency in certain key sectors and to specify fairly ambitious targets in all branches of the economy.

2.7. *Problems*

The growth of physical welfare, facilities and services, has not kept pace with our recent dynamic economic growth. Present living conditions in Pakistan are not necessarily due to neglect on the part of the government, but rather to its pre-occupation with tasks which are more urgent and thus assigned higher priority. The First and Second Plans, for example, had to be devoted to settling the displaced Muslim families from India who were squatting all over the urban areas. The Plans also aimed at creating the essential institutional and organisational framework which could provide some semblance of a local and provincial governmental network for this sector, some urgent water, sewerage and building and housing research, and initiate regional and urban planning.

The Third Plan then tried to initiate the first modest programme on a *curative* and a *preventive* basis. Unfortunately this soon had to be abandoned, due to sudden war with India, and in 1965-66, the sectoral programme was reduced to the provision of bare essentials. We are now completing this reduced hardcore programme of Rs. 247 crores (Rs. 2470 million); it is estimated that by June 1970 the programme will be executed to the tune of Rs. 200 crores, thus falling short by some Rs. 47 crores i.e. approximately 20 percent. This difference is not due to lack of capacity or faulty planning or programming, but to non- or untimely release of resources or by lowering the sectoral priority by the Provincial Governments at the time of preparation of the Annual Development Programmes and Budgets.

A review of the programmes carried out by executing agencies shows the Central Government to have made the best performance

(102 percent achievement in financial terms) with East Pakistan second (80 percent) and West Pakistan third (only 68 percent). West Pakistan's poor record is due to the fact that the Provincial Government has not yet been able to develop the much needed institutions and organisational framework despite heroic prodding and leadership by the West Pakistan Planning Board. Inter-departmental rivalries, duplication and bureaucratic red tape, coupled with a serious shortage of professional and sub-professional manpower, have created gigantic bottlenecks.

However, the overall national picture is far brighter than in 1955 (beginning of the First Plan period). A crude organisational framework has been developed, most emergency tasks have been completed, some water and sewerage problems are being tackled. The futility of simple slum clearance without adequate tie-in with work opportunities etc. has been realised. A preliminary national pilot programme for regional and urban development has been initiated. Building and Housing Research Centres are being developed. Government departments and ministries have learned that regional, urban and rural planning and development need inter-departmental and inter-ministerial cooperation.

The housing situation in the country has further deteriorated, density per room increasing from 3.1 persons in 1960 to 4.0 in 1968. Room, as used here, means any compartment large enough to be slept in, including bedroom, dining room, kitchen, living room, attic, servants' room, basement, corridor or covered verandah etc. The housing backlog in urban areas increased progressively: from a shortage of 600,000 dwelling units in 1960 to $1^{1}/_{2}$ million by June 1970 (this does not include the new needs for 1970-75). The water, sewerage and drainage position is alarming, hardly 10 percent of the population having access to properly treated, potable water. In large urban areas, not more than 30 percent of the population has access to piped water (of small quantity and questionable safety), in most cases from public standposts, and in very limited cases, by house to house connections. Most of the upper middle classes and higher income groups have piped water in their homes, but there is no guarantee about its safety (due to faulty treatment or poor chemical, physical and bacteriological testing etc.) or its continuous availability. However, the upper classes enjoy water at the rate of 20-30 gallons per capita per day, while the poorer classes do not have more than 2 to 5 gallons per day. In rural areas, the lack of a safe sewerage system means that most families suffer from hookworm and other gastro-intestinal diseases. In urban areas, water-borne sewerage is available to hardly 2-4 percent of the population, the rest using either the traditional disposal system or open drains and open spaces. Hardly 40-60 percent of the urban population have access to open drains for general drainage purposes. Transport problems are even worse, affecting industrial workers and urban dwellers, while faulty transport planning and vehicle control accelerates accidents and propagates lung and other diseases due to air pollution. Besides these miserable and diseased living conditions, the benefits of economic growth and development have been concentrated in certain developed regions, thus creating a further economic and social gap between the developed and depressed regions of the nation.

2.8. *Urban Growth*

In 1901, Pakistan had an urban population of hardly 3.2 million. Today it is 13 million and by 1985 will be 50 million. This growth will not be followed by growth of facilities and services, and gigantic problems will therefore have to be faced.

3. REGIONAL PLANNING AND DEVELOPMENT IN PAKISTAN

Two major findings need to be considered carefully while reviewing the problems and solutions of this sector. Economic development by itself does not create good living conditions and a liveable and functional physical environment. Economic growth and an increase in per capita income do not necessarily mean automatic improvements in physical living conditions or per capita or community welfare.

The second important lesson learnt by the Development Planners is that urban and rural areas cannot be planned or developed in isolation. They are not only organically related to each other, but form part of the bigger whole, i.e. the geographic, cultural, economic and administrative region. Abstract national planning efforts have to be translated into concrete programmes for regional planning and development which in turn must provide for rural and urban development. Any change in part of an urban area brings about simultaneous changes in other parts. Similarly, any change in part of the region affects all or some of the urban and rural areas which form the regional organism. Actually, the region is the most viable unit for integrating physical planning with economic and social planning.

Houses, physical facilities and structures have no meaning by themselves. People living within an area or a region, and their values, culture, and aspirations are far more important than physical structures or even physical or financial resources. In most developing parts of the world, where these facts are not considered sympathetically by national economic planners, regionalism is raising its ugly head. A National Plan not based on appropriate regional development plans is bound to create many socio-cultural and even economic problems.

As far as development planning is concerned, there is a movement away from the traditional concepts which propagated the gospel that if economic development could be brought about, developing countries would solve most of their problems. This naive theory has unfortunately failed. Regional planning and development, with an emphasis on the development of human resources, is now emerging as a possible new technique to be utilised within the framework of a comprehensive national development plan. In addition, we are increasingly realising that besides dealing with economic development, there is a need for creating new qualities of life. Whatever importance may be given to financial and physical resources, these lose their identity when compared to certain basic and vital qualities and potentialities of human resources. A nation possessing vast quantities of the basic resource which may be called 'the will to work' can surpass another nation with better financial and physical resources but lacking this basic resource.

Although the crisis in the physical planning and housing sector is partly due to the shortage or untimely release of resources, there is also a problem of planning methodology. Many problems and solutions demand an integrated approach with other related sectors. Policies, plans and programmes for water and power, transport and communication and industries broadly lay down the general framework for the overall physical development of a region. The general pattern and distribution of urban and rural communities is actually determined by these extraneous influences, and their meaningful development is impossible without effectively relating distribution of population and living facilities with the growth of economic activities and employment opportunities. Physical planning and housing projects therefore need to be coordinated with plans and programmes of agriculture, industry, transport and communication, and water and power. The most rational and functional administrative unit for achieving such an inter-sectoral physical coordination and optimum efficiency is 'the region'. If we consider a Division of the Provincial Government as a unit for regional planning we immediately see the confusion that prevails due to traditional approaches to development planning. If we put the yearly development budget of the Government for a particular Division on a geographic map, it becomes clear that sectoral investments cause various physical developments which have been simply viewed in financial terms and do not produce optimum efficiency. Factories may be located in one place while houses might be built in another, and the priority for community service and utilities may be accorded to a project in yet a third place. Had these regional investments been made in their physical and geographical context, it would have been possible not only to achieve a balanced and harmonious development and growth, but also optimum efficiency and economy. The first important need is to create viable planning regions in both provinces and then to initiate regional analysis and planning. It will then be possible not only to predict and control physical development but also to influence the achievement of pre-determined objectives.

The Physical Planning and Housing Sector of our Plans has so far been rather unsuccessful due to:

1. hasty decisions due to political or social urgency;
2. immature policies converted into plans and programmes without associating the relevant professional and technical experts;
3. low priority given to operational research and analysis;
4. lack of appropriate institutional frameworks;
5. lack of coordination;
6. shortage of manpower;
7. shortage of materials, machinery and equipment;
8. complete disregard of any process of evaluation and feedback.

Present legislation on physical planning is not conducive to regional planning and development. For example, in West Pakistan there are at least 23 various Acts and Orders relating to physical planning. Appropriate legislation for physical planning on regional and local levels should be enacted at an early date.

To conclude, a national policy must be formulated on urban and regional physical development. Not only the targets of various sectors must be known, but also where and how urban and metropolitan development is to be encouraged. Such a policy would provide a sounder basis for coordinating sectoral programmes. Two important corollaries will follow: a clear-cut policy for urban and metroplitan development will need to be followed by all related sectors, departments and ministries, and the national, provincial, regional and local economic development policies will need to be related to these overall urban and metropolitan growth policies.

In a recent article, Professor L. Rodwin mentions that economic development plans concentrate on capital use. They rarely plan for land use, decisions on which are left to private investors, local governments and to central government implementing agencies within the framework of capital allocation provided in the economic development plan. The assumption seems to be that if an appropriate allocation of capital is obtained, the proper allocation of management, labour and land will follow.

As a result, economists have generally neglected such questions as where growth should occur, on what scale, and over what period. Most economists now working on plans for economic development have been specifically trained and have only a marginal interest in the metropolitan or regional aspect of development. It is not surprising, therefore, that analyses of local or regional economic prospects, of feasible alternatives for development, or of the relations between the rural and urban sectors, have been negligible. The gulf between physical and economic planning further complicates matters. The low esteem in which local and regional studies are still held inhibits most top-rank graduates in economics and other social sciences from developing serious interests along these lines. Development economists also function in a different sphere of government, use esoteric language, utilise different methods of analysis, and generally distrust 'do-gooders', a class in which they often place city and regional planners. In developing countries the instinctive reaction of the economist to city planners is to wonder whether the economy can afford the luxury of 'the city beautiful' or whatever other frills he imagines the city planner is contemplating. The latter, on the other hand, not infrequently scorns the economist for limiting himself to convenient national aggregates and for misapplying textbook principles, without any real understanding of the effects of his decisions on urban and regional possibilities. Neither image is flattering or just, yet each continues to influence attitudes. This is in many ways an under-statement of actual facts. Rodwin has been kind and considerate and has presented the issues in a sophisticated framework. The actual situation is that fully-trained physical planners are either unemployed or under-employed, or in many cases are not properly utilised.

In the past city, town or urban planning was considered to be a branch of architecture, and a city or town planner was considered to be a city beautifier. Putting a plaza here, opening a boulevard there, inserting a fountain here and landscaping there; these were considered the prime activities of a city planner. This archaic concept of urban planning and development has now been abandoned. Urban planning is now seen as dealing with the whole organism of an urban area or centre. As such it is an inter-disciplinary exercise embodying social, administrative and physical sciences. The planning of an urban area thus becomes an effort at planning all sectors of the economy on a particular geographic scale, i.e., the particular urban area or centre. It thus becomes an inter and intra-sectoral activity.

Training in regional planning is even broader and more inter-disciplinary, and a trained regional planner should be able to perform the duties of a Development Commissioner for a Division or District. This requires a considerable amount of careful analysis and some minor restructuring of administrative arrangements.

Regional and urban planning cuts across three vital disciplines: public administration and political science, social and economic sciences, and physical and environmental sciences such as architecture, engineering, geography etc. Operationally it is a function of regional and local government, while substantively it deals with socio-economic and physical development. To consider a regional and urban planner as a sort of second class engineer or as a refined draughtsman for mapping out new residential colonies or industrial estates is essentially misusing a scarce resource.

These misunderstandings have caused a serious damage to the profession. Trained regional and urban planners are thus either under-employed, employed for wrong duties, or unemployed. One highly qualified regional and urban planner, after some years advanced training in the U.S.A., is currently employed on secretariat duties, dealing with postings and transfers of secretariat staff and other purely administrative duties.

The regional and urban planning and development function in actual practice is exercised by Commissioners and Deputy Commissioners. The problem thus has reached critical proportions, and needs careful analysis and dynamic new solutions.

After the First and Second Five-year Plans, the National Planning Commission was convinced that physical and social planning should be integrated with national economic planning. Education, manpower and social welfare sectors were strengthened. A National Manpower and Education Commission was established, and a Physical Planning Section was set up within the Planning Commission. These steps paved the way for launching some careful experiments in regional planning.

In pursuance of function IV of its Charter, the Commission has launched three National Pilot Projects at present being executed by the two Provincial Governments under close technical and policy level supervision of the Commission. These Pilot Projects in order of priority are:

(1) National Pilot Project Number I (NPP-I)
    "Location and Planning of Cities in East Pakistan".
(2) National Pilot Project Number II (NPP-II)
    "Regional Development Plan for Peshawar Valley".
(3) National Pilot Project Number III (NPP-III)
    "Development Plan for Karachi Metropolitan Region".

These Projects intend to integrate physical and social planning with economic planning and to establish a systematic methodology and practices for regional development planning as part of national and provincial plans.

4. PROBLEMS AND PROSPECTS

In Pakistan the concept of national physical planning was introduced for the first time in the Third Five-year Plan. This new development was made possible by the interest of the Chairman of the National Planning Commission, to whom a plea was made that a new concept of national planning was essential. After detailed research, analysis and discussion it was decided not only to create a Physical Planning and Housing Sector within the Planning Commission, but also to prepare the Third Five-year Plan within the conceptual framework.

The physical planning approach adopted by the Commission was based on the coordination and integration of sectoral programmes in terms of the most advantageous use of the land at a given level of development and the infrastructure required to service the land uses. Also included was an optimum utilisation of building materials and construction activities. This approach ensures that sectoral projects are built when and where needed.

The crux of the problem is the coordination and integration of sectoral programmes having a physical component. An important corollary is that the present budgetary type of planning should be further improved and made more important by analysis of the real and physical resources as well as the analysis and programme of physical coordination.

Although the approach adopted for the Third Plan is quite radical, some writers on development planning have suggested that budgetary planning and budgetary functions should not be the concern of national planners, who should address themselves fairly and squarely to the task of working out an overall development plan based on the available natural resources, in terms of the most urgent needs, and checked against the geographical analysis and problems.

It is clear that there is neither conceptual awareness of comprehensive rational planning nor any systematic administrative machinery for its implementation. The new concept adopted in the Third Plan adds another dimension to the national planning process by focusing attention on regional and local needs and development, as well as crystallising a comprehensive planning system well-integrated on local, regional and national levels. For the approach to be effective, a systematic and viable programme of regional planning and development will have to be initiated. Except for overall policy control and coordination, however, it will be necessary to stimulate local administrations and authorities for regional and local development and to delegate to them the necessary powers to implement the programme. Such a programme for the urban areas will pose challenges which have so far not been met in the rural works programme. In the rural areas is a spirit of community cooperation. The situation in the urban areas is somewhat different. During the process of urbanisation, rural immigrants who become industrial, commercial or white-collar workers go through a frustrating phase of adjustment to the new, unsympathetic and hostile urban environment. Many traits of cooperation, community action and an optimistic belief in the final results of such action are slowly submerged in their struggle for survival. Against this background, the manner in which a programme of urban works can be initiated and the latent energies of these people can be mobilised will be the key challenge to the Government. It may not be possible to immediately institute radical measures.

Such efforts are being carried out successfully in various parts of the world. In the United States, programmes were taken up all over the country during the depression period, and similar programmes are now being launched on a limited functions basis for under-privileged or problem groups in urban areas. In centrally planned economies like those of China and the U.S.S.R., programmes of this type form part of the planned efforts for national reconstruction. In both cases the energies of the urban population are mobilised either due to an acute crisis or by an intensive system of community education, value reconstruction and decentralisation as well as delegation of certain powers to local government. The important feature in these experiments is the sense of participation that the urban population has in these ventures. A partnership between the people and the Government cannot be created by executive order, by expanding the bureaucratic network, or by relying on an optimistic belief that eventually people will work out some solution for themselves. It requires intensive research and thinking and a deliberate programme outlined and tested on the basis of pilot projects.

The Rural Works Programme in Pakistan has been oriented towards certain types of rural development. The approach suggested here points to the need for an urban development programme within the overall philosophy of the Works Programme. This means integrating urban and rural development within a framework of regional development planning. The Works Programme, in this context, can make a dynamic contribution to the whole field of regional planning. Public expenditure, though relatively small, will act as a catalyst for bringing forth public enthusiasm on a coopera-tive self-help basis.

With regard to this suggestion it may be useful to consider the possibility of utilising the existing institutions of the Deputy Commissioner and the Commissioner instead of creating new planning and development units of provincial and regional govern-ments.

The Fourth Five-year Plan lays great emphasis on:

1. developing an institutional framework for regional planning and development;

2. enacting appropriate legislation for regional planning and development;

3. producing trained manpower for regional planning and development;

4. clarifying policies, plans and methodology by assigning top priority to the three National Pilot Projects at Dacca, Karachi and Peshawar:

5. establishing a Pakistan Centre for Regional and Urban Development (with the technical assistance of the U.N.) for providing support, operational and other technical assistance.

The following three policy issues also need attention:

(i) *Time Horizon or Scale for Physical Planning*. A five-year span is too short for physical planning and development; a 50 to 100 year span may be considered for the overall framework within which shorter span plans may be prepared. Such long-range planning should try to anticipate future needs and to cater for them systematically. If this is not done much larger resources will be needed to meet these needs or to correct the damage caused by short-sightedness. Cities should thus be planned on a long-range basis, so flexibly that they can continue to adjust to future needs and circumstances.

(ii) *Population, Distribution, Redistribution, Location of Economic Activities, Regional and Urban Development Policies, Selection of Growth Poles, etc*. Regional and urban development policies need to be spelled out more concretely within the national and provincial contexts with some examination of possibilities of decentralisation and dispersal of economic activities. Instead of slowing down or discouraging the growth of large metropolitan areas, it may be more desirable to select potential growth poles among the smaller and medium-sized urban centres and to encourage their growth and development. Attention must also be given to the development and physical planning problems and needs of villages.

(iii) *Need for An Integrated Approach*. Regional and urban development is closely linked with industrial location, transport, water and power and general economic development, and must be tackled within the broader framework. The sector deals with planning of the whole physical infrastructure for economic development.

Another vital area of concern is the utilisation of human resources, and youth in particular, for regional and urban development.

This is an area needing urgent attention. Housing, water supply, schools, transport, parks and recreation areas, shopping centres etc., are important and vital human needs and interests. No amount of government propaganda about economic growth or about postponement of consumption in the interests of growth will convince the people unless they are made part and parcel of the making and implementation of the Plan. This is all the more important as we do not have the priority to meet all the needs, nor could we do so even if we had the priority and financial resources. As we mentioned earlier, human resources not only create new resources, but can cause serious bottlenecks in the implementation of policies and plans if the people are not associated with these at various stages of their formulation.

In this respect, youth can play a significant role. The younger generation forms the citizens of tomorrow and represents a vital segment of the total human resources of a particular region or nation. So far, youth's role and place in national, regional and urban development is extremely limited. Young people are considered a commodity to be catered for, but not a resource to be exploited and developed. Children and youth receive attention in terms of health, education and recreation, to the extent that a national economy can spare resources for these sectors after meeting needs of economic development which are accorded higher priority. The potentialities of youth and children for urban and regional development may be briefly summarized as follows:

1. participation in simple programmes of slum improvement, creation or tending of open spaces and parks; participation in compaigns of neighbourhood and community cleanliness, etc.;
2. participation in simple organized handicrafts or skilled work as part of a neighbourhood or community workshop or trade school related to local needs etc.;
3. participation in organized recreation as well as arts and crafts workshops or festivals etc;
4. preparation for future citizenship by simple informal instruction

and learning by participation in community or city-wide functions especially organised for them;

5. parents can be informally but intensively trained to supplement other efforts, encouraging their children to participate and contribute to the programmes outlined above;

6. school and university curricula could include simple facts on regional and urban plans, objectives and goals, thus stimulating the interest of the younger generation.

Farreaching changes in the national education system are necessary to attain the following results:

1. to produce the right type of regional and urban planners;

2. to gear the energies and potentialities of youth to the national, regional and urban development plans and programmes;

3. to provide an intensive programme for civic education and citizenship;

4. to introduce a research programme for launching simple public works projects (for slum improvements, creation or maintenance of parks and playgrounds etc.) with the help of students and youths;

5. to make the whole educational programme more planning and development-oriented, catering to the developmental needs of the nation;

6. to make the whole educational system more responsive to (if not part of) a wider programme of national manpower and educational planning, as part of national and regional plans and programmes.

6

J. E. BANNERMAN

PROBLEMS AND POLICIES OF REGIONAL PLANNING IN GHANA

For some time now development planning has been quite popular with many developing countries of Africa, and Ghana is no exception. The question is: Why is planning so attractive to developing countries?

It must first be noted that planning is a policy and like all other policies, must have an objective. The objective of planning in the developing countries is economic growth and development. It is the nature of the development problem which induces developing countries to adopt a plan.

There is a conviction that the demands of development can be contained through balanced growth promoted nationally as well as internationally; and balanced growth is not possible without planning. The linkages must be worked out before any projects are undertaken.

The supply side of the problem requires large investments, involving structural changes which cannot be achieved without planning. As Prof. J. Bognar observed while addressing the Economic Society of Ghana in 1963: "The developing countries are especially in need of planning, for there the so-called spontaneous factors of the economy retard rather than help development. The vicious circle which is characteristic of the economic status of these countries... can be gradually modified only by purposeful effort and by comprehensive political-economic concepts embodied in plans."[1]

Development planning has received the official blessing of the United Nations and its agencies as well as of some world powers. Indeed, the decision whether or not to draw up a new Development Plan is almost preconditional to the grant of aid; prospective donors,

[1] J. Bognar, "The Importance of Devising Effective Machinery for the Implementation of Development Plans", *Economic Bulletin of Ghana*, Vol. VII, 1963, No. 4.

such as the World Bank and the Government of the United States, demand to see such plans.

The effect of the impressive rapid economic transformation of the centrally planned economy of the Soviet Union must not be ignored. In Ghana, during the Nkrumah era, the Soviet System had so much attraction for the government that the post of economic advisor was given to a Russian, Mr. Sedof.

1. HISTORY OF PLANNING

In Ghana, planning is often dated from 1951. However, in discussing the history of planning in Ghana, it is impossible to disregard Governor Sir Gordon Guggisberg's ten year programme for economic development (1919-29), the effect of which is a remarkably solid infrastructure of railways, schools, harbours, roads, water etc.

In 1951 a "Ten-year Plan for the Economic and Social Development of the Gold Coast" was launched. The same year, immediately after Dr. Kwame Nkrumah had come to power, it was decided that the Ten-year Plan should be implemented in five years, and it was accordingly transformed into a five-year development plan. The basic structure of the plan remained the same although some additions were made.

This plan which lasted until 1956, was followed by a Two-year Consolidated Plan (1956-58), regarded as a 'tidying-up operation', after which a Second Five-year Development Plan was put into operation in 1959.

After two years of implementation, the latter plan was abandoned by the Government. In its place was launched in 1963 a Seven-year Development Plan (1963-70), whose completion was designed to coincide with the tenth anniversary of the Republic and the end of the United Nations Development Decade. This plan is regarded by many as Ghana's first really integrated and comprehensive plan, drawn up after a thorough examination of the country's needs and resources; it was concerned with the growth of all aspects of the economy – infrastructure, agriculture, industry etc., and embraced all sectors – public, cooperative and private. This plan eventually proved to be over-ambitious, especially as regards the foreign exchange bottleneck; this was further constricted during the plan period by the unprecedented collapse of the world price of cocoa, the country's chief foreign exchange earner. No wonder that the military-police government suspended and eventually replaced this plan with a sort of 'consolidation plan' (1968-70), meant to prepare the ground for progress and with the sub-title: "From Stabilization To Development".

2. PROCESS OF PLAN FORMULATION

The process of plan formulation before the Seven-year Development Plan (1963-70) was very simple indeed. A circular from the Development Commission to government departments in 1957 sums up the process:

The first step to be taken in planning for the Second Development Plan is to obtain from all departments, through the Ministries, a list of projects which they desire should be considered for inclusion in the plan and which departments consider they will be able to undertake during the five years commencing June 1959.[2]

Plan targets were thus formulated essentially at the centre, only national targets being formulated, without any regional break-downs.

It has been suggested that this approach was necessitated by the state of the country's statistical data. While this is reasonable, it is also true that serious thought was not given to the need for region-alizing development plans.

The Seven-year Development Plan endeavoured to marshal information from the regions as regards their potentialities, and was to some extent based on regional resource appraisal. But as in the previous plans, targets were solely formulated at the centre for the nation as a whole. There were no targets for the regions and conscious regional policy formulation was lacking.

In this respect, the Two-year Development Plan (1968/69-1969/70) is similar to the Seven-year Development Plan. However, this latest plan approaches development by sectors, setting up appropriate policies for each sector. Also, there is some attempt at regional-ization at the implementation stage: the country's last two annual budgets include regional breakdowns of expenditure estimates. But the important point to note is that regionalization of policies has yet to be given serious consideration, and regional planning con-tinues to grope in the dark.

3. PLAN IMPLEMENTATION

Periodic reviews of plans are regarded as absolutely essential since

[2] Development Commission Circular No. SCR. 10100/Vol. IV, 31st December 1957.

conditions upon which targets are based are bound to change. This is one respect in which development planning in Ghana has proved unsatisfactory. It was noted in the introduction to the Seven-year Development Plan that: "This plan itself must be constantly reviewed as we gain more experience and collect more information."[3] Despite this observation and warning and despite serious changes, particularly in the country's foreign exchange position owing to persistent falls in the world price for cocoa, no reviews of the plan were undertaken. As we have already noted, the plan had to be abandoned in 1966 as unrealistic, especially as regards the availability of foreign exchange.

The current Two-year Plan, however, continues to review its policies and targets in consonance with changed conditions. The abnormally heavy rains of 1968, for example, prevented a large tonnage of the country's cocoa from leaving the farms on account of its disruptive effect on transport, thus affecting the expected foreign exchange earnings as well as the tax revenue from customs and excise. The plan had to be adjusted subsequently.

4. RESULTS OF GHANA'S PLANNING EFFORT

A significant effect of the approach to planning followed in Ghana in the past has been a legacy of extreme disparities in regional development. Ghana is divided into nine administrative regions which are also her planning regions: Western, Central, Eastern, Volta, Ashanti, Brong Ahafo, Northern, Upper and Greater Accra. The information on area, population, and population density of the regions in 1960 given in Table 1 shows a very high concentration of population at one centre.

Greater Accra with a mere 1.1 percent of the total area of Ghana commands 7.3 percent of the population, while the Northern Region with 29.4 percent of the total area commands 7.9 percent. The high concentration of urbanization in Greater Accra has of course taken place at the expense of the other regions through migration. Economic development in many cases necessitates progressive urbanization, either because increasing efficiency creates a surplus population on the farms or because there is need to attract

---

[3] Ghana Government, Office of the Planning Commission, *Seven Year Development Plan*, p. viii.

TABLE 1 *Area, Population and Population Density of the Regions of Ghana, 1960*

Regions	Area Sq. miles	Percent	Population thousands	Percent	Density persons per sq. mile
Greater Accra	990	1.1	492	7.3	497
Western	9,494	10.3	626	9.3	66
Central	3,656	4.0	751	11.2	205
Eastern	7,760	8.4	1,094	16.3	141
Volta	8,000	8.7	777	11.5	97
Ashanti	9,700	10.5	1,109	16.5	114
Brong Ahafo	14,900	16.2	588	8.7	39
Northern	27,122	29.4	532	7.9	20
Upper	10,478	11.4	757	11.3	72
All Regions	92,100	100	6,727	100.0	73

labour to urban manufacturing centres. The problem in Ghana presently is that the evolution seems to be taking the form of a wave of migration to the Accra-Tema metropolitan area and a few major urban centres like Takoradi and Kumasi, with the result that the amenities in these places are overtaxed. Nearly all of them are short of schools, houses, buses, water, hospitals, streets and other services.

The statistics on gross value added by regional origin given in Table 2 corroborate this point of regional disparities. The table shows a distinct concentration of Ghana's economic activity in Accra, and also in the Eastern, Ashanti and Western regions. Together, these four regions yield almost three-quarters of the value added of the economy, although their area and population are 34 percent and 61 percent respectively of the national totals. While the disparities may be attributed to the greater potentialities of the four regions, it is also true that lack of regional policies has been a contributory factor.

Further evidence of regional disparity is obtained from the statistics on regional distribution of some selected skills given in Table 3. It may be argued that the high degree of urbanisation in Accra and to some extent in Takoradi, Kumasi and Koforidua, accounts for the high concentration of the human capital of Ghana in these regions. However, in the specific case of Accra it is clear that the endowment of human capital is out of proportion to the region's share of the urban population. 25 percent of the urban population of the country lived in Accra in 1960, but it contained 34 percent of persons who had attended institutions of higher

TABLE 2 *Regional Gross Value Added by Sectors of Origin 1960 Percentage*

Region	Agriculture	Forestry	Cocoa	Mining & Quarrying	Manufacturing	Electricity	Construction	Fuel	Public Utilities	Services	Public consumption	All
Accra	1.3	0.1	—	—	3.9	0.3	22.5	1.5	1.6	58.7	9.9	100.0
Western (including Central)	12.3	8.6	9.8	11.4	2.6	0.4	7.0	1.0	5.5	36.9	4.6	100.0
Eastern	24.9	4.3	13.7	14.6	0.7	0.2	5.9	0.3	0.5	31.1	3.7	100.0
Volta	42.7	3.3	9.9	—	—	—	6.3	0.3	0.3	31.9	5.4	100.0
Ashanti	17.2	5.2	21.1	4.5	2.5	0.1	7.4	0.8	0.8	35.6	4.7	100.0
Brong Ahafo	34.6	8.7	26.7	—	0.3	—	4.2	0.3	—	22.2	3.1	100.0
Northern (including Upper)	54.9	4.4	—	—	0.3	—	10.1	0.5	0.5	22.9	6.4	100.0
All Regions	20.8	4.8	10.9	5.3	2.0	0.3	10.1	0.8	1.9	37.4	5.7	100.0

Source: Birmingham, Neustadt and Omaboe, *A Study of Contemporary Ghana*, Vol. I. (London, 1966), p. 93.

TABLE 3 *Regional Distribution of Selected Skills, 1960 percentages*

Region	Higher Education	Directors & Managers	Book-Keepers, Accountants & Cashiers	Mechanics	Electricians	Drivers
Accra	34.1	51.9	58.3	21.2	34.2	18.4
Western (including Central)	20.5	17.3	14.4	29.3	29.6	23.0
Eastern	12.9	6.1	5.4	12.1	10.5	18.4
Volta	8.5	2.8	3.1	6.9	2.6	7.7
Ashanti	16.2	20.6	13.8	23.0	18.9	21.7
Brong Ahafo	3.4	—	2.3	3.5	2.8	6.4
Northern (including Upper)	4.3	1.4	2.8	4.0	1.5	4.4
All Regions	100.0	100.0	100.0	100.0	100.0	100.0

Source: *Ibid*; p. 101.

learning, 52 percent of directors and managers and 58 percent of bookkeepers, accountants and cashiers.

Strongly related to the regional distribution of modern skills is that of man-made capital (Table 4). This is no less concentrated than the human resources. Ashanti, East, West and Accra account for 82 percent (or 87 percent including cocoa) of the capital stock of Ghana. Accra alone has one-third of the total stock, mainly comprising buildings and constructions. Almost half the value of con-

TABLE 4 *Estimated Regional Distribution of Capital Resources, 1960 at 1960 Prices*

Regions	Total Capital Stock NC Million	%	Capital Stock excluding Cocoa NC Million	%
Accra	752	32	752	47
Western (including Central)	462	20	318	20
Eastern	260	11	136	8
Volta	118	5	66	8
Ashanti	440	19	190	12
Brong Ahafo	194	8	44	3
Northern (including Upper)	100	4	100	6
Total	2,328	100	1,606	100

(Note: Original capital stock figures in £G)

Source: *Ibid*, p. 102.

structions in Ghana can be credited to Greater Accra. Its share in general equipment excluding rural implements, aircraft, ships and vehicles is about 44 percent.

The problem of imbalances in regional development has been recognized in Ghana for some time now. Launching Ghana's Seven-year Development Plan in Parliament in 1963, the President observed: "The development of Ghana has hitherto not been sufficiently balanced between different parts of the country. It is the deliberate policy of this Plan to correct this imbalance."[4]

The Two-year (Stabilization) Plan also recognizes this problem. It notes "... [Ghana] should seek to achieve a more equitable distribution of income between regions..."[5]

Of late, this problem has so much forced itself on national consciousness that the last military regime created a Ministry for Rural Development. The present Government also has established a special Ministry in charge of Social and Rural Development. It is too early to pass judgment on the effectiveness of this Ministry, although another school of thought suggests that the solution to the problem lies in "a devolution of policy and... decision-making on District and Regional Authorities..."[6]

Indeed, the present Two-year Development Plan appreciates the need for such an approach. It notes:

The geographical aspects of planning have not yet received much attention. The physical planning department of the Ministry of Economic Affairs provides a link with the Regional Planning Committees, thereby giving a spatial dimension to a development plan. The combination of physical and economic planning on a regional level will help the regions to define their structural problems and to identify their needs.[7]

The main weakness in the existing system is that responsibility for drawing up the regional development plans does not rest with the regional planning committees but with the various ministries, largely operating independently of one another. The resultant 'regional plans' are no more than a collection of uncoordinated projects, which bear no evidence of regionalization of policies.

This brings us to a discussion of the planning machinery as

4   Ghana Government, Office of the Planning Commission, *Seven-year Development Plan*, p. xiv.
5   Ghana Government, Min. of Economic Affairs, *Two-year Development Plan*, p. 2.
6   J. A. Peasah, "Ministry of Rural Development", *The Legon Observer*, Vol. IV, No. 9, p. 13.
7   Ghana Government, Ministry of Economic Affairs, *Two-year Development Plan*, p. 20.

operated in Ghana. Until 1961, the ministries and departments were "largely responsible for their actions..."[8] Indeed in many respects, the earliest Development plans could be considered as having been motivated mainly by the desire to "bring order into... government expenditures".[9] There were no special considerations for 'linkages' between projects, nor were there any specific policies designed for the regions.

In 1961, a Planning Commission was established to draw up the country's Seven-year Development Plan. There were 29 members, all but two being Ghanaians; most of them were civil servants appointed for their expert knowledge in certain fields of activity. In addition, there were a few technical experts from overseas.

The Commission set up a number of committees, each to deal with a specific area. Thus there were committees for education and manpower, health and nutrition, infrastructure, finance, works and housing, agriculture, industry etc.

Although this new machinery may be considered an improvement on the earlier one since it ensured some degree of coordination between the various segments of the plan, it also suffered from the malaise with which planning in many countries has been afflicted: the thinkers were not the doers.

It has already been stated that in his speech on launching the Seven-year Development Plan, the President referred to the need for a balance in regional development. However, it was not going to be easy to achieve that objective since the regions were not directly involved in the process of plan formulation.

The National Planning Commission was a central agency and the committees formed to help it were also basically 'central' – there were no regional representatives. The Plan was therefore essentially prepared by the centre using data supplied by the central ministries. There was very little participation of the regional population; and yet the population as a whole was expected to implement the plan. Under such circumstances, it was difficult to effect a proper balance between the development of urban areas on the one hand and the countryside on the other, since the information on which the plans were based related mainly to urban areas.

The planning machinery of the country obviously needed further examination, and it was not surprising that in 1966 Mr. Albert

8 Birmingham, W., et al., *op. cit.*, p. 462.
9 *Ibid.*

Waterston, a World Bank expert, was invited to advise on the reorganisation of the planning machinery. The recommendations contained in his "A Practical Programme of Planning for Ghana" were accepted by the government. In addition to the existing central agency, Waterston recommended the establishment of programming units in each of the big spending ministries and departments for the preparation of sector programmes, covering agriculture, industry, lands and mineral resources, education, works and housing, health, communications and forestry.

Essentially, the programming unit:

(i) sets up standards and criteria for operating departments or other units in the respective economic sectors to follow in preparing and carrying out projects;

(ii) formulates the overall development programme and the recurrent budget for the sector or sub-sector on the basis of directives from its head;

(iii) prepares alternative development policies for the consideration of the organization's heads after consulting the various operating heads of departments or other units;

(iv) sets up standards for operating departments and units to follow in reporting on the progress of projects;

(v) on the basis of reports from operating units, prepares regular, timely and reasonably complete reports and evaluations of its organization's overall programme;

(vi) coordinates the technical assistance programme for its organization; and

(vii) acts as the liaison between its organization and the central planning agency.

For liaison purposes, the heads of all programming units were to constitute an Inter-Ministry Planning Committee, chaired by a high official of the Central Planning Agency. An official of the Budget Office was to be present at the Committee's meetings in order that his Office should be fully acquainted with its activities.

The functions of the Committee were to include the formulation of uniform criteria and standards for formulating projects, sector programmes and plans, and for a consistent reporting on their progress.

In formulating this planning machinery for Ghana, Albert Waterston made the mistake to which most economic planners are prone: concentration on sectoral analysis and national accounts to the complete neglect of regional planning. The latter is now accepted as critical for strengthening a national economy, enabling full and efficient use of productive resources over the whole country, as well as helping improve economic and social conditions. Sectoral planning is admittedly an effective tool for development, but it is applied more successfully within the framework of regional policies.

Recognizing the need for a balance in regional development, the Government of Ghana decided in late 1967 that in addition to the Central Planning Agency and the sectoral programming units, regional planning committees should be established in all the nine administrative regions. "In order that this process [of planning and implementing development projects and programmes] is not limited only to those Ministries in Accra ,but that it should be extended to all parts of the country, it has been decided to establish Planning Committees in the Regions, whose function will relate mostly to the regional aspects and requirements of our economic development."[10] This gave concrete expression to the Government's intention of pursuing a policy of more balanced regional development in the country. It also reflected the Government's view that a good plan originates at the grassroots, where it should be prepared by regional committees.

The membership of the Regional Planning Committee is as follows:

the Chairman of the Regional Committee of Administration (Chairman)
the Regional Administrative Officer
the Regional Heads of all Government Ministries and Departments
the Chairman of the Regional Employers' Association
the Head of the Trades Union Congress in the Region
the Clerks of Urban/Municipal Councils in the Region
the Chairmen of the Urban/Municipal Councils in the Region
two or three persons representing leading commercial, industrial, banking institutions in the Region
a professional Regional Planner (Secretary).

All of these people are to attend as ex-officio members. In addition, provision was made for the inclusion of public spirited people in the

---

10 Mr. E. N. Omaboe, Commissioner of Economic Affairs: address at the inauguration of the Eastern Regional Planning Committee, 20th January, 1968.

regions, such as university lecturers, enlightened farmers, energetic private businessmen, professionals such as engineers, lawyers, doctors etc. in private practice in the Region, zealous heads of leading religious organizations, influential and patriotic women, and secondary school teachers. Public spirited persons are "those desirous of seeing the Region develop at a more rapid rate of growth than has been possible in the past".

The specific functions of the regional planning committees include:

– to collect data on all local resources for purposes of regional development planning;
– to submit proposals on the utilization of available local resources to the Ministry of Economic Affairs (now Economic Planning Division, Ministry of Finance and Economic Planning) and to the relevant Ministerial Sectoral programming units;
– to coordinate regional development activities;
– to implement regional development projects, whether or not sponsored by government, private enterprise, cooperatives or self-help ventures;
– to initiate local and regional development activities;
– to report regularly and timely on a quarterly basis on all activities on the economic development of the Region to the Ministry of Economic Affairs.

The methods by which the Government hope to achieve a balanced regional development include greater emphasis on agriculture which is important in all regions of the country. "In addition, studies will be pursued under the aegis of the Central Government, in order to reveal the economic potentials of the various regions. Efforts will be made to encourage the siting of some new factories in suitable parts of the country outside the present main industrial areas."[11] Another tool which the Government hope to rely upon is the budget. In each budget, a certain amount (N¢ 2 million in the last budget) is to be set aside out of which the regions can finance projects of particular regional significance.

It is two years since these regional planning committees were inaugurated in the various regions of Ghana, accompanied by the general hope that at long last planning in Ghana was to be placed

11   *Ibid.*

on a proper footing. Unfortunately, this has not been the case, for several reasons.

The apparent ineffectiveness of the regional planning committees resulted from a sterile approach to regional planning. Under the existing system, regional planning committees are not shown the limits of their resources. Moreover, they are not directly responsible for formulating regional plans. Regional committees receive copies of the estimates of expenditure prepared by the regional departments for the parent ministries in Accra. They may make recommendations, but sometimes these are rejected by the parent Ministries. In their present role, regional committees are best described as discussion forums, "information bureaux and project inspectorates".

The basic fault is that the regional committees have been imposed on a system in which they have no place – a sort of 'ministerial system' which provides for the formulation of plans by programming units in the various ministries. Under the present arrangement, the regional committees serve the sectoral planning units when it should be the other way around. Sectoral planning is certainly an essential tool; however, in a country such as Ghana where regional planning has been adopted as a policy, one would have thought that the sectoral programming units would be organized within the regional planning committees. A new approach is clearly required.

It has been stated elsewhere in this paper that planning should start from the grassroots, so that those for whom plans are made might participate in identifying their own needs and in making policies. To do this it is suggested that:

1. the Central Planning Agency presently based at the Ministry of Finance and Economic Planning in Accra be reconsitituted;
2. the regional planning committees be similarly reconstituted to function as bona fide agencies of the above Central Agency in Accra;
3. district as well as local planning committees be set up to function as local branches of the regional committees.

These planning agencies should be made up as follows:
(i) a team of professional planners with background training in various disciplines;
(ii) representatives of the regional planning committees. Since these committees will be regional branches of the central planning agency and regional plans (with modifications) will partly constitute the

national plan, it is important that the regional committees be represented;

(iii) representatives of the ministries, public corporations, research organizations and financial institutions in the country. Almost invariably, these will be affected by whatever programmes and policies are formulated and should therefore be represented on the Central Planning Agency. The inclusion of financial institutions will enable their expertise to be called upon in formulating the monetary policies to be pursued;

(iv) representatives of private business groups in the country. The idea is to seek their views on certain policies as well as to acquaint them with proposed government policies so that they can fit in their own programmes.

The Regional Planning Committees should include the following members:

(i) the Regional Chief Executive;

(ii) the Regional Administrative Officers;

(iii) a team of professional regional planners with background training in economics, geography, sociology, engineering, agriculture, law, political science etc. This is necessary since regional planning is an inter-disciplinary profession;

(iv) representatives of the district planning committees. Since the district plans (properly examined and reviewed) will partly constitute the regional plan, it is necessary that they should be represented;

(v) regional heads of ministries and public corporations;

(vi) representatives of the regional branches of the Chamber of Commerce, Trades Union Congress, Manufacturers' Associations etc. This is intended to facilitate private business by integrating it into the plan of the appropriate district. This should guarantee, for example, the facilities required for successful operation of viable private business.

The District Planning Committees should comprise the following members:

(i) Members of Parliament from the District, whose presence should provide a link between the government and the people;

(ii) representatives of the local planning committees;

(iii) Paramount Chiefs in the district;

(iv) the District Ministerial Heads;

(v) one or two regional planners.

The Local Planning Committees should consist of the following members:
(i) the local chief;
(ii) the Members of Parliament representing the area;
(iii) the Chairman and Treasurer of the City, Municipal or Local Council;
(iv) the regional planner(s) in the district.

The establishment of District and Local Committees is meant to ensure that plan formulation starts with the grassroots.

In order that the regional committees prepare internally consistent plans, the limits of available resources should in the first instance be made known to them. This is indispensable since planning consists essentially of matching objectives with 'possibilities'. This is to prevent regional plans being hacked and mutilated on the gronds that there is no money so that thcy are ruined before their implementation starts. To overcome this problem, it is suggested that:

1. the whole planning exercise could start with the allocation of resources among the various regions accompanied by a statement of guidelines. Allocations could be computed, for example, on the basis of (a) existing levels of development in the various regions, (b) population, (c) the potential for development – allocations being inversely proportional to (a) and directly proportional to (b) and (c);
2. subsequently, the regional planning committees should work out allocations to the district planning committees, after setting aside part of the regional allocation to projects which, by reason of large-scale economies etc., are better undertaken at the regional level, e.g. a specialist hospital.

The district committees will do the same *vis-à-vis* the local committees, also after setting aside part of the allocations for projects which, for reasons of size and scale, are better undertaken at the district level, e.g. health centre.

It has already been stated that the original allocations to the regional committees by the Central Planning Agency should be accompanied by some guidelines, e.g. national priorities. Armed with information on the funds at their disposal (both from government and from their own resources e.g. rates, levies etc.) and the priorities and guidelines stated by the Central Planning Agency and the regional and district planning committees, the local planning bodies would work out their development plans which will then be submitted to and examined for internal consistency by the district planning committee. The various local plans coordinated (together with the projects worked out by the district planning committees) would form the district plan.

The various district plans will go to the regional planning committees and will also be examined and coordinated (together with projects designed by the regional planning committees) to produce a regional plan.

The resultant regional plans from the regional committees together with projects which, again by consideration of size etc., will have to be designed and planned by the Central Planning Agency, after proper coordination and examination as to their internal consistency, will form the national plan.

The virtues of this approach are as follows:

1. the national development plan would essentially be formulated by the people who are ultimately charged with its implementation. These will include the departments, corporations, private companies and the people at large. The requisite enthusiasm for the successful implementation of the plans will therefore be available;
2. since those on the scene would be largely responsible for formulating the plan, the plans should be reasonably related to the environment at each place and time. This is indispensable for the success of the plan;
3. the age-old problem of imbalanced regional development, which is the root cause of tribalism, would be contained since every region would have its due share of the nation's resources and would be primarily responsible for deciding how to utilize it.

IV

PARTICIPATION IN DECISION MAKING

7

H. J. A. MORSINK

REGIONAL PLAN FORMULATION AND POPULAR PARTICIPATION WITH SPECIAL REFERENCE TO LATIN AMERICA

The Governments which voted in favour of the United Nations Resolution calling for a world-wide programme of research and training in regional development considered as one of the motivations for sponsoring regional development the urgent need to promote modernization in the cities and the countryside.[1]

Governments define in various ways the actual meaning and content of the term 'modernization'. A growing number of governments and politicians consider that modernization implies a gradual or abrupt transformation in the social structure of society, and a general democratization of the process of decision-making in society.

Some government leaders and politicians recognize the obstacles impeding their nation-wide efforts aiming at social transformation and democratization. Some have therefore capitalized on regional development to supplement general nation-wide measures with specific action programmes, concentrating on selected regions and explicitly aiming at a profound transformation of the social structure of society in those regions. An outstanding example of this approach is the planned development of the KOSMET region in Yugoslavia over the past decades.[2] In this case, a change in the political and social system at the national level preceded the formulation of policies and the implementation of action aiming at a transformation of the social system at the regional level.

Other governments have recognized wider popular participation as one of the ultimate goals of development, but their leaders have not yet defined its meaning and content in operational terms,[3] and

---

[1] United Nations Economic and Social Council Resolution 1086 C (XXXIX).
[2] See Miodrag Nikolic, "Autonomous Province of Kosovo and Metohija", *Medunarodna Politika* (Belgrade, 1965, No. 5, 43 pages).
[3] ECLA, "Popular participation and principles of community development in

no single broad policy can be discerned as the central one in relation to popular participation in the life of the nation.[4]

At the same time, the overall political climate in many of these countries remains unresponsive to effective involvement of the entire population in the economic, social and administrative and political decisions facing the nation in its process of development. The majority of the people have long been excluded from the tasks of government and the furthering of development.[5] Moreover, while "present lines of economic growth and social change are of a nature to exclude rather than foster popular participation", "there is only lukewarm support in central policy and decision-making layers for creating instruments of local institutional change and participation."[6] Attitudes prevailing in key-groups such as the local power-elites, local business circles, the church, the military, the press, have not yet generally evolved to a point where vigorous support to further democratization is being given. Generally, in these countries, the prevailing centre-local relationship, between the capital city and the rest of the country and between the central Government and authorities at lower levels, has not facilitated any initiative toward broadening the basis of democracy.[7]

It is in particular in relation to this latter group of countries that professional persons dealing with regional planning are currently opening discussions on the broad issues of models for the society of the future.[8] Recent discussions sponsored by the United Nations pointed to a high degree of consensus among specialists from Eastern Europe, Western Europe and Latin America as regards the ultimate goal of social transformation and democratization of society in regional planning and in regional plans.[9]

In practice, however, there is an increased risk that goals in regional policies and regional plans become ambivalent in a situ-

relation to the acceleration of economic and social development", *Economic Bulletin for Latin America*, Vol. IX, No. 2, November 1964, p. 227.

[4] ECLA, "Second United Nations Development Decade" *Social Change and Social Development Policy in Latin America* (1969), p. 370.

[5] ECLA, "Popular participation", *op. cit.*, p. 228.

[6] ECLA, "Second United Nations Development Decade", *op. cit.*, pp. 352 and 375.

[7] ECLA, "Rural Settlement Patterns and Social Change in Latin America", *Economic Bulletin for Latin America*, Vol. X, 1965, pp. 1-22.

[8] UNRISD, *Goals in Regional Policies and Objectives in Regional Planning* (Geneva, 1969, 56 pages).

[9] Rubén D. Utria, "Draft Report of the Workshop on the Sociology of Regional Development" held in Geneva on 11, 12 and 13 November 1968 (United Nations Research Institute for Social Development, 1969, 51 pages).

ation where government leaders and politicians have not yet defined their concept of wider popular participation (and in fact, may wish to use planned social change in order to prevent upheaval) while, on the other hand, the planning profession may wish to insert progressive democratic ideas into the future model. In order to get their goals accepted in such a situation, planners may feel tempted to promise simultaneously (but to different groups in the region): preservation and change; past and future. Goals presenting such different faces may at first obtain common consent almost without scrutiny. However, it may prove difficult to translate such goals into concrete, quantified, objectives and targets, It may even prove more difficult to implement such goals as various groups gradually discover the points on which the plan contradicts their group interests and *their* view of popular participation.

Whether or not wider popular participation is among the explicitly recognized goals of regional planning, any public planning, including regional planning, is universally considered to be more valid and effective the more it is (a) rational, (b) comprehensive and (c) reflecting the interests of those for whom the plan is made.

Here the question arises: to what extent do regional planners, including those who aspire to a complete transformation of social structure, meet these three criteria in their formulation of regional policies and regional plans?

Regional development planning as a profession is only now emerging and hardly any evaluations are available to allow this question to be answered. However, a closely related professional specialist of established academic standing is the city planner, whose claims towards building for a new society at city-scale show a remarkable resemblance to the claims of today's regional planners towards constructing a new society at a regional scale. Evaluations have been made of the professional performance of city planners and of the plans they produce.

a) A sociological evaluation of western town and country planning (in particular in the United States and Great Britain) was made by Ruth Glass.[10] This evaluation points out that in the planning profession the 'planners', namely, the architects, engineers, surveyors and administrators, are all specialists in their own field, used

---

[10] Ruth Glass, "The Evaluation of Planning, Some Sociological Considerations" in *Regional Planning* combined Nos 12 and 13 of *Housing, Building and Planning*, UN, 1959, pp. 51-57.

to a mechanistic model of thought, and that each one considers planning as a new professional label added to the previous one. As regards the reflection of the people's best interests in the plans, Ruth Glass notes that planners in Great Britain under-estimate the people's desire and capacity to change, stress the preservation of the status quo, take their own subjective preferences to be objective and universal, and easily call the interests of some groups 'the public interest'. It should be noted that this evaluation focused on a country with a universally recognized high standard of training and professional competence among its planning profession.

b) Thomas A. Reiner, after analyzing 20 city plans presented during the period 1896-1947 by world-famous town-planners, concludes with regard to their logical consistency that in many cases the conclusions simply do not follow from stated assumptions; that often neither goals nor assumptions are clearly stated; that often also neither the source nor the degree of certainty of the goals are identified and, finally, that there is sometimes even confusion as to whether the plan is intended as an actual plan of action or only as a logical demonstration of theoretical possibilities. As regards comprehensiveness, Reiner notes that sometimes the entire economic or social situation of the planned city is left out of consideration, and that in general there is little recognition by the planners of the limitations of their approaches. Insofar as some regional planners today pretend to accurately reflect the wishes of the population by mixing their political views with their professional thinking, it may be interesting to note that, in the city plans he reviewed, Reiner could not detect a consistency of approach according to the political bias of the authors.[11]

c) Françoise Choay analyses the basic ideas and ideals which have inspired town and country planners, including Walter Gropius, Le Corbusier, Camillo Sitte, Ebenezer Howard, Raymond Unwin, Frank Lloyd Wright, Eugène Hénard, Iannis Xenakis, Patrick Geddes, Marcel Poéte, Lewis Mumford and Keven Lynch. She brilliantly demonstrates to what extent in various parts of the world planners have taken their own subjective preferences and value-systems to be objective and universal. In her conclusions she warns the citizen not to be misled by the myth of 'scientific' town and

11 Thomas A. Reiner, *The Place of the Ideal Community in Urban Planning* (University of Pennsylvania Press, 1963, 194 pages).

country planning. The idea itself of scientific town and country planning is in her opinion one of the myths of the industrial society.[12]

These short notes from some current evaluations of the contribution made by town and country planners confirm the urgency of raising the same question among regional planners: to what extent do regional planners take their subjective models for the future of society in certain regions to be objective and universal in the sense of reflecting the true interests of the population at large? It is true that there is a growing feeling that construction of models or of 'preconceived schemes of social progress' is not feasible, and that attention should focus on the identification and definition of values and goals to guide planning as a continuing and open-ended process.[13] However, this recognition does not in any way diminish the urgency of this basic question, which can be re-formulated as follows: how can regional planners ensure that their plans become more rational, more comprehensive and more truly a reflection of the people's aspirations, needs and demands?[14]

At present, most regional planners are located in national civil services, mainly in national capitals, and a few in capitals of regions or districts. These regional planners deal mainly with problems of disaggregation of national targets and with problems of aggregation of local targets into intra-regional plans within the framework of the directives contained in the national plan. These notes focus on the question of popular participation in relation to the formulation of intra-regional or mono-regional plans and policies.

The view has been expressed that the region is the level where the forces behind social problems orginate, where specific solutions can best be found, and where efforts can best be pooled to implement the suggested solutions.[15]

This view does not exclude that there may be a clear conflict of interests among political and economic forces operating in the region. For instance, conflicts among established forces within the

12 Françoise Choay, *L'Urbanisme, utopies et réalités, une anthologie* (Paris: Editions du Seuil, 1965, 448 pages).
13 ECLA, "Second United Nations Development Decade", *op. cit.*
14 "How public opinion and professional expertise should be institutionalized is an open problem in some countries." Quoted from: Antoni R. Kuklinski, "Growth Poles and Growth Centres in Regional Policies and Planning, and Institutional Perspective" (Toulouse, 19-24 May, 1969, 7 pages).
15 Rubén D. Utria, "Development as a Social Phenomenon and its Implications for Social Policy and Programmes at the Regional Level" (Geneva, November 1968, 46 pages), in particular pp. 31-35.

region (e.g. between importers and businessmen, between crop farmers and livestock producers)[16] and conflicts between the regional 'establishment' and newly emerging forces.[17]

In relation to formulating a regional plan, some of the following groups will have interests to promote or to defend:[18]

a) the government, represented by its planning office and by local offices of vertical central government organizations (e.g. ministries and agencies for public works, agriculture, mining, education);
b) local politicians, representing to some extent the interests of local power élites, big landowners, large industries, business and utilities, etc.;
c) service institutions, including government sponsored banks and credit institutions;
d) foreign technical assistance in the region;
e) medium and smaller private enterprises, perhaps represented in a chamber of commerce;
f) the large majority of the population: the adult male population, mainly peasants and labourers, perhaps represented in peasant and labour organizations; adult women, and youth.

These groups differ:

a) in the amount and type of political power, social prestige and economic resources which they can marshall to buttress their aspirations concerning the content of the regional plan;
b) in their interests in relation to the plan (big business: e.g. profit and sometimes non-economic prestige behaviour; small land-owners: e.g. defence of old rights; government: e.g. protecting tax

---

[16] ECLA, "Popular participation and principles of community development", op. cit., p. 231.

[17] It is interesting to note that some recent United Nations papers concerning regional planning and development planning suggest explicitly an analysis of social change in terms of possible social conflict between groups, collectivities and other categories among the population, for example:
a) ECLA, "Social change and social development policy in Latin America", 1969, op. cit., in particular pp. 352-64 on conflicts between "collectivities"
b) Hubert J. A. Morsink, "Five Fields for a Sociology of Regional Development, Suggestions for a United Nations Programme", (UNRISD/68/C.46, 1968, 20 pages), in particular pp. 10-13 dealing with "Social Transformation" and the role of power.

[18] Cf. the following article: Bernard Le Compte, "Eléments pour une recherche sur l'Organization de l'Aide (interne et externe) au développement rural", in Développement et Civilisations, June, 1969, pp. 8-23.

values; protecting land for public use; promoting economic development);

c) in their internal organization and external relations (e.g. local government offices may show lack of coordination between different agencies; small farmers may not at all be organized);

d) as to whom the group is responsible (foreign technical assistance experts to foreign government or international organizations; a big corporation to the parent company and to stockholders; small enterprises only to themselves).

As regards the degree of internal organization and the impact of external relations of collectivities, the ECLA study *Social Change and Social Development Policy in Latin America* (1969-376) presents a most valuable analytical framework for their classification. This study also provides several examples of the importance of such organizations and associations in obtaining a voice for categories of the population hitherto excluded from active participation in the process of decision making in public affairs.

The inclusion of these groups and interests in the process of plan formulation will have the following advantages for the regional planners:

a) it provides the planner and all participants with more information about the interests to be represented in the plan;

b) it may assist the planner in a more realistic formulation of goals, objectives and targets;

c) it may assist the planner to make a better allocation of means;

d) it will make people aware that the regional plan is not being imposed by outsiders formulating a plan "chez nous, sur nous et sans nous"; in that sense it may promote identification of the population with the plan;

e) it may help mobilize resources available within the region in terms of finance, land, labour and commitments;

f) as regards commitments, it may facilitate progress in mutual trust and understanding to a point where several parties participating in regional plan formulation may be willing to commit themselves contractually to perform their tasks as envisaged in the plan;

g) even without such contractual commitments, it may facilitate early adoption of the plan at the regional level;

h) it will encourage continuous evaluation of the plan and its implementation by all concerned insofar as this implies an element of continuing mutual control or general supervision by all those who participated in the formulation of the plan.

In all these respects, an effective inclusion of these groups makes the process perhaps more rational, certainly more comprehensive, and definitely more democratic. Some governments are becoming aware of this. For example, the Government of France, fully recognising that the success of regional development efforts depends on popular participation, drew up its plans for regions of Brittany and the Massif Central in close consultation with industry and with agricultural, trade union and local organizations.[19]

When discussing popular participation in plan formulation, it seems useful to distinguish between participation in the sense of expressing an opinion without taking responsibility for its implementation; and participation in the sense of accepting a responsibility for its implementation in terms of finance, labour, or moral commitment. This distinction permits us to see more clearly the difference in maximum participation which each group can possibly be allowed to enjoy. On the other hand, even when participation means only an exchange of views and opinions, such participation in plan formulation should be real and effective, as distinct from a ceremonial 'pseudo-participation' on ineffective committees or boards whose decisions will be ignored, mislaid, or otherwise made ineffective.[20]

With regard to organizational structure for wider popular participation in the process of plan formulation at the regional level, several solutions can be tried within the region of their jurisdiction by existing regional planning offices and agencies:

a) an *ad hoc advisory council*, with some members appointed and others elected, directly or indirectly. The council's elected members could be chosen from among the general public or from special interest groups as listed above;
b) *public hearings* on draft regional plans prepared by the regional planning office;
c) a *permanent advisory council*;

---

19   See ECOSOC E/CN.5/SR.414 (22 September 1966, p. 11).
20   See United Nations: European Social Development Programmes: Seminar on Rural Community Development, Madrid, 21-28 April 1968. *Final Report* (New York, 1969), p. 73, on different forms of pseudo-participation.

d) a *people's spokesman* assigned and paid by the regional planning office to take the initiative in exploring the demands of all groups in the region in order to transmit them to the regional planners for consideration. This official would be open to public suggestions as to the content of the regional plan. He would be in close contact with all groups mentioned above. An essential characteristic of his function would be that he would be free to take the initiative in making or transmitting suggestions to the regional planning officers.[21]

A study published by ECLA indicates some of the obstacles to any of these solutions, such as: the sparseness of population and the topographical barriers limiting contacts between rural populations and urban centres; the feeling of superiority prevailing among urban residents towards the rural population; the direct intervention of hacienda management in public affairs while isolating the resident workers from such public affairs, and the suspicion among large segments of the rural population that any official activity is a subterfuge for some new exploitation, Especially important for any attempts towards more widely involving the population in regional plan formulation at the regional level are the observed attempts by the rural population not to link with *municipio* or district level authorities in order to avoid abuse, and to link directly with the national level.[22]

The question arises, therefore, whether any of these four suggested institutional solutions can bring about wider popular participation in regional plan formulation, or whether perhaps a more gradual preparation of the ground would be called for.

This preparation might consist of:

a) accepting any of the four suggested forms step by step, for example as regards: the *issues* to be discussed or the *stages* of plan formulation at which consultations are held; as regards the *groups* being consulted; as regards the *degree* of consultation of these groups, etc.

21 Compare suggestions recently made for a *Tribunis Plebis* in city government. See, for instance, "Popular Participation and Representation" chapter V of a forthcoming publication by the United Nations Public Administration Division on *Administrative Aspects of Urbanization* (Second draft of Chapter, 1969, 28 pages).
22 ECLA, "Rural Settlement Patterns and Social Change in Latin America", *Economic Bulletin for Latin America*, Vol. X, 1965, pp. 1-22.

b) finding other and more modest institutional solutions for wider participation of the groups listed above.

Whatever solution will be adopted, the State through its civil servants will have to play a key role in two respects:
a) in providing the general framework and guidelines for the formulation of the content of regional plans;[23]
b) in promoting wider popular participation in the regional planning process through information, education and organization of all partners involved in the process of development.[24]

[23]   United Nations, *Local Participation in Development Planning* (New York, 1967, 64 pages).
[24]   See ECLA, "Social change and social development policy in Latin America", 1969, *op. cit.*, p. 376.

8

PIETER C. J. VAN LOON

THE PROCESS OF REGIONAL POLICY FORMULATION IN THE NETHERLANDS

1. INTRODUCTION

To provide a better understanding of the Dutch perspective I shall begin my examination of the regionalisation of national policy in the Netherlands with a brief – partially historical – description of the system of public administration. In my examination itself I intend to distinguish three periods:

   i. 1949 – 1959
  ii. 1959 – 1969
 iii. 1970 and the future.

1.1. *Central, Provincial and Municipal Government*

1.1.1. *Central Government*

Economic affairs are dealt with by three ministries, namely the ministries of Economic Affairs, of Social Affairs and Public Health and of Finance. Naturally, the Ministry of Agriculture and Fisheries also fulfills an important socio-economic function and since the agrarian crisis in the 1930s agrarian affairs have been more centralised than have those of other government branches.

On the social side the Ministries of Education and Science, and of Culture, Recreation and Social Work contribute fundamentally to social planning, other essential components of which are provided by the Ministry of Social Affairs and Public Health already mentioned, and also by the Ministry of Housing and Physical Planning.

The Ministry of the Interior is responsible for the supervision of provincial and local government, for stimulating administrative reforms and for changes in administrative boundaries. The Ministry of Housing and Physical Planning is, as its name suggests, primarily responsible for physical planning.

On several occasions Government policy has been stated as directed towards a realisation of the following goals:
- an increase in prosperity;
- full employment;
- a stable financial situation;
- a just distribution of income;
- equilibrium in the balance of trade.

Its efforts are also oriented towards the formulation of a social policy that aims at improving the well-being of the national population. Economic development is fundamental to our ability to achieve these ends.

The central aim of the structural policy is a rapid economic growth which can be maintained for a long period. Proceeding on the proposition that the rapidly growing working population should largely be employed in industry, the emphasis lies on the industrialisation policy, which is related with the promotion of exports and productivity. The industrialisation policy is based on five-yearly forecasts regarding the industrial development; regularly Parliament takes note of it, when the Government explains its expectations and measures in this field in the so-styled Industrialisation Notes. The measures are aimed particularly at the preservation of a high and stable level of investments – which is pursued through investment facilities – and at a sound spreading of industries over the whole country.[1]

1.1.2. *The Provinces*[2]

Even in the 18th century the Netherlands was not a state in the modern sense of the word. It was really a loose confederation of the Seven – sovereign – United Netherlands (the rather loosely fanned bunch of arrows held by the lion in the Netherlands coat of arms is an excellent symbol of it) around which some other provinces which were not yet regarded worthy of participating in the confederation as full-fledged partners also grouped themselves. These provinces now constitute together the eleven provinces of the Netherlands. They are autonomous administrative units, whose powers have been laid down by the Constitution and by the law.

In view of their considerable independence during the era of the Republic of the Seven United Netherlands, the Constitution of 1814 sought to curtail the autonomous powers of the provinces as strictly as possible. As autonomous administrative units these provinces at first developed very little initiative of their own: financially they

---

[1] Prof. A. Kleijn, "The Administrative Organisation of the Netherlands' in *Planning and Development in the Netherlands*, No. 1, 1962.
[2] This section is based on the text of Kleijn *ibid*.

were simply not capable of it. However, their administrative powers have increased continually since then. Various kinds of institutions were established at a provincial level, in close conjunction with the provincial administration which itself became active in the fields of health and economic and social affairs. However, their chief administrative role remains that of an intermediary between the Government and the municipalities, and as guardian of the municipalities which fall under their control.

1.1.3. *The Municipalities*

Notwithstanding their provincial guardianship, the Netherlands municipalities – and especially the towns, which have long had an important share in the administrative task – came to play an increasingly important role in the course of the 19th century. The roughly 1,050 municipalities (whose numbers were gradually reduced to some 975 by 1960 as a result of border corrections and annexations) constituted, as it were, administrative laboratories, within which all kinds of new tasks for public administration were conceived, worked out and implemented.

The importance of many of these tasks was in time recognised by the central government and embodied in some new acts which compelled *all* municipalities, including those which had so far shown no or insufficient initiative of their own, to undertake responsibility for their execution. The Building and Housing Act of 1901 which contained the first regulations with regard to physical planning is a case in point.

Thus administration in the Netherlands has been organised according to a hierarchical three-tier system under which the provinces, in the course of the years, have gradually gained influence and under which the nature of the municipal task has changed considerably. Whereas formerly the municipalities held an autonomous position, issuing and carrying out regulations on their own initiative, their tasks have now assumed a more executive character.

2. REGIONAL POLICY DURING THE PERIOD 1949-1959

2.1. *Population increase and the decrease of employment in agriculture*

In 1949 the first industrialisation memorandum was adopted by the government. At the time the country was faced with an unexpected increase in population growth (the so-called postwar bulge) and unemployment was anticipated for when these people would enter the labour market. The decreasing employment opportunities in agriculture were taken seriously into account. The Ministry of Agriculture, supported by farmers' organisations and farm-workers, pleaded for the use of more modern agricultural methods, for mechanisation and rationalisation in order to increase agricultural production. But alternative employment had to be made available in order to facilitate the transfer of the farmers' sons into other sectors. There was also a fear that there was going to be a deficit on the balance of payments and this had to be in equilibrium at any cost before the Marshall Plan terminated in 1953. It was against this background that the first regional industrialisation programmes emerged.

2.2. *Aspects of the first stage of regional industrialisation*

2.2.1. *Areas with surplus labour*

The first industrialisation memorandum discussed in the States-General (the Dutch Parliament) emphasised the importance of industrialising the areas that had surplus labour. One of the considerations that was mentioned was that separating workers from the agricultural environment in which they grew up might have serious social and moral consequences. The moral dangers were usually illustrated with examples of the moral deterioration of workers from North Brabant who had migrated to Rotterdam before 1940.

The Government would only support the industrialisation of certain rural areas on condition that favourable factors for settlement should exist, or be developed. Throughout the period (1949-1959) it was thought that industrial settlement could be achieved if a number of hampering factors of a formal and material nature could be eliminated – the stepping stone theory. The 1955 industrialisation memorandum made clear the fact that the existence of surplus labour could not be countered by making an immediate offer of employment.

It was in this memorandum that a paragraph was devoted for the first time to social planning in development areas as a means of providing an impetus to the process of economic development. The social climate was to be improved so that it would attract entrepreneurs and management officials from elsewhere and so that they would be willing to settle in the depressed areas of the country.

2.2.2. *Infrastructural facilities*

Government support was provided in the following areas:
- in preparing industrial sites for construction;
- in linking these sites with the existing road system;
- in expanding connections for gas, electricity and water supplies;
- in the construction of industrial housing;
- in the construction of industrial plants.

It is not surprising that the municipalities in development areas began to compete for industries. The industries that were set up received subsidies for the construction of factories and other industrial buildings. It became a competition between some 90 municipalities.

2.2.3. *Education and occupational re-training*

From the start of these regional policies special attention was given to vocational training and occupational re-training. The Ministry of Education and Science encouraged enterprising teachers to enter primary education and promoted opportunities for technical vocational training which was very often to be completed in industrial schools. The Ministry of Social Affairs and Health also saw to the establishment of workshops for vocational training which provided resettlement training, especially for older people.

However, although this training undoubtedly encouraged the development of a more technically oriented social climate among the young, the industries that could be attracted to these areas were usually too small to produce the type of results that had been expected.

2.2.4. *Social aspects of industrialisation*

In terms of its social climate the Netherlands after 1945 was still an agrarian nation. Outside the main industrial centres there was a predominant agrarian sphere where norms and behaviour patterns were still based on rural relationships. Churches and religious groups struck the key-note but also in non-religious agrarian areas, attachment to earth and nature was strongly felt. The youths and older people who went to work in industry were looked upon as outcasts by the local community. It took courage to go against this dominant behavioral pattern.

In provinces such as Noord-Brabant, Drente and Friesland which felt strong regional attachments, attempts were made to plead for industrialisation with the leaders of the main denomination groups. Joint efforts were made to take care of possible moral and social consequences by means of certain measures of social guidance both for individuals and for families.

But the Central Government never tried to support this social movement even though it was based on regional characteristics and directed at the province as a regional entity. It remained aloof and possibly afraid of regionalisation (territorial decentralisation) from below. That there was a provincially inspired movement in support of industrialisation can nevertheless be illustrated, for example, by the welfare plans for the province of Noord-Brabant.[3]

In 1947, the late Bishop Bekkers described the religious-ethical aspect of the Brabant industrialisation as follows:

Industrialisation poses great dangers religiously and ethically. Industrialisation is necessary in order to find means of support for a growing population. However, there is the danger of a division between religious and temporal life. Many people come from agrarian backgrounds. They are not sufficiently able to cope with the degenerative tendencies of industrial life. It is important to establish the industry in the villages because then the people will remain under the protective influence of the familiar environment. The desirable contact with the earth will remain.

There were warnings during this period against moral decay of young girls working together with men. Thus he continued:

In 1946, I led a social movement against employment of female conductors on buses, because of the threat of moral decay. This was done at the request of the collaborating Roman Catholic Church, the Dutch Reformed Church, the Calvinist Church and the Humanist circles.

We may say in summary that the social climate in the Dutch development areas of 1949 showed barriers which were social-

---

[3]   Proposals for the welfare plan for the province of Noord-Brabant No. 1, October 1957; No. 2, March 1949; No. 3, also March 1949.

psychologically and social-structurally analogous to the case of other European development areas.[4]

However, a fundamental difference may be distinguished. In the different European development areas a lack of motivation is frequently mentioned as well as a lack of interest in innovation and a resistance to improvement and social change. Indeed, there seems to have been a counter-current running against any form of adaption and change.[5] But in contrast the strength of effective social elements in the religious and social life of the Netherlands at this time introduced motivation and inspiration into the Dutch development areas. Supportive social development was thereby taken up in order to make possible economic development in favour of the population. The negative effects of social change in the microsphere were taken care of as far as possible. A severance of existing norms and familiar behavioral patterns may have been feared by the social leaders in these regions but they nevertheless became social pioneers.

2.2.5. *The joint efforts of local, regional and national forces in the social field*

It seems useful to look at the causes of this break-through of inspiration and motivation. In some agrarian provinces provincial bodies for community organisation were set up during the agrarian crisis. They were led by socially motivated pioneers who were prepared to act against the government policy. Moreover, after World War II, there was a general willingness on the part of these pioneers to join hands and to work together. The need for a dynamic social approach to the stimulation of industrialisation presented them with a challenge, and in the face of it the different religous denominations and humanist circles decided to collaborate in provincial bodies for social development.

In 1952 a new Ministry, the Ministry of Social Work, was created through a political power game. It was manned on the whole by young functionaries who had no idea yet of official tradition or of the power game in inter-departmental relations. The first Ministers of

---

[4] Cf. report on the "European Seminar on Social Research and Community Development in European Problem Areas", Palermo, Sicily, 8-18 June 1958 (United Nations in Geneva).

[5] Cf. P. C. J. van Loon, "International Aid to Developing Countries", *Maandblad Economie*, Vol. 6, March 1952; "The Human Factor in the Economic Development of Backward Areas", *Economisch en Sociaal Tijdschrift*, VI. 3, June 1952; "Increased Effectiveness of International Cooperation", Ch. 3, Part V, of *Welvaart, Welzijn en Geluk* (Hilversum, 1963) (all written in Dutch).

Social Work, Mr. van Thiel, and Miss Klompé, felt personally called upon to inspire social adaptation for industrialisation. They also established contact with national leaders of the many denominational groups, agricultural organisations and various organisations in the field of social work.

Yet, in some areas, it appeared as if certain local religious leaders were not prepared to yield to pressures from administrative centres. The Minister of Social Work enabled churches and humanist organisations to appoint special counsellors for the developing areas. But these were exclusively concerned with putting in motion local religious and social groups. In the sphere of municipal government in the agrarian areas social work had as yet been given neither shape nor form. Hence, efforts took place with the approval of the burgomasters, but without the involvement of the municipal apparatus in influencing this social adaptation. The municipal administration came into action only when preparations were made to provide housing, village centres, clubs etc. The social movement itself remained a free enterprise of religiously inspired leaders and their groups.

Thus the first efforts to stimulate social action were both manifold and dynamic, and social life was subjected to the influence of many powers and changing circumstances. On the other hand it was to a certain extent limited because television, the modern communication medium, was missing. Local and regional press associations devoted all attention to social development, however, and provided space in their papers for the various local leaders.

At the rural level the Ministry of Social Work, in consultation with representatives of the churches and social organisations, decided to undertake social research through a number of sociological research institutes which were organised along denominational lines. The social researchers' discussions on the more isolated areas led to a better awareness of existing social problems and provided in a sense the first signs of a consciously organised participation by the local population. As a result of these new efforts in research and participation a new form of cooperation developed between the Ministries of Social Affairs and Health, Agriculture and Fisheries, Education and Science and Economic Affairs.

This found expression in the formation of an Interministerial Committee for the Development Areas which both advised ministers and reviewed plans.

After 20 years, I have come to the conclusion that the impetus of this social movement was established only because the local social leaders knew themselves to be completely and unconditionally backed by the population. These social leaders – ministers of religions, teachers, leaders of farmers' organisations etc. – appealed to feelings of self-respect, responsibility and active participation by preparing and executing measures designed by the people themselves. The rallying-cry could still be used that local conditions were insufficiently developed and that the social-cultural standards of the population should be raised. There were improvements in social-hygiene through the more rapid creation of health centres, increases in the number of district nurses, the promotion of creativity and initiative through clubwork etc.

Government support through the provision of infrastructural facilities may be seen as a regionalisation of national policy. But the regionalisation of national policy pursued by the Ministry of Social Work in collaboration with the national churches and humanist organisations was a much more drastic regionalisation in the eyes of the population than were infrastructural measures in the economy.

However, industry also played a decisive role in that it organised, albeit in consultation with local leaders, the process of social adaptation within the factories. The industrial leaders who set up their enterprises in these areas also acted as social pioneers and with great imagination. The influence of young women's education in industry produced a chain-reaction in village communities. Young people taught their parents new developments in areas such as hygiene and living conditions. The presence of social leaders in industry was the decisive link in the impetus towards strong industrialisation in Emmen, Drachten and the south-east of Noord-Brabant. Development in this sphere, through the collaboration of church leaders, factory managers, farmers' leaders and government authorities, must have made a strong impact on the rural population of the 1950s.

Whether this process of systematic, socially guided adaptation can be labeled social planning remains an open question. But it would seem wise to consider it a social movement which was deeply rooted in the population.

The conclusion to be drawn from this short examination of the social movement to adapt the population to industrialisation may be that it was the combined actions of private forces at the national, regional and local levels, that was decisive and that the functioning of government authorities should be seen only as a lever.

2.3. *Effects of the policy*

Although this approach to regional problems during the 1949-59 period was one of one-sided enlightenment in certain areas that had surplus labour, results were nevertheless achieved. During this period the number of jobs in industry increased by 53 percent and grew from 30,000 to 45,600.

3. THE PERIOD 1959-69: A DECENTRALISATION POLICY

3.1. *Introduction*

Throughout this period the government was confronted by a continuing concentration of population in the western part of the country and national policy was directed towards achieving a more balanced distribution over the different regions. It was nevertheless a policy of regional concentration. Measures were taken to encourage the establishment of industries in the different regions, but they were to be concentrated in certain nuclei. It was thought that this would more rapidly create an industrial climate in these areas. The choice of nuclei was based on the so-called regional analyses of the provincial economic institutions and the provincial services for physical planning. Requirements for recreation and tourism were also improved in these areas.

In the considerations of the Ministry of Economic Affairs it was time and again pointed out that the fact that certain areas were lagging behind in terms of their general economic development would lead to the emigration of young people from these areas and result in an increased ageing of the population and impoverishment of its social life. This would aggravate further the problems of developing these areas and would be harmful to the development of the national economy. On the other hand, the central government was also aware that international economic ties were pointing to an expansion and further concentration of economic activities in the western part of the country. The 8th industrialisation memorandum of 1963 placed the Netherlands in a West-European context. The then Minister of Economic Affairs, De Pous, maintained that: "In essence this concerns one unified area favourable for the establishment of industries. The improvement and construction of main roads will more and more emphasise this fact".

Moreover, in announcing the general trends of the economy in

his New Year's Speech 1970, the Chairman of the Socio-Economic
Council also mentioned that Dutch trade movements were running
almost parallel to those of other West European industrial countries and that in general this curtailed the possibility of executing an
independent economic policy. This view is also taken in the second
report on physical planning of 1966 which summarises the aims of
physical planning as the promotion of a physical structure which
can optionally serve in dispersing the population growth. The
report formulates four objectives of national policy:

- to prevent regional labour surpluses;
- to prevent long-distance commuting;
- to prevent strong migration, which could drain economic
  and social life outside the western part of the country;
- to prevent too great a congestion of housing and traffic
  in the concentration areas to the detriment of recreation
  and environmental hygiene.

In as much as an independent economic policy cannot be seen as
feasible, so much more should a policy regarding the objectives of
physical planning be regarded as dependent. In fact, are they physical planning objectives? They have a social character and might
thus be seen as an aspect of social planning – I prefer to say of
socio-economic development planning.

3.2. *Incentives and measures by which to improve the social and economic climate*

3.2.1. *Infrastructural provisions*

In this period (1959-69) emphasis was placed upon freedom of
industrial location. 312 million guilders were voted for infrastructural improvements. In addition the budget of the Ministry of
Roads and Waterways allocated the sum of 110 million guilders
for roads and bridges which were particularly intended for opening
up the development areas.

Industrial location in these areas was stimulated by granting
progressive premiums for the building of factories (from Dfl. 30
to Dfl 60 per m^2). A 50 percent reduction in the price of land was
given to entrepreneurs who were willing to build on specified sites.
In certain cases subsidies were also granted to cover 25 percent of
the expenses of the machine park.

An interesting fact, however, is that economic conditions had curtailed investments in industrial buildings outside the development areas. An average delay of 2 or 3 years before government approval was received for the building of a new factory meant that an entrepreneur needed 4 or 5 years to realise his investment plans. And then it must be remembered that some applications were concerned with modernisation plans, with mechanisation and automation of production processes that could rarely be executed in existing factory buildings.

3.2.2. *Social incentives*

3.2.2.1. *Migration policy.* Financial assistance was given towards removal expenses incurred by workers who accepted employment in a factory in a development region. Employees who would move with a firm from the west of the country to a development region were also helped with their removal expenses.

3.2.2.2. *Training allowances.* In addition to workshop training and re-training, a training allowance was granted to industries which supplied in-service training to workers who were threatened with unemployment as a result of structural changes in the economy.

3.2.3. *Social infrastructure*

During this period there was general agreement that the social infrastructure of the various regions was in need of improvement. The Ministries of Culture, Recreation and Social Work and of Social Affairs and Public Health subsidised the building of theatres, sport halls, service centres, health centres, neighbourhood centres, lending libraries and other recreational facilities.

3.3. *Regional problems and the dispersion policy*

In its 1968 report, the Social Economic Council stated that notwithstanding the recovery in industrial production and the favourable results achieved in the building and agricultural sectors in 1967, employment still decreased by 1 percent. This indicates a reduction of labour needs due to rationalisation of the production process, a shift towards investment in depth, and also an accelerated process of international division of labour. Conurbation Holland shows a general scarcity on the labour market. In the north unemployment is considerable, as it is in Zeeland and part of Overijssel. Noord-Brabant and Limburg have also shown relatively high unemployment figures during the last few years. Moreover, a noticeable regional affiliation restricts the mobility of the population. The following areas can be distinguished.

3.3.1. *Reconversion areas*

These are areas in which existing industry has insufficient economic opportunities and where changes are necessary in the structure of the regional economy. Limburg springs immediately to mind, where the mines are closing down. The textile industry in Central Brabant has little future perspective. The leather and shoe industry is also undergoing serious difficulties. There is good reason to believe that other industries will also encounter structural problems if they persist in retaining their traditional familial character. As a rule, structural difficulties can only be prevented by increasing concentrations and mergers. According to the Ministers of Economic Affairs, and Social Affairs and Public Health, this will affect regional development as a whole.

During this period Limburg and Central Brabant were appointed reconversion areas. Here are mostly older industries which are labour-intensive and whose products have a low income elasticity. These factories have sometimes to reduce their staff fairly drastically. The personnel then have to be re-trained for new jobs, and this has already proved to be the cause of considerable difficulties particularly for the older workers.

3.3.2. *The North of the country*

The entire Northern Netherlands has been declared a developing area. On January 12, 1968 a special memorandum was submitted to the States General regarding the development of this region.

3.3.3. *Lelystad – a bridging function*

Professor van den Berg has pleaded for a connection between the industrial area of North Holland and the north of the country.[6]

6 Prof. G. J. van den Berg, "Condition planning in the West Netherlands", in *Bouw* 6 December 1969.

The industrial development of Lelystad as the centre of the polder-ised area of the IJssel Lake can be considered as offering such a bridge and roads have already been constructed which considerably reduce the distance Amsterdam-Groningen. Enterprises which move from Conurbation Holland to Lelystad are given a premium of *f* 10,000 per male labourer moving with the industry. This incentive is regarded by the central government as a means of reducing the population concentration in Holland.

3.3.4. *Land consolidation areas*

Under 1.2.1. we mentioned that agricultural policy and care for the agrarian population in the Netherlands is more strongly centralised than in the case of other sectors. The Ministry of Agriculture and Fisheries has its own service for the use and management of re-parcelled land holdings – the State Cultivation and Technological Service – which also acts as a sectoral planning service. In co-operation with the agricultural sector and the employees' organi-sations, the Ministry has created an Agricultural-Economic Insti-tute which undertakes various economic analyses and which, in cooperation with a network of experimental stations, gives scientific support to the extension services in the form of data on crop growing, prevention of pollution, and crop ripening for export. A circle of research institutes has sprung up around the Agricultural-Economic Institute mostly situated near the Agricultural University of Wageningen which has partly an international function.

However, despite the integration of national and regional policy in this sphere – with due allowance for international policies of the E.E.C. – signs of friction have made themselves felt. In particular, in the IJssel delta, along part of the Veluwe coastal strip and between the great rivers where consolidation is normally in progress, some areas appear to lag behind. A policy of social incentives has been aimed at these areas, consisting of special subsidies for the pro-vision of various social amenities.[7]

3.3.5. *Development areas with industrial nuclei.*

Although more and more areas have been designated as problem areas, the number of industrial development nuclei has been retained

---

[7] J. W. Vriezen, "Regional Welfare Policy", in *Agrarian Information*, May 1969.

at the same level, namely 21 primary and 26 secondary nuclei. But the fact that their number is so large has meant that they have been subjected to ever more criticism as being liable to create poles of attraction rather than poles of animation.[8]

The fact that so many centres qualify for development incentives can probably be traced to the policy's origins – i.e. to the basic idea of combatting regional labour surpluses, particularly in areas where population growth and the mechanisation of agriculture prevented the automatic assimilation of the labour supply. Infrastructure was provided with the same aims in view. Moreover, because of the nature of the planning process, and particularly of policy formulation, local interests were weighed against each other in the competition for available funds. Choice was not based upon an analysis, while it appears that the theoretical analysis of the influence of interconnected factors was considered quite irrelevant. The social movements of national, regional and local nature described under 2.2.5. no longer exist. The motivation to change was no longer present among the population, and innovation from below was not therefore to be expected.

3.3.6. *Urban centres*

In 1969 a decision was taken to extend social welfare policy to the rapidly growing urban centres, which had frequently proved to lack social facilities for recreation, sport, and various social gatherings. In The Hague, Rotterdam, Apeldoorn and Enschede the central government decided to experiment by providing new residential areas with the social facilities that the local population wanted. It is not yet known whether this experiment will be based on a thorough multidisciplinary population research or whether the government will make do with bringing together the various local experts who traditionally sit in local committees for public health, social work, youth affairs, sport and recreation, and by holding incidental hearings. Nevertheless, this is an extension of the old regional policy and ushers in a new trend.

But if the trend is to be followed systematically an agglomeration policy must be opted for. The question then arises as to whether the present policy of regional dispersion offers sufficient basis from which to embark on a new policy. Popular participation is now even

8 M. C. Verburg, "Regional Dispersion Policy and Physical Planning", Report for the Political Economy Association, 22 November 1969.

more essential than it was in 1949, yet neither the municipalities, nor the provinces, nor the state has so far shown any sign of developing new ways by which to make this possible.

The population research carried out in 1949 focused on the social structure as a whole; but should this be repeated in its old guise? The question is whether sociology, psychology, planology and other disciplines have not advanced so far that an entirely new approach is feasible. It seems out of date to make do with district hearings over particular problems. Allowance must now be made for the younger generation which has so far been rather neglected. Youth should be given the opportunity to find its own motivation for modern social participation. Will this chance be given? Youth organisation representatives in the various youth councils are approaching retirement age, which seems to signify that each category in the entire system of popular representation should be thoroughly revised.

The consideration of social equipment within the framework of the new regional welfare policy for the seventies has so far ignored the question of social environment. This requires some explanation. Is some sort of a taboo placed on shaping a new living climate? "The planners cannot agree as to how new houses can best be distributed according to type. Studies carried out in the Rotterdam agglomeration, known as the Rhine Estuary region, have shown that an ideal distribution can only be of real value if not only the expense is taken into account but also the varying needs of the population, which ought to be known. Research has shown that part of the population prefer one family houses and that others prefer to live in high apartment blocks. Nevertheless, low apartment buildings continue to be built, although they are far less appreciated".[9]

3.4. *The effects of the dispersion policy 1959-1969*

In some regions the dispersion policy has undoubtedly been effective. Unfortunately however, there is little sense in discussing increases in industrial employment since developments show that many industries are still in serious structural difficulty. It is no

[9] R. F. Geijer & L. A. Welters, "Productivity and Regional Labour Relationships; an analysis of research results, documentation and literature regarding living and work in the Rhine Estuary Area" (Parts I, II, III, IV, 1969). This research was carried out under the aegis of the Foundation for the Labour Situation Research in the Rhine Estuary Area and of the Ministry of Economic Affairs. Industry and representatives of popular organisations participate in this Foundation.

longer merely a case of absorbing a fairly large population growth or surplus agricultural labour; it is now a question of deciding in which respects Dutch regional policy, with industry as its spearhead and radiating factor, is in need of revision.

The economist Verburg (see footnote 8) writes that Dutch regional policy is efficient in its instruments but that it needs refinement. Government policy should still be directed towards infrastructural improvements, but should promote the formation of agglomerations. This is a new dimension for the Dutch. Agglomeration forming has not been analysed as a direct policy objective for physical planning in the Netherlands. The question is whether it is possible to change to a new policy without quantitative analyses, without further multidisciplinary reflection and without modern system-theoretical bases.

Our conclusion is that Dutch regional policy has retained its pragmatic character and has shown great ingenuity. This has enabled considerable expansion in the industrial and services sectors. However, preparing the policy to be followed during the seventies requires analytical reflection, after which the objectives must be reformulated.

4. THE FUTURE – POST-1970

In this section attention will be paid to a series of interconnected factors and structural processes which may not have been given sufficient systematic consideration in Dutch planning and policy.

4.1. Policy in the field of science development

As yet scientific policy is a rather underdeveloped field in the Netherlands. Universities are still organised along traditional lines and multi-disciplinary research and education is defective or, in many cases, is only in the initial exploratory stage. The various disciplines still tend to overestimate the relevance of their own contribution and to underestimate the relevance of co-operation with others.

In contrast to this, however, the spectacular progress now being made on the borders of the present scientific disciplines means that training in the field of interdisciplinary communication is particularly significant. Examples of this trend are particularly evident in the field of public health. But it is also making itself felt in the scientific substructure with which this report deals – namely socio-economic development planning.

In the Netherlands we are presently setting up a "Central Organisation for Scientific and Technical Data". All ministries and government institutions concerned with communications are represented on its governing body. This is an important initiative, but its effect will depend on its working methods and upon the interpretation of its scientific and technical data, both by researchers from various disciplines and by policy experts. My own experience has been that analytical laboratories are rarely able to add a generalist dimension to the plan because they are too aloof from daily policy and are not conversant with the actual problems of integrating the various policy areas. Small analytical laboratories incorporated into government policy centres may possibly be more effective in planning and policy preparation than more or less isolated centres.

The integrated planning of a number of inherently meaningful planning sectors is anyway inconceivable without systematic work in the field of research and development. In 1968 a Scientific Policy Council was set up in The Netherlands. This council, which advises the government in its efforts to achieve an integrated scientific policy, is primarily concerned with trying to break through traditional attitudes to the allocation of central finances for research and development. A planning substructure must then be created in these policy areas with the aid of focused multi-disciplinary research. The 1970s should see a joint effort on the part of the universities, business community and TNO institutes to provide more coherence and integration in their research efforts. There should be a systematic search for connections between different techniques, methodology and results as characterised by theoretical systems approaches.

4.2. *Health and Environmental Planning*

4.2.1. *Evolutionary sciences*

One of the most important remedies against abuse of science is that the scientists develop a profound awareness of the ethical import of their work, that is to say, of the functions of science in the totality of human life. In the 1970s one hears of manipulation of genetic properties of man and its applications. Medico-biological discoveries in cellular biology and molecular biology put the connections and mechanisms within human reach. In the future the quality of human life will be less protected by individual medical intervention and affected more by structural inventions with regard to 'being'. But at the same time the environment is affected by industrialisation, urbanisation and the application of chemical substances and other synthetics so that not only the environment is threatened but also the biosphere.

4.2.2. Health planning

In the coming decade health planning should acquire a different dimension than in the past when it consisted mainly of combatting endemic diseases and providing health care throughout the country. Future planning will depend on experts from many disciplines in which biochemists and biophysicists will play an important role.

The development of psycho-hygiene is another element of health planning. What are the needs of man and modern society? What causes uneasiness and frustration in the western world where welfare objectives and human well-being have been achieved? In the 19th century the West still knew a hunger for developing its countries. When food and clothing had been provided human endeavour was directed at achieving social security. Now that social security has been achieved mankind seems to have acquired a feeling of imprisonment. The science of psycho-hygiene will have to develop in order to come to macro-planning for human health. While uneasiness and feelings of imprisonment are emerging, the threat against the environment begins to acquire serious proportions, physically as well as psychologically.

4.2.3. Planning for environmental health

Flora, fauna and communities are threatened by technology. At the same time, man is threatened by air, earth and water pollution, by noise and by radiation. Analyses are made of the toxity of certain foods, stimulants and medicines.

The Netherlands is vulnerable on this account because of its location. Eighty years ago the Rhine brought down the equivalent of 50 kilograms of salt per second. In 1966, this had increased to 300 kilograms of salt creating a permanent lack of oxygen and a threat to agriculture.

There are a great number of planning aspects to these problems. As a rule it is not possible to prevent air pollution, waste disposal, destruction of waste products such as plastics at the local level or even the regional level. National and international measures are needed. Development of the environment which had not been foreseen in the 1950s makes demands on developmental research and necessitates intensive multi-disciplinary and international collaboration. It also demands rethinking on factors of growth and even on the factor of economic growth.

4.2.4. *Economic growth*

The developments of mankind and of the human environment are forerunners to a period in which question-marks should be placed on the type of expectations that formed a basis for growth-rates in the past. In highly industrialised countries a greater part of economic growth will have to be devoted to measures for the redress of the external effects of this growth and consequently of promoting and maintaining 'livability'.[10]

One may also ask whether the economic growth rate should not be purposely lowered in order to achieve this end.

The future will show whether Holland will escape from these dilemmas. But if choices are not made in the short term, the chances are that not only its socio-economic development but health and environmental standards will suffer. The threat to health has already become a very real problem.

---

[10]   Dr. J. D. De Pous, New Year's speech, Socio-Economic Council 1970 – Par. medium-term.

9

M. DATTA-CHAUDHURI

REGIONAL PLANNING IN INDIA

I. INTRODUCTION

Proper assessment of the planning technique actually practised in an economy is possible only in the context of an analysis of the political and administrative framework in which economic policy decisions are made. Planning techniques, after all, are nothing but a method of formulating a set of policies to be carried out by the particular organizational set-up. After formulating a consistent set of social and economic objectives and given the institutional, behavioural and technological constraints on the economic system, the planning authority is supposed to formulate a programme of action for the various economic agencies, which together constitute the planning machinery for the economy. These agencies, which operate at various levels – national, regional or sectoral – need to have clearly understood relationships among themselves to facilitate smooth flows of information and an orderly transmission of commands throughout the system.

The political organization of the country sometimes imposes significant limits on the nature of the planning process. In a country with a federal constitution, for example, where the federating units enjoy a considerable degree of autonomy, the national planning machinery must be geared to the task of integrating and harmonizing the development objectives of the various subnational units. In such a situation, regional planning ceases to be merely a technique of translating the over-all national development objective over geographical space, possibly with a certain degree of decentralization; it becomes also an integral part of the process of national plan formulation.

The Indian Union is a federation of autonomous States. The Constitution of the country prescribes respective spheres in which the Central and State Governments are assumed to exercise exclusive authority. There are also important spheres in which the central government shares authority with the State governments. During the period since Independence, the country has undergone an almost continuous process of redefining the geographical boundaries of the different States in order to make each one cover a territory inhabited by a more or less homogenous social group. Today, on the whole, each State represents one linguistic group.

Throughout this period, Centre-States relationships remained an extremely sensitive and potentially dangerous area in the political process of the country. Until recently and with minor exceptions, the Congress Party controlled the government at the Centre and in all the States. The party tried as far as possible to conceal potential areas of conflict between the Centre and the States, preferring to resolve them informally within its ranks.

The structure of economic planning, both national and regional, reflected this important fact of the country's political life. Rational planning implies the considering of alternative problems, making a choice on the basis of certain socially accepted criteria, and evolving a hierarchy of decision-making apparatus on the different levels to implement the policy implications of these choices. In the 1950s, the Indian planning process tried to specify the alternatives regarding the allocation of resources among different sectors of commodity production, as well as those regarding the techniques of production, applying economic analysis in an attempt to reach a rational solution. However, the process almost deliberately side-tracked all questions concerning interregional conflicts of interests. The objectives of planned development were stated in such a fashion as to hide all questions of choice inherent in the planning process of a multi-regional economy. Because the same political party controlled all governments, it could afford to make the process of formulating both Central and States' plans a cooperative and almost informal venture. Conflicts naturally developed, but no formal machinery for their resolution was established.

Although the Indian planning process did not try to find a rational solution to problems of regional allocation (in fact, it made no attempt to state these problems realistically), actual decisions concerning the regional allocation of resources had to be made. In practice, except for the few cases in which non-institutionalized political bargaining provided the solution, the allocation problem was solved by analogy with solutions of other choice problems concerning commodity composition and choice of techniques.

During the last three years, however, important political changes have taken place. The Congress Party has lost control of more than half of the State governments, even though it retains control at the Centre. The old system of informal and cooperative planning is no longer possible. The entire planning machinery is undergoing drastic change, with the intention of introducing greater autonomy for the States in formulating their Plans and of specifying the rules for inter-State resource allocation. A clear picture of the new situation has yet to emerge, thus making it rather difficult at present to assess the regional planning techniques as practised in India.

Although the coordination of State and national planning represents the most important aspect of the regional planning problem in India, planning apparatus have been set up for regional planning at the lower levels. *Panchayati Raj* were instituted to initiate a process of planned development at the local level using local initiative. Their field of activity was largely confined to agriculture, community development and rural infra-structure. In certain cities such as Calcutta and Bombay, metropolitan planning organizations were created to prepare master plans for land-use in the cities. With the present move toward greater decentralization in the planning process, the Planning Commission has prepared a scheme for introducing regional planning at the district level in order to formulate comprehensive area development plans for the districts. A district is chosen as the geographical unit largely because the present system of data collection does not go below this level.

In the past, *ad hoc* regional development organizations have been sometimes set up to prepare development programmes for geographical areas which covered territories belonging to different States. The most outstanding example of such an organization is the Dandakaranya Development Board, which was set up to develop Dandakaranya, a thinly populated hill area in Central India extending over three districts belonging to two States, Orissa and Madhya Pradesh, for the specific purpose of settling refugees from East Pakistan, Except for such special programmes, regional planning in India has been more or less for regions defined in terms of political and administrative boundaries.

2. THE EXISTING PLANNING MACHINERY AT THE NATIONAL AND STATE LEVELS

The formulation of a five-year plan has been a complex, partly formal and partly informal process involving three distinct stages. During the first stage, which begins about three years before the commencement of the new Plan, the Central Planning Commission initiates studies relating to the state of the economy in order to identify principal economic, social and institutional areas in which action is necessary. The results of these studies are communicated to the Central Government and then to the National Development Council.[1] These initial discussions help in the formulation of certain broad, tentative features of the Plan, e.g. the aggregate growth to be aimed at and a few broad guidelines regarding priorities in the allocation of Plan Outlay.

In the second stage, the Planning Commission works out the general dimensions of the Plan in the light of these parameters. The usual techniques for working-out commodity balances and sectoral allocation of investments are those based on certain inter-industry investment allocation models. At this stage, officials of the various ministries responsible for the different sectors and representatives of private industries are brought in to constitute several working groups to review the programmes of the different sectors in the light of more detailed information. State government officials are simultaneously advised to set up their own working groups, which are expected to remain in informal contact with their counterparts at the Centre. After all these studies and the subsequent discussions at several levels, a draft outline of the plan indicating the programmes for the different sectors of the economy is formulated by the Planning Commission.

In the next stage, the Planning Commission holds detailed discussions with the State governments regarding estimates of resources likely to be made available to them, measures for mobilising additional resources, and proposals for the sectoral programmes of the States. Since the Central government controls the tax collecting machinery for almost the entire non-agricultural sector of the economy and since most foreign aid is channeled through the

---

[1] The National Development Council is the highest planning authority in the country. It consists of ministers in the central government in charge of the economic ministries, members of the Planning Commission and the Chief Ministers of the States.

Central government, the State governments are largely dependent on Central assistance for their development plans. The Centre can thus exercise a fair amount of control, although informally, over the precise formulation of State Plans. In fact, many projects included in a State Plan are so-called 'approved schemes'.

3. LOCATION OF INDUSTRIAL PROJECTS

The Constitution of the country gives Central government almost exclusive powers in promoting and regulating large industries, transport and communication. A substantial part of the allocations in the Five-year Plans consists of investment projects undertaken by the Central government in the industrial field. The Central government has also exercised a fair amount of indirect control in guiding private investment in industries.[2] Obviously, the locational choice for these industries has profound implications on the pattern of regional growth in the country. Moreover, industrial location offers considerable scope for improving the efficiency of resource-use by way of proper location planning. For reasons described in Section 1, however, these questions of choice were not brought out in the open in discussions concerning India's planning strategy.[3]

There is evidence to the effect that the government's industrial licensing policy has often favoured small-sized plants in less industrialized areas, resulting in obvious efficiency losses due to the sacrifice of economy of scale. Freight rates for the movement of bulk commodities – mostly industrial raw materials such as coal – on the government-owned Indian Railways were deliberately kept low, partly for historical reasons but partly because of the pressure applied by industrial users located far from the sources of supply. The low costs of transportation of these bulky industrial inputs further induced dispersal of industries over the country.[4]

[2] Recent studies of the operation of the Indian government's industrial licensing policies (for regulating private investments) reveal that the system has failed almost completely in guiding private industries in the desired direction. See Government of India, *The Report of the Committee on Industrial Licensing* (New Delhi, 1969).

[3] A notable exception is a paper entitled "Regional Allocation of Resources in India" by L. Lefeber, published in P. N. Rosenstein-Rodan (ed.), *Capital Accumulation and Economic Development* (London: Allen & Unwin Ltd., 1964). This paper was originally submitted to the Perspective Planning division of the Indian Planning Commission in 1961.

[4] See L. Lefeber and M. Datta-Chaudhuri, "Transport Policy in India" in P. N. Rosenstein-Rodan (ed.), *Pricing and Fiscal Policies* (London: Allen & Unwin Ltd., 1964).

With regard to locational decisions concerning direct industrial investments by the government, locations for heavy industry projects were apparently chosen largely on grounds of efficiency. But the locational choice for small industries, particularly for the Industrial Estates programme, was largely based on the regional dispersal principle.[5] This is an imperfect generalization, of course. In some cases, strong political pressure caused heavy industrial projects to be located in backward areas at considerable cost in terms of overall resource-use in the economy. An obvious example is the locational decision concerning an inefficiently-sized refinery in the State of Assam, situated far from the markets for its products. Similarly some industrial estates were located near big cities. Incidentally, most industrial estates located in backward areas showed poor performance. This was largely because policy planners failed to understand adequately the economic forces governing location of industries.[6] A few programming exercises on the location, scale and time-phasing of certain industries or industrial groups were made by independent economists, but it is not clear whether these studies had any influence on the decision-making process.[7]

4. NEW CHANGES IN THE FRAMEWORK OF STATE PLANNING

In the changed political circumstances of the country the informal and cooperative planning method is fast becoming ineffective. The

[5] The planner's choice was divided between commodity composition and technology. On the one hand, capital-intensive heavy industrial projects were undertaken on the grounds that (a) insufficient foreign trade transformation possibilities might constrain the growth of the domestic industrialization programme by creating bottlenecks in the supplies of producers' goods and (b) these public sector industries would generate sufficient reinvestment funds for future growth. On the other hand, labour-intensive small-scale industries were promoted for creating short-run employment. A similar dichotomy in the field of locational choice was possibly accepted by analogy. The choice in the case of heavy industries was made on the grounds of efficiency for the growth programme. But locational choice for small industries was largely dictated by distributional considerations.

[6] For a detailed discussion on the Industrial Estates programme see M. Datta Chaudhuri and L. Lefeber *Regional Development in South East Asia* Chapter XI (Forthcoming) UNRISD, Geneva.

[7] See A. S. Manne, *Investment For Capacity Expansion* (London 1966) and M. Datta Chaudhuri, "Regional Specialisation in Metallurgical and Machine-Building Industries in India in the Framework of a Planning Model for Optimum Use of National Resources", *Indian Economic Review*, Oct. 1967.

Planning Commission in a recent publication has recognized this fact, saying that "the whole approach of directing the development effort in the States through Centrally-assisted 'approved' schemes has been given up." It is felt that the tying of Central assistance with such schemes had led in the past not only to the distortion of States' priorities, but also to a tendency to apply these schemes everywhere without due regard to the variety of conditions existing within the States.[8] The implications are obvious. The States should work out their own development strategies based on their own assessment of development potentials and objectives.

Two sets of problems have to be solved for this decentralization scheme to be successful. Firstly, the rules governing the distribution of the investment fund, which to a large extent accrues to the Centre, must be clearly formulated.[9] Secondly, appropriate policy instruments must be evolved for Central planners to apply in regulating the over-all commodity balances in the entire economy and also regarding the use of certain scarce resources such as foreign exchange. Obviously, the Central government will have to rely more on fiscal policies (tax-subsidy measures) than in the past. But these may not be sufficient in view of the wellknown difficulties in market conditions of underdeveloped economies. The planning machinery will have to be reorganized to handle new problems arising from the necessity to harmonize State Plans.

How are State plans to be formulated in the new situation? The States' planning machineries are not of uniform quality. The level of sophistication shown by the planners in formulating State plans has been so far rather low. However, the Government of West Bengal recently published a fairly sophisticated exercise which may provide some clues to the evolution of State planning techniques. The methodology of West Bengal's planning is outlined below.

To summarise, the regional plan would have to consist of the following major elements:

a statement of social goals and objectives expressed in explicit, qualitative terms with a measurable quantitative dimension.

[8] Planning Commission, Government of India, *Guidelines For The Formulation Of District Plans* (New Delhi, 1969), p. 2.
[9] In 1968, the National Development Council agreed on a formula for the distribution of non-development funds to the States from Central revenues. This is based on several criteria like population, per capita income, past performance in resource mobilization, etc.

a comprehensive demographic projection of future regional population and its urban component, wherever possible in relation to its locale.

a quantitative projection of future economic activity by major sectors and industry groups and their desired spatial distribution.

a spatial plan, showing the organisation of urban places in the region.

a design policy statement, outlining in broad terms the desirable configurations of major urban developments and spelling out regional goals, objectives and standards with respect to urban form, urban density, and urban structure.

a transportation plan designed to accommodate and facilitate the projected needs and the proposed spatial organisation of economic activity and urbanisation.

a projection of the total cost of the proposed plan and a programme for its financing.

a programme for administration and governmental organisation for plan implementation, including drafts for the necessary legislation.[10]

This does not detail the techniques used in formulating the Plan. For example, "the quantitative projections of future economic activity by major sector and industry groups" would require assumptions regarding (a) the pattern of interregional trade flows and (b) the time pattern of the volume of investments. The State planners of West Bengal at one stage tried these projections on the basis of a gravity-type two-region input-output model – West-Bengal and the rest of India being the two regions. Inter-regional commodity flows were related to production and demand in the two regions. West Bengal was postulated to have the same rate of growth for its domestic products as the entire country (as suggested by the Perspective Planning Division of the Indian Planning Commission). But all these are as yet in the nature of academic exercises. The actual techniques to be used have yet to be evolved. Moreover, the techniques actually used by the different State Governments are likely to show wide variations.

5. THE NEW SCHEME FOR DISTRICT PLANNING

The Planning Commission is currently trying to persuade the States

---

[10] CMPO, Development and Planning Department, Government of West Bengal *Regional Planning For West Bengal* (Calcutta, 1965), p. 7.

to adopt the area development approach in the formulation of State Plans. The idea is to make full allowance for the variety of conditions existing in the different physico-geographical and economic regions of the State. The district is chosen as the regional planning area because the various machineries for data collection have been using it as the ultimate reducible unit.

District plans, according to the Planning Commission, should be formulated along the following lines:

The first objective of the formulation of district plans is to set forth a long-term perspective indicating the economic activities to be established in different sub-regions of the district and the measures to be taken over the next 15 or 20 years to develop (and conserve) natural resources, build up infra-structural facilities and social services and foster the growth of towns and cities in a manner that would help the district to develop in the pre-determined direction. The second objective is to prepare an integrated programme of action for the next five-year or one-year period on the basis of a careful analysis of the existing conditions and a realistic assessment of the immediate problems, short-term priorities and available resources.[11]

A Perspective plan or a short-run programme need to be based on a careful survey of the situation in the district regarding the natural resource base of the region, the socio-economic conditions of the people, and the administrative machinery necessary for the execution of any development programme. The Planning Commission has prepared a set of detailed forms for systematic collection of the necessary statistical information. Detailed statistics are to be collected under twenty-six different heads to cover all relevant aspects of socio-economic development for the district. These 26 categories are:

Land Resources and Utilization,
Vegetation Resources and Utilization,
Water Resources and Utilization,
Mineral Resources and Utilization,
Livestock Resources and Utilization,
Communication System,
Marketing Facilities,
Storage and Processing Facilities,
Banking and Credit Facilities,
Canal Irrigation System,
Power Distribution,

[11] *Guidelines for the Formulation of District Plans*, p. 13.

Educational Facilities,
Medical and Public Health Facilities,
Drinking Water Facilities,
Veterinary Facilities,
Agriculture,
Horticulture,
Animal Husbandry and Dairying,
Large-scale Industries,
Modern Small-scale Industries,
Other Small Industries including Handloom, Powerloom,
    Sericulture, Coir, Handcrafts and Village Industries,
Backward Communities,
Institutional Structure – Cooperation,
Institutional Structure – Panchayati Raj Bodies,
Institutional Structure – Local Self Government,
Employment.

On the basis of this information, planning officials at the district levels are to prepare development schemes, specifying in each case (a) the objectives, (b) the activities envisaged, (c) the financial, physical and personnel inputs required, (d) the physical results expected from year to year, (e) the quantum of private and institutional resources likely to become available towards its execution and (f) the manner in which the schemes would be reviewed, coordinated and synchronized with other schemes and periodically evaluated. Next, these schemes are to be arranged in such a manner as to provide a feasible time profile of a development programme. For each period, inter-relationships among the various parts of the different schemes will have to be examined to maintain the internal consistency of the total programme. The production, demand and supply implications of particular inputs and resources will have to be aggregated to bring out the total implications of the entire development programme of the district during any period.

However, for some sectors, e.g. power development and electrification, programmes of contiguous districts will need to be harmonized. The State planning machinery will have to coordinate the programmes of the various districts in formulating the State Plan.

6. THE IMPLICATIONS OF MULTI-LEVEL PLANNING

To operate efficiently, a multi-level planning process is a tremendous task, requiring a competent and flexible planning machinery. If the total available resources were given at any regional level, it would be possible to prepare a proper development Plan for the region.[12] But the total resources are not given. Part of the investment fund may be raised locally, but a sizeable contribution will have to come from the national machinery for resource mobilization. It is not desirable to allocate investment funds only on grounds of justice regarding regional distribution because among other things, population is not entirely immobile. Distributional justice is meaningful only in the context of distribution among people. If people are prepared to move from place to place in search of higher income and welfare, it makes little sense to tie the allocation of investments to geographical areas. Neither is such tying up efficient from the point of view of overall use of resources.

However, rational use of the country's resources is feasible only when the various opportunities for the use of these resources are known. The full potentialities of certain development schemes become apparent only when viewed from close quarters. Therefore, ground-level planning efforts are often more efficient in formulating development schemes which are consistent with the endowment of the place and the needs of the people.

But it is not easy to devise an institutional machinery which can efficiently explore development potentials and also exercise social choice consistent with the objectives of efficiency and distributive justice. Current political developments in India are improving the situation in the former sense by decentralizing the planning process. The need to devise a mechanism of rational choice is correspondingly becoming more and more important, but the major innovation in this field is yet to come.

---

[12] Even there, estimations of interregional trade flows would present some tricky problems.

JEAN PAELINCK

TECHNIQUES OF REGIONAL PLAN FORMULATION: PROBLEMS OF INTERREGIONAL CONSISTENCY

1. INTRODUCTION

The formulation of regional plans, although possibly stimulated by national authorities, relies essentially on prospective thinking by regional bodies. The reasons for this are manifold:

– local people will have the greatest share in the benefits of growth and development that will eventually take place in their region;
– more than national technocrats, they are in a position to evaluate the various factors that prevent their region from growing at a desirable pace;
– adequate information can be easily collected through the local channels which often are more readily accessible to the local boys than to some group of outsiders sent down to them by a central planning agency.

The trend is in this direction, and can only be applauded by democratic society. Let us join the cheering and develop our further thoughts along three lines:

– what should be the ingredients of a reasonable regional development programme?
– how can the macro-economic consistency of such programmes be tested, if necessary?
– how can the sectoral consistency of such programmes be tested, if necessary?

2. THE LOGIC OF REGIONAL PLANNING AND POLICY

We shall only draw attention to one main point in the economic reasoning underlying a regional programme.

In our opinion, the logical thread leads from a set of feasible targets for the region to a set of necessary policy measures. In all cases, targets have to be sectorally specified, and this can be done by means of a medium-term one-shot or a long-term multi-stage programme. An example of this could be the following.

$$\text{Minimize } I = \sum_i i_i p_i \tag{1}$$

s.t.

$$p^*_i \leqslant p_i \leqslant p_i^{**} \tag{2}$$

$$\lambda^* \leqslant \sum_i l_i p_i \leqslant \lambda^{**} \tag{3}$$

$$\rho^* \leqslant \sum_i \rho_i p_i / \pi \tag{4}$$

$$A \underline{p} = \underline{e} \tag{5}$$

where: I = total investment;
p_i = production levels (the starred variables indicate lower (*) and upper (**) bounds;
i_i = marginal capital coefficients;
l_i — marginal labor coefficients (the starred λ's indicate lower and upper bounds;
ρ_i = marginal income coefficients (ρ^* is a lower limit to per capita income);
π = total population.

Equation [5] is a regional model, where $\underline{p}$ is the vector of production levels, and $\underline{e}$ some other variable;[1] model [5] might be, for example, an attraction model.[2]

In this simple form, the model guarantees a desirable product-mix (equation [2]), a minimal feasible employment level (equation [3]) and a minimal income per capita (equation [5])[3].

Exercises of the sort described above are no longer academic and should form the normal basis for some kind of consistent regional plan formulation.

[1] Endogeneous too; they might be targets for policy efforts.
[2] L. H. Klaassen and A. C. Van Wickeren: "Inter-industry Relations: An Attraction Model. A Progress Report", H. C. Bos (ed.), *Towards Balanced International Growth* (Amsterdam: North Holland Publishing Company, 1969).
[3] For a more sophisticated version in terms of geometric programming, see J. Paelinck, "Programming in Minimal Investment Viable Industrial Complex for a Development Region", to appear in *The Role of Growth Centers in Regional Economic Development* (New York: Free Press, 1970).

It is only *after* such a plan has been selected that measures of economic policy should be promoted, and possibly negotiated with the central authorities. In other words, we consider as a logical error the current tendency for local pressure groups to ask for certain types of infrastructure, fiscal aid, etc., *before* any uses of these media have been specified. We do *not* deny, however, the difficulty in selecting the adequate bunch of such measures that should lead a region toward the desired goals. As far as we know, our action rests most of the time on casual empiricism, although efforts towards a systematic theory of the efficiency of measures of regional economic policy have recently been undertaken.[4]

One final point, leading up to our main argument. Policy actions in different regions are *not* independent; we think that all sorts of *spin-off effects* exist between regions. In view of this fact, also known through casual empiricism, a model for testing the consistency of plans drafted independently by local bodies becomes a necessary complement to the purely intraregional allocation techniques.

3. MACROECONOMIC CONSISTENCY OF REGIONAL PLANS

A useful model for testing the macroeconomic consistency of separate regional plans should obligatorily include the following elements:

1. an explicit description of the local investment dynamics;
2. a dynamic setting for the relevant variables;
3. policy measures as part of the exogenous variables;
4. some formulation of possible spin-off effects.

The following model[5] tries to encompass these phenomena; its purely 'interior' version will first be given.

$$\Delta E^S = a_1 I + b_1 \Delta (w^* - \overline{w}) + c_1 \Delta S + d_1 \qquad [6]$$

$$I = a_2 \Delta \pi + b_2 \Delta J + c_2 \qquad [7]$$

$$\Delta \pi = a_3 \Delta (w^* - \overline{w}) + b_3 I + c_3 L + d_3 \Delta S \\ + e_3 \Delta R + f_3 \qquad [8]$$

---

[4] Cfr. J. Paelinck (ed.), *L'efficacité des mesures de politiques économique régionale* (Namur: Faculty of Economics, Research Centre, 1967).
[5] An extension of the Klaassen-Kroft-Voskuil model; the initial version ("Regional Income Differences in Holland") appeared in *PAPRSA*, X, 1962.

$$\Delta E^d = a_4 (\Delta P_n + M) + b_4 \Delta (w^* - \overline{w}) + c_4 \qquad [9]$$

$$M = a_5 \Delta (w^* - \overline{w}) + b_5 \Delta J + c_5 L + d_5 \qquad [10]$$

$$\Delta J = a_6 \Delta A + b_6 \Delta U + c_6 \qquad [11]$$

$$\Delta (w^* - \overline{w}) = a_7 (\Delta E^S - \Delta E^d) + b_7 \Delta S + c_7 \qquad [12]$$

$$\Delta C = a_8 \Delta (w^* - \overline{w}) + b_8 \Delta S + c_8 \Delta A + d_8 \Delta U + e_8 \qquad [13]$$

The symbols are explained in the table hereafter.

Symbol	Meaning	States
Δ	time-difference operation	—
E^S	supply of jobs	endogenous
I	investment	endogenous
w^*	wage-level	endogenous
$\overline{w}$	average national wage-level	exogenous
S	structural variable	exogenous
π	profits	endogenous
J	attractivity	endogenous
L	relative distance of a region	exogenous or policy
R	financial stimuli	policy
ΔP_n	natural population increase	exogenous
M	net migration	endogenous
E^d	supply of labour (demand for jobs)	endogenous
A	town-and-country planning measures	policy
U	degree of urbanization	policy
C	per capita disposable income	endogenous

As to the equations, [6] is a supply-of-jobs equation, [7] determines the regional propensity to invest, [8] defines regional profits, demand for jobs is expressed through [9], migration through [10]; equation [11] defines regional attractivity, equation [12] determines the regional wage-level; equation [13] fixes the level of regional per capita disposable income.

A useful reduced form is equation [14] hereafter

$$\Delta E^S = \alpha \Delta S + \beta L + v \Delta R + \delta \Delta A + \varepsilon \Delta U + \xi \Delta P_n + \eta \qquad [14]$$

expressing local employment as a function of certain exogenous and policy variables. [6]

On the other hand, the model is an 8th order system of non-homogeneous linear difference equations of first order with constant coefficients; it can be written as

$$A\underline{y}_t = B\underline{y}_{t-1} + Cx \qquad [15]$$

or alternatively as

$$\underline{y}_t = A^{-1} B\underline{y}_{t-1} + A^{-1} C\underline{x} \qquad [16]$$

where $\underline{y}$'s are the vectors of endogenous variables, $\underline{x}$ the vector of exogenous and policy variables, plus the constants.

Spin-off effects can now be introduced, a simple hypothesis being that they occur only between neighbouring regions. A simple case would be the comparison of the following models [7]

without spin-off
$$I_i = a X_i \qquad [17]$$

with spin-off
$$I_i = a X_i + b \Sigma I_j, \; j \, R_e i \qquad [18]$$
$$j \neq i$$

where R_e denotes the neighbourhood relation.

The main difficulty is that b can be positive or negative; in other words, a region can either *stimulate* or *break* the growth process in a neighbouring region. A proposal, to be submitted to a subsequent test, is to fix the sign of the spin-off effect by *a priori* considerations; this can be done, as in the reduced-form equations the effect appears as the sum of some relevant exogenous variables. Another refinement consists of considering different intensities for positive or negative spin-offs. All depend finally on the available degrees of freedom in the statistical tests.

If spin-off effects are considered at all, as they should be in our

$$\begin{bmatrix} & \vdots & & \vdots & & \vdots & \\ ----&\vdots&----&\vdots&----&\vdots&---- \\ & R_{ii} & \vdots & R_{ij} & \vdots & \\ ----&\vdots&----&\vdots&----&\vdots&---- \\ & R_{ji} & \vdots & R_{jj} & \vdots & \\ ----&\vdots&----&\vdots&----&\vdots&---- \\ & \vdots & & \vdots & & \vdots & \end{bmatrix}$$

---

[6] Equations of this form are in the process of being tested at the Netherlands Economic Institute.

[7] I = investment; X = some exogenous variable.

opinion, the matrices A and B of equations [15] and [16] become totally connected, as is shown above.

R_{ii} and R_{jj} would be the purely intraregional matrices, R_{ij} and R_{ji} the spin-off matrices.

The model as it stands now describes a $n^2 X 64^8$ first-order linear dynamic process; negative spin-off effects can account for long-term cyclical effects, typical in the process of multiregional development where take-off, fast growth and stagnation are simultaneous and alternating development patterns.

The uses of the model just exposed are obvious. On the one hand, the reduced-form equations of type [14] allow the computation of, for example, total investment and net migration, which totals could be compared with those of a national plan; figures in excess of a certain percentage of these plan totals might induce national officials to re-discuss certain assumptions underlying regional plans.

On the other hand, the dynamic version [16] including spin-off effects, allows to compute longer-term effects of present policies, and to detect possible dynamic disequilibrium implicit in the proposed policy measures.

4. SECTORAL EXTENSION OF A CONSISTENCY-CONTROL MODEL

It is not difficult to extend the model described in section III in such a way that sectoral consistency tests can be performed.

Let us start from the following hypotheses exposed in terms of population and employment variables:[9]

H.1.: there exist certain dynamic attraction tendencies between activities present in a region, on which tendencies the future spontaneous growth of the region is based;

H.2.: the attraction takes place on the basis of demand and supply phenomena on the regional level;

H.3.: these attraction phenomena exert themselves across regional borders;

H.4.: the spin-off effects defined under H.3. are a function of the 'openness' of a region;

H.5.: the tendencies just described are of medium term.

[8] n = number of regions.
[9]   This is an extended dynamic version of the Klaassen attraction model mentioned above.

For sector i, the dynamic intra-regional attraction can be described by the following equation:

$$E^i = a^{ii} E^i + a^{ij} E^j + b^{ii} E^i + b^{ij} E^j + c^i P \qquad [19]$$

In this equation E^i describes the increase in spontaneous employment induced in sector i through the previous existing industrial structure,[10] possibly 'augmented' through known investment projects, on the basis of supply attraction (coefficients a^{ij}) or demand attraction (coefficients b^{ij} and c^i); P stands for population.

Once more a set of these equations can be written in matrix-form as

$$\underline{e}_t = G\underline{e}_{t-1} + \hat{H}p_{t-1} \qquad [20]$$

Spin-off effects can be introduced by the following equation, written for a region A:

$$\Delta E^i_A = a^{ii} E^i_A + a^{ij} E^j_A + b^{ii} E^i_A + b^{ij} E^j_A + c^i P + \underset{R}{\Sigma} d^i_R \Delta E^i_R \qquad [21]$$

if we limit R to contiguous regions.

The simple hypothesis is that a fraction of employment, generated by investment projects in other regions, spins off to region A – in a positive or negative way, once more.

Regional interdependence, at the sectoral level, is expressed through system [22]:[11]

$$\begin{bmatrix} \underline{e}_A \\ \underline{e}_B \end{bmatrix}_t = \begin{bmatrix} G_{AA} & G_{AB} \\ G_{BA} & G_{BB} \end{bmatrix} \begin{bmatrix} \underline{e}_A \\ \underline{e}_B \end{bmatrix}_{t-1} + \begin{bmatrix} \underline{ex}_A \\ \underline{ex}_B \end{bmatrix}$$

where $\underline{ex}_A$, $\underline{ex}_B$ stand for exogenous vectors.

Once more, G_{AB} and G_{BA} express the interregional dynamic links; possible long-term regional and sectoral dynamics (take-off, fast growth, stagnation) are encompassed by the system.

5. CONCLUSIONS

We would like to conclude this short study with a number of statements on the operational virtues of the proposed models.

---

10   j stands for all other sectors with which sector i has input and/or output relations.
11   Reduced to two regions for the sake of simplicity.

S.1.: optimal regional plans can nowadays be computed; the problems consist on the regional level:
- of the difficulty of taking into account the effects of other regional plans;
- of fragmentary knowledge of the efficiency of regional policy measures;

S.2.: only the use of an overall interregional model, probably estimated by some sort of cross-section device, can remedy the state of affairs described in *S.1.*;

S.3.: simple models, alluded to in *S.2.*, are now on the market; they function on the macro- and the sectoral level;

S.4.: data are available to implement these simple models;

S.5.: no experience is known to us where consistency checks based on *S.1.–S.4* have been systematically used; there is an urgent need for experimentation in this field.

V

THE ADMINISTRATION OF REGIONAL DEVELOPMENT

11

PIERRE VIOT

THE PROCESS OF INTERREGIONAL PLAN FORMULATION IN FRANCE

1. INTRODUCTION

After the failure of the regional reform proposed to the French in the Referendum of April 1969, the future of the region remains uncertain. It is quite difficult to foresee when and how a region endowed with real powers will find its place into the political and administrative organisation of France.

1969 constituted a broken off stage in an evolution which started about 20 years ago and which was characterised by a progressive transformation of institutions. 1950: the first official reports on regional planning. 1955: a series of laws establishing new bodies. 1960: the adoption of the regional framework by the principal administrative bodies of the government. 1963-64: on the one hand administrative organisation for carrying out the national tasks of "aménagement du territoire", on the other, the establishment of a regional organisation with limited powers: the Regional Prefect and the Committee for regional economic development (CODER).

This development by stages did not take place without clashes or interruptions. In a country where tradition shows a strong tendency towards political and administrative centralisation in decision making, it is not easy to introduce the regional dimension. Nevertheless, one has seen the development of the idea that an extreme centralisation involves serious inconveniences for the efficacy of the political and administrative system. Economic and social policy is progressively characterised by the increasing concern to differentiate these interventions in geographical space and to decentralise a part of the responsibilities. Thus the guidelines of a national development policy for regions and of the "aménagement du territoire" are gradually appearing.

After 20 years of experience it is possible to draw up a balance of the progress realised in the formulation of this policy. This study, which will be limited to interregional aspects and dwell upon the preparation of the national 6th Plan now in progress for the economic and social development (1971-1975), will successively examine:

- the role of the central bodies of the government
- the process of the preparation of the national plan
- the definition of long term guiding regional development policy decisions
- the regionalisation of the medium term national plan.

2. THE CENTRAL GOVERNMENT ORGANISATIONS RESPONSIBLE FOR "AMENAGEMENT DU TERRITOIRE".

The present organisation of "aménagement du territoire" at the national level has been laid down in the decrees and resolutions of February 14, 1963. The principal characteristic of this reform is that the main aspects in this field came under the responsibility of the Prime Minister. Two principles have justified their attachment here: the need to assure co-ordination between economic planning and physical planning or "aménagement du territoire" and particularly to carry out coordination of the investments of the different administrations with regard to the objectives of "aménagement du territoire".

Before the reform, the Minister of Housing was responsible for "aménagement du territoire" matters. Under his authority was a Directorate of "aménagement du territoire" and the Higher Council of the Department of Housing included a section concerned with these activities. But this department met with difficulties when wanting to give an interministerial character to the policy of "aménagement du territoire", because of insufficient co-ordination between the different offices; moreover, the problems that were involved were studied in a different manner from those of economic planning, and this led to contradictions between the two policies.

2.1. *The main organisations*

The present organisation comprises: the inter-ministerial committee for "aménagement du territoire", the two organisations attached to the Prime Minister and the central services of the ministries.

RELATIONS BETWEEN THE INSTITUTIONS OF THE 'L'AMENAGEMENT DU TERRITOIRE' (AdT)

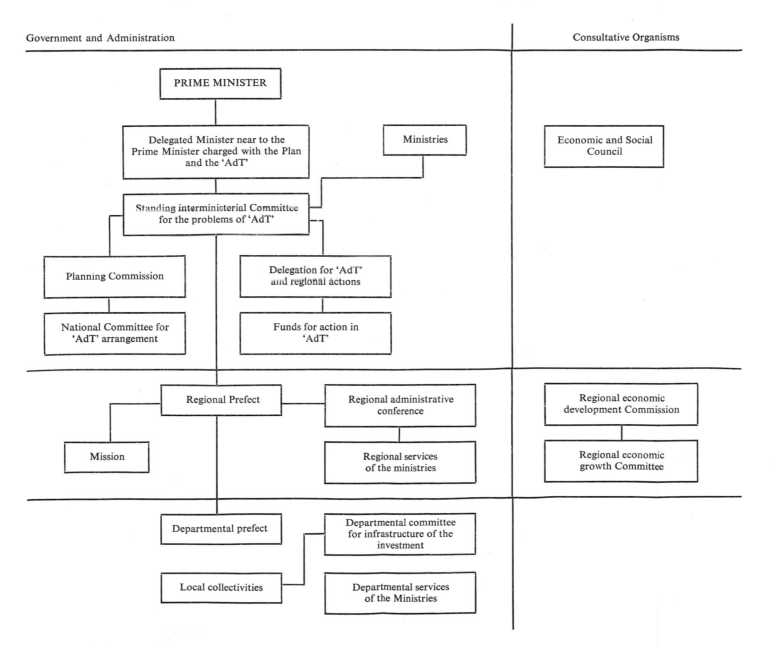

2.1.1. *The interministerial committee*

In order to assure co-ordination between the ministries, an inter-ministerial committee for the solution of regional and "aménage-ment du territoire affairs" was set up by the decree of November 19, 1960, comprising the ministers involved under the presidency of the Prime Minister. This body either makes decisions which do not have to be submitted to the Council of Ministers or prepares materials for the latter's decision.

2.1.2.

Besides the Prime Minister two organisations have powers in the field of "aménagement du territoire" (see chart):

(a) The "Commissariat Général au Plan", which used to be under the jurisdiction of the Minister of Finance, was attached to the Prime Minister in 1962 and was made responsible in February 1963 for the field of "aménagement du territoire"; and

(b) the "Délégation à l'aménagement du territoire et à l'action regionale", created in February 1963, which shows similarities with the "Commissariat Général au Plan" in as far as it is also a 'light' organisation (some twenty executive bodies) which should not serve as a substitute for the ministries but play a role of encouragement.

2.1.3. *The Ministries*

Through the February 1963 reform, the government has wanted the action of the different offices to be oriented in future to the pro-motion of "aménagement du territoire" and regional activities. Certain ministries play a particularly important role. To mention briefly a few:

– The Ministry of the Interior (adjustment of prefectoral institutions to new tasks, reform of the departmental and community organi-sations, infrastructure of local communities).

– The Ministry of Economics and Finance: the Directorate of the Budget looks after the regionalisation of the budget; the Directorate of the Treasury is concerned with Government aid to enterprises; the General Directorate of Taxes is responsible for fiscal reduction; the Directorate of public accountancy is responsible for establish-ment of an accounting system for government and local community investments in each region; I.N.S.E.E.[1] is responsible for regional statistics, regionalisation of national accounts (the I.N.S.E.E. participates very closely with all regional and urban planning activities, and with the preparation of the national plan). Finally the Ministry of Economics and Finance has expressed an increasing preoccupation with reinforcing the activities of its external services (increase of the means of regional organisations of the I.N.S.E.E.; intervention of the chief treasurers and paymasters of the region in the preparation of the development programmes etc.).

– The Ministry of Infrastructure which is mainly responsible for housing, the infrastructure of cities and transportation, and which is actually reorganisating its central services and deconcentrating certain tasks in its regional and departmental services.

– The Ministry of Agriculture which has competence in the field of rural "aménagement" (infrastructure of rural communities, directing rural activities, etc.).

Being represented by their field services in the regions and departments, the ministries play a very important role in "aménagement du territoire". Nevertheless, we will pay special attention to the two recently created organisations which have no regional or local representative: the "Commissariat Général au Plan" and "l'Aménagement du territorie" Delegation. They actually ensure a mission of interministerial co-ordination which constitutes one of the essential aspects of the entire policy of "aménagement du territoire".

2.2. *The role of the "Commissariat Général au Plan" in the field of "aménagement du territoire"*

Since the texts of 1963 have asserted the principle of unity between economic planning and "aménagement du territoire" as a necessity, the "Commissariat Général au Plan" intervenes in three cases:

(a) defining the national policy of "aménagement du territoire": it is in charge of the proceedings concerning studies on the formulation of this policy and of integrating the conclusions in the medium term plans.

To this end, the "Commissariat Général au Plan" is assisted by the National Committee of "aménagement du territoire", which is one of the committees of the plan. The first report of the Committee,

[1] Institut national de la statistique et des études économiques.

published in September 1964 and submitted to Parliament with the options of the Fifth Plan, determined guidelines which are still essentially valid. The objectives of "aménagement du territoire" of the Fifth plan have actually been determined on the basis of this report.

(b) Regionalisation of the Plan: the "Commissariat Général au Plan" in charge of the regionalisation of the plan sends instructions to the "Préfets" of the regions, determines objectives and financial amounts by region, establishes priorities and choices of projects. These various tasks are executed in close cooperation with the different ministries. The resultant documents are the "tranches régionales" or regional sections of the plan and the urban programmes. In order to ensure this interministerial coordination, a specialised committee was set up in 1965 (the Committee on Plan Regionalisation) presided over by the "Commissaire Général au Plan" or his representative. Its composition is purely administrative and its role is to give advice on the definition and execution of the regional sections of the plan.

(c) Execution of the plan at the regional and local level: the "Commissariat Général au Plan" proceeds with the execution of the regional sections and urban programmes; it relies for this on the annual reports on the execution of the regional sections prepared by the Prefects of the Regions.

2.3. *The role of the "Délégation à l'aménagement du territoire et à l'action régionale"*

The "Délégation à l'aménagement du territoire et à l'action régionale" (DATAR) has since its establishment in February 1963 worked in two directions:

(i) it participates, in close cooperation with the "Commissariat Général au Plan", in drafting and defining the national policy of "aménagement du territoire": in this capacity it holds inquiries and samples, organises meetings and guides prospective studies (whose results are published in the "Revue 2000"); very recently it has taken the initiative of preparing a general scheme for the "aménagement" of France;

(ii) for the execution of this policy it plays a stimulating role, encouraging and coordinating. The "Délégation" carries out this task even more efficiently, as it is charged with preparing the deliberations of the interministerial committee for the problems of the "aménagement du territoire" and sees to their execution. This enables it to perfect and coordinate governmental decisions in the field of "aménagement du territoire".

We will emphasise four aspects of the role of the "Délégation".

2.3.1. *Regionalisation of the Budget*

Applied since 1963, the regionalisation of the budget realises the coordination of public investments with regard to the objectives of the "aménagement du territoire". This regionalisation includes: the analysis, definition and regrouping of public investments by region, whether they concern direct operations or subsidies promoting organisations for operations specified at the national or regional level or separate operations indicated by aggregates. Three important points are:

– first, it is an instrument of interministerial coordination, especially for operations depending on various administrative bodies and consequently on various ways of financing;
– next, it is able to control implementation of the regional sections of the plan, as the annual budgetary subsidies can effectively be compared with the multi-annual programmes;
– finally, it is a means for information on financial support by the State for each region; in fact, this is the subject matter of an annex which is published together with the law on finances and which moreover contains statistical indicators on the development of each region.

2.3.2. *The Capital Fund for the "aménagement du territoire"*

The decree of February 14, 1963, establishing the "Délégation à l'aménagement du territoire", set up at the same time the FIAT[2] for the financing of complex infrastructural operations that are considered necessary for the implementation of the policy on the "aménagement du territoire". The credits of the FIAT constitute a very appreciable means for action, although it is only complementary to the activities of the different ministries. Indeed, it would be wrong and completely opposed to the concept of a policy for the

---

[2]   Fonds d'intervention de l'aménagement du territoire.

"aménagement du territoire" to consider it otherwise. The resources of FIAT represent only a little more than 1 percent of the total available funds for infra-structure, i.e. 220 million francs for 1968. It in fact provides the government with the means to complement or group infrastructure as defined in the regional perspective by each of the ministries during the carrying out of the budget.

As a result, the actions taken by the FIAT, have been based on the following criteria:

– as a means by which to start urgent operations whose continuation will be taken over by the competent department;
– as a means of complementing complex operations calling on different means of financing while the possibility of furnishing a supplement does not exist outside of the FIAT.

The criticisms aimed at the FIAT see in it the danger of an over-splintering of activities or investments, questionable priorities, etc. The funds appear to be a means of financing those projects whose urgency only appears during periods in which they cannot be financed through normal channels. It steps in in particular with regard to infrastructural problems, e.g. roads, telecommunications, urban and rural infrastructure, tourist development infrastructure, etc. In addition, the FIAT is allowed to conduct surveys, to create a system of accumulation of data and regional observatories, and to initiate research on specific new techniques, etc.

2.3.3. *Special bodies for interministerial coordination at the central level*

The following bodies are situated near the "Délégation"

– Permanent Secretariat for the Study of Water Problems;
– Interministerial Committees for National and Regional Parks;
– Interministerial or other similar groups, working for the regions but located in Paris: Languedoc-Roussillon, Corse Fos, Aquitaine, Bassin parisien;
– The Central Group for Urban Planning;
– The Committee for Decentralisation of Private and Governmental Establishments;
– The Central Committee for Renewal of Rural Zones.

The "Délégation" also plays an active role in the distribution of subsidies for regional industrial development. This is particularly important in the hundreds of matters related to new industries and in its participation in the interministerial committee for affairs concerned with industrial adaptation and decentralisation.

2.3.4. *The Creation of New Bodies in the Regions*

These are particularly the following bodies: those studying the planning for metropolitan areas (OREAM); the Commissioners for Industrial Conversion and the Industrialisation Bureaus, the Commissioners for Rural Renewal. The "Délégation" has contributed much in the formation of these bodies and continues both to guide and to financially support their activities.

3. THE PROCESS OF PREPARATION OF THE SIXTH PLAN IN THE FIELD OF "AMENAGEMENT DU TERRITOIRE" AND REGIONAL DEVELOPMENT

After limited experience with the Fourth Plan a systematic effort was made during the preparation of the Fifth Plan to proceed with regionalisation. The process that is planned for the Sixth Plan mainly uses methods applied for the previous plan, while trying to correct the insufficiencies and gaps. As in the Fifth Plan, the Sixth Plan requires the vote of Parliament on two successive texts: first the options of the Plan in spring 1970, then the Plan itself in the spring of 1971. Regionalisation has been organised in line with these two essential dates. Three periods have thus been distinguished:

3.1. *The First Period* (until the beginning of 1970)

The first period covers the preparatory work for the drawing-up of a report on the options of the Sixth Plan. This work is being placed at three levels:

(a) The work of the national Committee of the "l'Aménagement du Territoire". A draft made by the "Commissariat Général au Plan" and the I.N.S.E.E.: it contains per section of activity long term perspectives which can be brought to regional levels. It constitutes a general framework, first of all assuring the coherence of the different perspectives formed by the regions of the large agglomerations, then defining the general guiding lines for the policy of "l'aménagement du territoire".

(b) The tasks of the regions: reports on regional aspects and advice by the regional economic development committees (CODER). The regions are invited to participate in preparatory work for the document on the options of the Sixth Plan insofar as it concerns problems of "l'aménagement du territoire" and regional development. Thus the CODER already had to formulate advice concerning these issues at the very beginning of spring 1968. In 1969 a report on regional directives was established by the Prefect of the region and submitted to CODER for advice.

(c) The socio-economic tasks at the level of metropolitan areas and urban agglomerations.

These tasks have as object to bring out the perspectives of long term development (up to 1985) of metropolitan areas and the principal agglomerations.

Their elaboration constitutes the first phase with a view to the establishment of the different documents for urban planning: schemes for "aménagement" plans for the land use and programmes for modernisation and infrastructure for the Sixth Plan.

3.2. *The Second Period* (from spring 1970 until spring 1971)

At the national level this second period will start with the adoption by Parliament of the options intended for the orientation of the final tasks. At the regional or local level this second period will be devoted to the elaboration of the following documents:

(1) Draft programmes for the modernisation and infrastructure of the principal agglomerations for the Sixth Plan.

Starting from the long-term perspectives established during the first period the question will be to present:

a) Propositions related to infrastructure, indicating the major operations and the global financial amounts for each sector, and specifying the responsibilities for execution of works.

b) The results of the financial studies: projections of operational and investment expenses, cost and time schedule of the operations, proposed means of financing.

As for the Fifth Plan, the preparation of these programmes will concern all agglomerations of more than 50,000 inhabitants to which will be added agglomerations which do not reach this population figure but for which the establishment of a medium-term programme will be of special interest.

(2) Regional Propositions for the Sixth Plan.
Established by the Prefect of the region and submitted to CODER before the vote on the Sixth Plan, they will contain:
a) Proposals of the region as to infrastructure with, for each sector, an indication of the most important operations, their cost and interest, the others being treated more globally. These proposals will result from a first synthesis of projects for programmes in modernisation and infrastructure and needs in infrastructure as evaluated for the other urban or rural communities; projects elaborated under the direct responsibility of the central office and of interest to the region concerned will also be incorporated into this report.
Indications on the financial restraints per sector as well as concerning the financial capacities of local authorities will allow the elaboration of these proposals. The priorities formulated at the regional level can thus be taken into account for the final national choices of the Sixth Plan.
b) Proposals of the region on matters of economic activities: these will be presented per branch of activity: agriculture (orientation of the production, transformation of structures, training, rural renewal, etc.), industry (decentralisation, reconversion, professional education, industrial zones, etc.) They will thus put the emphasis on all actions which, because of their importance and their continuity, must be examined within the framework of medium-term evolution.

3.3. *The Third Period* (from October 1970 until March 1971)

This will be a question of drawing consequences from the vote on the plan for the establishment of the regional sections and urban programmes for modernisation and infrastructure for the Sixth Plan. The content of the programmes of the local authorities will be so determined with the choice of operations which are politically and financially feasible.

4. DEFINITION OF THE LONG TERM OPTIONS OF REGIONAL DEVELOPMENT POLICY

With the preparation of the Sixth Plan, long term studies of eco-

PLANNING CALENDAR FOR THE SIXTH PLAN

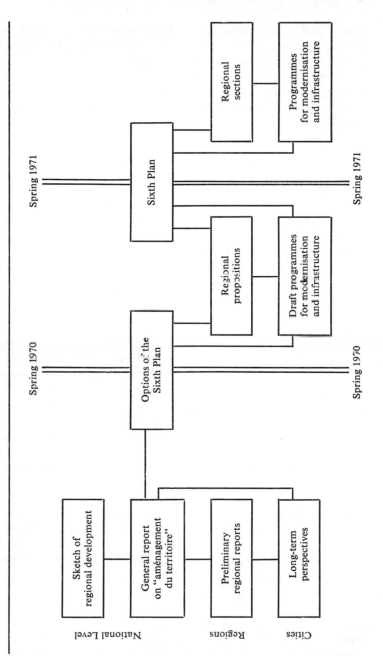

nomic and social development have been actively carried on. Studies reaching as far as 1985 had already been undertaken in 1964 when the Fifth Plan was being worked out; these were continued in 1968 and 1969 in different fields: consumption, recreation, labour force mobility, etc. Here we will only indicate the long term work which is particularly interesting with regard to "l'aménagement du territoire".

4.1. The 1985 regional outline

The regional outline consists of long term perspectives expressed in total population, active population and internal migration figures, which describe the long-term evolution of large zones of the territory. For the Sixth Plan research has been carried out in eight different regions of "l'aménagement du territoire"; it has not yet resulted in the formulation of hypotheses for development. Consequently we will adhere to comparable proceedings realised during the preparation of the Fifth Plan for which a simplified pattern was set up which distinguished the East, West and Parisian Region, and an attempt made to determine how industry and population would be distributed between these three regions in 1985.

In order to do this it was necessary to have an over-all perspective view of the French economy over 20 years. This was drawn up at the time of the proceedings of the 1985 group, which was installed in the "Commissariat Général au Plan", and the outcome was published as an annex to the report of this group. In this outline growth hypotheses were formulated in connection with the evolution of the total and active population to 1985, of productivity, gross production and household consumption. Starting from this general outline the "Commissariat Général au Plan" worked out a model for the distribution of the active population for 26 branches in the East, West and Parisian Region. It was presented as a "study on the localisation of industry and habitation in three major zones in 1985".

It is for instance pointed out that for the industry "motorcars and bicycles" 168,000 out of a total of 356,000 employees in 1985 would be found in the Parisian Region, 103,000 in the East and 84,200 in the West. Of course these only represented a hypothesis which might be useful for the selection of objectives. Reckoning with the uncertainties of the future, the scope of the hypotheses was also kept as wide as possible. But such a method also offered the advantage of usefully guiding the preliminary discussions on choices. Two examples will clarify the importance of this method.

4.1.1. *First example: the Case of the Parisian Region*

It was necessary to formulate a hypothesis for the long-term development of the Parisian Region because it was unreasonable to adhere to the longstanding doctrine, officially accepted in France yet continuously contradicted by the facts, that the capital would cease growing. The National Committee for "aménagement du territoire" forecasted an increasing growth of the Parisian Region, but less than that of the provincial towns, or, in other words: the growth of the Parisian Region will not exceed 36 percent (from 8.4 to 11.6 million inhabitants, approximately) while the other localities will together show a growth of 54 percent (from 21.1 tot 32.5 millions). In fact, extrapolation of the tendencies from 1954 to 1962 for the Parisian Region in 1985 would not lead to 5 million jobs – corresponding with a population 11.6 million – but to 5.7 million with a population of 13 million. With the hypothesis of 11.6 million the 'decrease in growth' of the Parisian Region amounts to approximately $1^1/_2$ million inhabitants.

4.1.2. *Second example: the Case of the West*

Here ten regions in 1962 represented 23.7 percent of the total industrial employment of France. It was necessary to make a long-term hypothetical forecast on the development of the total and active population of this zone based on important displacements of agricultural labour. While it had more than half of the total population of France at the beginning of the 19th century, the West did not have more than a third in 1962. It was necessary to assess to what extent this relative decline would continue.

What number of jobs should be created in the West to counter the situation of imbalance caused by outmigration and, consequently, what effort of reduction should be conducted in the Parisian Region and the East? The studies made as far as 1985 gave an answer to this question: in order to reverse the stream of migration so that the West would not suffer any decline in population until 1985, it would be necessary to create there, from 1962 until 1985, 60 percent of the total new industrial jobs in France. As the tendencies of the recent past have shown that its creation of new industrial jobs represented 25 percent of the total in France, it was hardly possible to make a sharp changeover to 60 percent. Between 25 and 60 percent various hypotheses on development could be expected. Thus the model 1985 gave a background for further study.

Starting from the overall picture thus drawn up, other long-term studies have been undertaken. Hypotheses have been formulated on population concentration in the seven regions crossed by the economic axis North Sea – Mediterranean. Similarly an essay on the geographical structure of French industry has led to the conclusion that from now until 1985 almost all the regions would suffer a very important decline in their specialisation as regional industrial activities would be increasingly diversified.

The aim of these models for the future is not to fix "ne varietur" an objective for spatial demographic balance in 1985, but rather to study the probable imbalances in various hypotheses and to elucidate the choices on the level of the objectives and the means.

4.2. Prospective urban studies

In the first place these contain a study of the whole territory by the "Groupe de Prospective Urbaine du VIIème Plan" whose conclusions have recently been worked out. The latter's purpose was to explain the urbanisation phenomenon: the urban population, which actually includes two-thirds of the total population, will represent approximately 85 percent of this total towards the end of the century. Further studies were also made by the "Organismes d'études d'aménagement des aires métropolitaines (OREAM)" created in 1967 in six large urban zones: Marseille, Metz-Nancy, Nord, Basse-Seine, Lyon-St. Etienne, Basse-Loire. After having edited a 'White paper' on the long-term perspectives of the metropolitan area, each OREAM is engaged in preparing perspective plans for "l'aménagement". These bodies are also making far-reaching studies on such subjects as: problems of employment and industrial change (Metz-Nancy, Nord), urban forms and mediterranean patterns of living (Marseille), etc. Thus the policies of "aménagement du territoire" are increasingly emphasising the modernisation of the major provincial towns to balance the growth of Paris.

4.3. Interregional Studies

Preliminary work has emphasised the growing solidarity between the regions within geographical complexes. Therefore studies have been made to complete the regional picture. The following studies are significant:

– Atlantic front: This research foresees the development of the West as an element in the international maritime economy, brought about by the revolution in sea-transport. Therefore traditional heavy industries are not likely to create the basis for industrial development in the West. The initial conclusions of the study-group recommend actions granting priority to light industries, and especially to more technically developed activities. (The development of electronics in Bretagne and the airspace-industry in the South-West are already pointing in that direction).

These conclusions also stress the necessity of avoiding ecological damage in the West in order to preserve all opportunities for the development of activities connected with tourism.

The Rhone-Mediterranean axis: In this zone which comprises Lyon and Marseille, recent developments have been extremely rapid; the chances are such that the rhythm of growth of these regions will remain high not only as a result of the increase in heavy industries (around the new port site of Fos-Marseille), but especially because of advanced technological industries and research activities.

The study of this area shows the necessity of carefully watching a wellbalanced spatial distribution as this zone is threatened by overpopulation (12.6 million inhabitants in 20 years as compared to the present 9.5 millions).

– The Atlantic-Mediterranean axis: The development of an eco-. nomic axis along the Garonne-valley and its continuation seems much more uncertain over a longer period than that of the Rhone-mediterranean axis. It has also led to consideration as to which activities could over the years take root in the growing metropolises and network of cities, and ultimately in the infrastructures demanded by the industrial development of the axis.

4.4. *Towards a general outline of 'aménagement' in France*

At the end of 1968 the preparation of a general outline or scheme of 'l'aménagement' was officially undertaken which was to go further than merely formulating long-term objectives such as had come up during the preparation of each separate national plan. This outline will consist of long-term perspectives for the "aménagement du territoire" based on the following concerns:

1) The outline must be an instrument of permanent and systematic research into the territorial 'aménagement'. It seems that for the moment the publication of a perspective plan for France for 1985 as a sort of charter which would lay down the desirable distribution of people and activities as well as the localisation of infrastructures has been brushed aside. Such a document would have the serious inconvenience of binding certain options over a long period in which periodical revision would be necessary. There is need for the utmost flexibility in choosing the right course. The strength of the general outline would thus be less in a proposed plan than in the fresh ideas which its development would put forward and its being constantly under discussion.

2) The general outline must be the point of convergence of other long-term studies. Certain administrative bodies have already for some years been working out development prospects for the area in which they are responsible and are now giving these works the form of 'sectorial perspective plans'. In the near future projects of these perspective plans regarding highways, harbours, navigable ways, air-connections, telecommunications, statistical centres, will especially be realised. Still other plans will concern the evaluation of natural resources, the protection of living conditions, informative services, scientific research, sources of energy, etc. All these long-term studies will soon result in proposals for decisions concerning collective infrastructural projects. The increasing importance of major infrastructural projects will considerably raise the risk of rash decisions of an unco-ordinated nature even though they will have a strong influence on the location and living conditions of people.

3) The general outline should ultimately provide occasion to use new techniques for prospective studies. The following studies are being utilised:
a) 'scenario' techniques: it should be possible to forecast, with the help of geographical 'scenarios' and a number of hypothetical combinations, the long-term tendencies in development. Various 'future images' could thus be drawn up to show the distribution of human activities. It would be possible, for example, to study the

situations created by a France, populated by approximately 100 million inhabitants, by developing almost exclusively the maritime zones or the valleys (In which regions would the French prefer to live? Will they be more or less attracted by the major urban concentrations? etc. etc.).

b) analysing techniques: these would permit a better evaluation of the efficacy of the main categories of activity, the study of their mutual repercussions and their coordination in due time. It would especially be possible to use the techniques developed in the central prospective and evaluation department of the War Ministry and in the Ministry for Economic Affairs and Finance for the rationalisation of budgetary allocations.

c) technological research: analysis of the effects of technological innovations on policies for the "aménagement du territoire": study of the risks of obsolescence of infrastructure, examination of the guiding-lines for applied research to promote the aims of these policies.

d) information technology: the media of information technology, which have permitted the systematic collecting of local statistical data, should permit a better appreciation of the results and the significance of future decisions. The development work of the general outline for "l'aménagement du territoire" of France will probably take a great many years and might become the object for drawing up several schemes, which will be published and discussed according to the advancement of the studies.

5. MEDIUM-TERM REGIONALISATION OF THE NATIONAL PLAN

The Regionalisation of the Plan occupies an essential position in the policies for "l'aménagement du territoire". It is in fact an intermediate stage, in two senses:

> – in time: it represents the medium-term (5 years in French planning) and is situated between the general planning scheme (long-term) and regionalisation of the budget (short-term).
> – in space: it is the hinge on which the national plan and the local plans (urban localities of rural zones) are revolving.

In many countries regional planning has been developed in the last

20 years. Two distinct types should, however, be distinguished.

In certain countries it has been interpreted as the regionalisation of national planning as is the case in France, where the term "tranches régionales" (regional sections) is significant; in other countries regional planning is not yet integrated into the national plan (the latter sometimes even does not exist). Then one can speak of autonomous regional planning. It is clear that these two types often correspond to different political and administrative systems.

In France the regional sections are defined as the geographical projection, on regional level, of the prospects for population distribution (total and active) and public investment objectives of the national plan. Without going into the technical mechanisms of their preparation we will survey their principal characteristics:

(1) Just as the national plan is preceded by a document on the options of development, likewise a report on guidelines for each region has preceded the development of each regional section. Moreover, in the planning calendar regional studies must be carried out early enough to be taken into account while making national planning choices: in this respect progress has been made in the transition from the Fifth to the Sixth Plan.

(2) Regional planning implies at the same time the study of regional development forecasts (mainly concerning labour) and the distribution of public investments; these two aspects are interrelated, as infrastructures must not be planned nor created independently from regional development objectives. The capacity of the regional sections is not exhaustive as the technical instruments that are available for regional planning do not allow us to proceed towards a geographical study of all important magnitudes of the plan. Present-day regional planning in France is selective in two respects:

– first the regional and urban forecasts which have been drawn up for a medium term do not cover all the problems of development. Thus greater stress is laid upon the investigation of production factors and conditions in the region than on market research, which only bears real significance for a number of branches of industry. The balance of employment only serves to diagnose the local labour imbalances which do not appear in the combination of figures on national level.

– secondly public investment programmes do not contain a detailed enumeration of all the infrastructural operations to be realised during the execution of the plan. The regional section only fixes the global investment expenditures for small operations, whereas the more important ones are mentioned in multi-annual lists in order of priority.

(3) Regional planning distinguishes three categories of public investment according to their national, regional or local character. The responsibilities of the Regional Prefects and of the CODER entrusted with the setting-up of the regional sections is different for each category; it is smaller (remarks) in the case of the national infrastructures (about one half of the total) and larger (proposals) for the regional and local infrastructures. But experience gathered from the Fifth Plan has shown that this division into three categories could only have real practical significance if it would bring about a change in the present-day regulations concerning the redivision of responsibilities and financing. In the present system regional and local investments largely depend upon the decisions of the central administrative powers, particularly because of the subsidies to local authorities.

(4) Regional Planning is set up within a financial framework adopted on a central level: the Regional Prefects enjoy freedom of action to some extent (changes or substitutions) within this framework which is indispensable in order to ensure complete coordination between the national plan and the regional sections. (In all other planning systems the addition of 21 regional sections would have largely exceeded the financial possibilities of the Fifth Plan). The problem is to know whether or not this financial framework should remain comparatively detailed (amounts fixed for the infra-structural categories within each public investment sector), which makes it particularly compulsory for the regional and local authorities.

(5) The regional sections cover investments financed by the State as well as those financed by local communities, and consequently those that are financed by both: this is the reason why they include task-performing authorisations drawn from the State budget (thus facilitating the linking-up with the annual budgeting of the State) as well as operations which mobilise all the other available sources of financing. This was necessary in order to obtain a complete view of

public investments, but at the same time proved to be a source of difficulties as the intentions of local communities regarding investment matters had to be found out even when these were of small practical value for the setting-up of working-programmes.

The criticisms formulated against regional planning in the Fifth Plan were mainly aimed at the period of regional consultations which was considered too short. Moreover, the margin of choice left to regions within the financial framework defined by central administrative bodies was considered to be equally insufficient.

But in spite of these difficulties it can be said that the regional actions have had two important advantages: primarily they have promoted the introduction of a better assessment in establishing standards for the geographical distribution of infrastructures: further they have, in spite of the narrow limits, united the regions and local communities in the preparation of choices for the plan and the setting-up of infrastructural programmes, thus opening-up the possibility of an increasing decentralisation. The application of clearly decentralised methods might prove to be the original hallmark of preparations for the Fifth Plan. But this progress will be impossible without the revision of institutions which must now be thoroughly examined.

It is clear that regional planning cannot be summarised in one simple operation of geographical division of the national figures of the plan, but that it also implies a distribution of responsibilities on various geographical levels for economic and social policies. That is the reason why the progress in planning in France has amply contributed towards the serious and firm belief in the importance of regional reform. After the failure of the referendum of April 1969 it is very difficult to forecast the future stages of this reform. But the experience acquired during the setting-up of the Fifth and Sixth Plans at least serves to emphasise some problems that have come up in France as a result of the development of present-day regional and local institutions:

– *the geographical (physical) framework of regional planning:* the majority of the 21 existing regions are considered too small to serve as a basis for the conception and realisation of full-fledged regional development policies within their own boundaries. It is therefore suggested to decrease the number of regions, to 8 or 9 or 12 at the most. We have indeed been able to observe, that the setting-up of the Sixth Plan would entail quite a number of studies covering a larger territory than that occupied by the 21 regions. But contrary to the opinions of those responsible for planning and "l'aménagement du territoire", who are often supporters of the idea of reducing the number of regions, there are others who for either political or administrative reasons are in favour of maintaining the 21 regions.

– *the powers of regional authorities:* the existing regional bodies have practically no power of decision with regard to the state-budget or local finances. This is the reason why ultimately regional planning does not sufficiently involve the decentralised regional authorities, because for the greater part it is mainly being realised with the aid of advisory organisations like the CODER. Whereas some wish to maintain the idea of a region being simply a link between the central government and the local authorities there are others who, on the contrary, consider that this linking-up is ineffective, and that the region should become a territorial unity having its own field of competence and budgetary means.

– *the role of local authorities in regional planning:* the most important improvements should be anticipated from a closer cooperation of local authorities in planning. Those responsible for the Sixth Plan therefore emphasise the necessity of improving the urban or rural programmes, which should form the basic stages of planning both for estimating the needs and financing and for coordinating the infrastructures. The proposals formulated in recent years with regard to a communal rearrangement should permit the establishment of new intercommunal stages, better adapted to the tasks of planning and "l'aménagement du territoire". The progress of physical and economic planning is creating new groupings, new communities which hitherto could only be dimly perceived on the level of regions, towns or rural areas. This progress will, however, only result in the creation of solid and durable institutions if it is accompanied by continuous efforts in the field of information and education. Therefore regional planning policies being actually executed in various countries should, instead of remaining a matter for specialists, be open to the wide participation of citizens.

12

K. PORWIT

TECHNIQUES OF INTERREGIONAL PLAN FORMULATION IN POLAND

This paper deals with the techniques of planning as they relate to long-term economic development programmes for the regions and the various branches of the economy and also to medium-term plans. Interregional aspects of these techniques will have to be considered against a background of a multidimensional system of planning (i.e. plans which vary in time and scope will be considered together). In line with the main theme of the paper basic techniques and procedures used in planning will be reviewed, but no specific formalised model will be considered in detail.

Planning is a systematic process which has various consecutive stages, each of which serves a specific purpose. Planning procedures applied at the various stages are based on a cooperation between various organisational units (on the levels of management). These units have to compile data which reflect past experiences and estimates of the future, and to utilise such data for decision-making. Depending on the time available and on the level of management, these decisions either directly start some action or indirectly influence action undertaken by others.

In this procedure regional aspects of the economy must be considered in many ways:

(a) the coordination of regional contributions to national growth by the CPA;
(b) the planning of activities in the regions through the drawing-up of programmes of activities in a region by the regional planning agency;
(c) the planning of local activities by branch planning agencies.

These problems will be discussed as follows: Section 1 will be devoted to the presentation of basic principles which serve as guidelines to practical solutions; in section 2 attention will be drawn to the main features and tasks of long-term and medium-term approaches; section 3 will be a description of the main problems to be solved in the long-term programmes of development; section 4 will indicate the characteristics of medium-term planning and the approaches applied in implementing such plans.

1. BASIC PRINCIPLES

Practical solutions must be based on a consideration of theoretical planning principles which aim at optimal development of the national economy and its particular sectors and regions. Consequently, the following problems must be considered: (a) the formulation of development targets and the place of regional targets in the whole structure of planning; (b) the most efficient way to reach such targets (i.e. a way which would ensure the optimal utilisation of resources); the role of regional approaches in the tasks of finding the solution to this problem; (c) how to organise the decision-making process and effect the implementation of decisions, giving due consideration to such matters as the efficiency of the information media and the managerial apparatus.

The necessity of an approach based on the principles of system analysis should be emphasised.

1.1.

As already stated planning is a systematic procedure which aims at the implementation of several specific targets. Consequently, it is necessary to: (a) specify quantified targets; (b) specify potential variants of reaching such targets (i.e. variants of utilisation of various resources); (c) find out the resources available for reaching such targets; (d) check whether some variants will make it possible to reach the targets; (e) revise the targets if some of the resources are not fully utilised or prove insufficient for reaching the targets; (f) find out which variant is optimal (in the sense of allowing the 'best set' of targets to be reached with the available resources); (g) organise the instruments which will ensure operational implementation of the variant finally chosen; (h) supervise the processes of implementation in order to find out eventual discrepancies and to set in motion adaptive activities.

Within the whole framework of planning we have to be aware of
the interdependence among particular targets and the conditions
for their implementation. Examples of such interdependence are as
follows:

(a) there is a hierarchical order of targets, i.e. there are targets of the
highest order (related to overall social development objectives)
and targets which are conditionally valid (they have to be revised
if this proves desirable from the point of view of priority targets);
(b) particular targets of the lower order are horizontally interdependent (i.e. the feasibility of implementing target A depends on
the implementation of target B etc.);
(c) at any given time horizon certain constraints limit the possibility
of reaching higher targets and are impossible to overcome; in the
longrun it is possible to launch programmes to overcome such
constraints, and this means that the reaching of certain targets
depends on the availability of time;
(d) sets of activities to be implemented by particular organisational
units, and which might lead to the formulation of organisation-
oriented programmes must be identified (i.e. targets and ways of
implementing them); such programmes will not necessarily be
identical with problem-oriented programmes; consequently, there
is an overlapping interdependence between:
– problem-oriented programmes, which should lead to the solution
of a comprehensive problem (very often related to the activities of
various organisations), and
– organisation-oriented programmes, which in a sense, are secondary in relation to the former.

1.3.

It is clear from the above that we have to deal with a very large and
complicated system, whose complexity is due not only to its size,
but also to its following features:

(a) the system covers all aspects of social, economic, political and
technological development of society and its welfare; consequently,
various phenomena, some of which are hardly quantifiable, must
be taken into account;

(b) it has to deal not only with the future but also with activities which have to be started now in order to obtain immediate results; consequently, it is a system which operates under conditions of uncertainty;
(c) it should lead to the implementation of certain predetermined objectives; it must therefore contain strong elements of normative, deterministic nature and cannot be based primarily on adaptive principles of self-regulation.[1]

1.4.

Taking these factors into consideration it must be pointed out that planning and management problems related to the large system can be solved in such a way as to allow:

(a) the application of the principles of decomposition (i.e. to consider particular sub-systems within a procedure which consists of iterative steps, vertical and horizontal information flows, and ensures the influence of overall criteria of rationality on a macro-scale);
(b) the combination of quantifiable and non-quantifiable criteria for the appraisal of certain problems;
(c) an adequate use to be made of various techniques of analysing, projecting, forecasting, programming and controlling[2] various kinds of problems and activities (in the sense of using a technique for the kinds of problems for which it is best suited).

1.5.

The planning and management procedures which were mentioned under 1.4., have the following characteristics in practice:

(a) they demand the cooperation of many people (grouped in the various planning agencies and organisational units) and also need adequate data processing equipment (DPE);
(b) all the actors taking part in planning and managerial procedures must use a common language (with regard to definitions, classi-

---

[1] In other words, it is not sufficient that the system should allow immediate problems to be solved. It must be simultaneously guided by the necessity to attain future objectives. This does not mean that self-regulating mechanisms can be neglected.
[2] We have in mind here direct techniques of control as well as those based on indirect mechanism of prices, financial and fiscal instruments, material and non-material incentives, etc.

fications, etc.); it is equally desirable that they use commonly accepted methods and criteria for appraisal and decision-making;[3] (c) the ability of all these people to cooperate efficiently depends on the adequacy of their knowledge based on their training and their experience with regard to techniques, and on the motivation to act according to the requirements of the whole system.

It follows that the efficient working of planning and managerial procedures depends, among others, on:

– the amount of effort exerted with regard to such prerequisites as manuals, unified classification rules, various aspects of data processing and conveying systems;
– how much emphasis is placed on education and training of personnel;
– the operation of a set of principles regarding performance indicators, incentives, financial instruments etc., which would create adequate motivation for the people involved to act according to certain expectations.[4]

1.6.

It has been necessary to outline some basic features of the whole system of planning and management (see 1.1. – 1.5.) because it is impossible to discuss any planning technique without an explicit statement concerning the part of the system it serves. Thus, for instance, forecasts based on econometric projections may be considered useful for the purposes of medium-term demand analysis, but cannot be of much use in appraising alternative variants for a set of investment projects or for drawing up an operational programme for their implementation. Similarly the techniques of comprehensive structural analysis based on inter-industrial input-output or linear programming models can be easily criticised if looked at from an angle of locational problems of a given branch, but they may prove indispensable at the stage of the planning

[3] This postulate meets some difficulties, in as far as there exist various conflicts between criteria of choice based on different understanding of interest (short-term versus long-term, social interest of a wider scope versus direct interest of a narrow group etc.).
[4] Any procedure which is based on decomposition principles and information flows pertaining to the future should have built-in devices to counter possible tendencies towards biased information.

procedure where major strategic lines for inter-branch and inter-regional proportions of development are considered.

Moreover, these various techniques have not only to serve various purposes, but have also to be mutually interdependent to be efficient in their application. This means that conditions may be more favourable for solving problem A with technique X if, simultaneously, problem B has been solved with technique Y. Thus, for example, a study of probable technological trends using appropriate forecasting techniques would also help us to undertake a structural study for the choice of strategic development proportions with the help of appropriate mathematical programming techniques. The latter would in turn give a better idea concerning future ratios of outlays (e.g. in terms of accounting prices), which may facilitate the analysis and choice of a set of industrial projects made with the aid of cost-benefit techniques, industrial complex or other appropriate mathematical programming techniques (such as: integer programming).

Only against the background of the whole system can one appraise the practical sense and usefulness of macro- and mezzo-economic models (regional models being an example of the latter). Such models do not give an answer at an operational, micro-level (i.e. they do not tell what particular products should be produced and sold, whether to build a new plant (and if so where) or to extend and modernise an existing one). It would not be worthwhile to execute programmes based on such models for purely academic purposes, in order to arrive at elegant solutions, if there were no possibilities of using these results for policy-making purposes. This means that macro- and mezzo-accounts should help to influence specific, more detailed activities. These solutions should then serve as a source of information, either for indirect policy instruments or for particular micro-calculations in a direct form of output (sales targets, resource limits or accounting price ratios).

Looking at the system as a whole, one can understand why it is useful and even necessary sometimes to make tentative estimates of exogenous factors as well as of some relationships (e.g. inter-industry input-output coefficients), and to make calculations based on such unsafe assumptions. This approach is often criticised by people with an engineering background for whom a calculation not based on detailed technological norms and designs is something similar to crystal gazing. The point, however, is that there are problems which cannot be solved on the basis of technological and "safe" information. The necessity of solving such problems arises in the initial stages of long and medium-term planning when policy variants are considered and not at those stages where operational implementation programmes for separate projects are made. We may consider, for example, the initial stages of branch development programming in which one of the problems that have to be tackled is the formulation of locational policy. Each branch would tend to solve this problem on the basis of an appraisal of past and future locational factors, and would be unable to allow for possible changes in locational factors which result from decisions made by other branches or by the regional authorities responsible for the development of infrastructural facilities. No branch can expect all other branches and regional authorities to provide detailed information concerning future activities, because they are all in a similar situation i.e. dependent on projects to be undertaken elsewhere. It would not be sensible or realistic to organise the procedure of planning in such a way as to require every branch or region to prepare many variants of detailed programmes and to adopt an iterative procedure on such a basis. Tentative estimates and a more aggregated approach make it possible to work out this procedure, whereas detailed programmes come later after basic proportions have been mutually coordinated.

1.7.

Following the characteristic stages of the planning procedure (as listed under 1.1.), it might be useful to indicate the main problems relating to regional planning:

(i) The task of specifying the targets (objectives) at the national level involves the following: (a) determination of an intertemporal schedule for satisfying the needs of the society; (b) determination of proportionate needs (of individual consumers, households and of society in general); (c) the formulation of policy in relation to the proportions in which the needs should be satisfied through the market or in the form of free (non-payable) services; (d) the laying down of policy in relation to the instruments which would shape the commodity structure of consumers demand on the market; (e) the formulation of policy with regard to distribution as it affects the major social-professional groups and the population of particular regions of the country; (f) balance of payments policy.

All these problems must be considered, appraised and solved at the national level. The structure of an important category of targets (listed under [c], [d] and [e]) is directly related to the preferences of the population, as expressed by its representatives in the respective regional and national authorities. Regional points of view will then play an important role in the task of setting all such targets and in deciding their proportional regional allocations. Similarly specification of these targets from the point of view of the regions in which they will have to be implemented is an important basis for balancing procedures which will match demand and supply, especially regarding local (hardly transferable) goods and services.

This defines the first category of interregional planning techniques, viz. the techniques concerned with consumption and all other indicators of the general welfare of the people.

(ii) The task of appraising available resources and their optimal utilisation involves the following: (a) population forecasts; (b) forecasts and analysis of particular natural resources; (c) appraisal of existing stock of capital and infrastructural facilities and the efficient way of utilising them; (d) forecasts, analysis and estimates of potentially feasible technologies as described by the respective input-output and similar technological co-efficients; (e) balancing of future demand and supply in the main branches, with regard to groups of products and services, labour, capital, and foreign exchange; (f) analyses and choice of technological variants and foreign trade, made with the use of cost-benefit or comparative cost techniques.[5]

Most of these problems must be tackled in a way which allows the explicit introduction of the elements of space.

A distinction is made in Poland between productive branches and services which are directly supervised by the respective regional authorities, and other branches under the supervision of central government agencies. The regional aspects of planning take the following forms:

– *territorial planning* in respect of the first of the two categories mentioned above;

[5] The tasks listed under (e) and (f) are sometimes combined into a comprehensive optimising programme.

– *territorial coordination* of certain activities relating to both categories (especially investment activities, which will be described in section 4 below);
– *Regional planning* in the sense of planning of all kinds of activities in a given region based on the proportional allocation of national development projects.

Regional approaches consequently play an important role in planning techniques and procedures which aim at an efficient utilisation of resources. According to the institutional forms of planning, this is being done in a more comprehensive way in terms of more aggregated development proportions (regional planning), and in a more detailed way in certain branches (local and small-scale industries, services, infrastructural facilities, covered by territorial planning) and in the coordination of certain aspects of key industries and territorial activities.

Similarly, there is a body of statistical data which corresponds to the classification of activities described above. This allows each region to make a comprehensive analysis of past developments and thus get an overall picture of interregional proportions at the national level.

1.8.

The characteristic features of planning, outlined under 1.4. and 1.5. above, give rise to important questions related to the role of particular lower subsystem levels of management within the overall decision-making system.[6]

In approaching such questions, the following interpretations of participation at the lower levels may be considered:

– the first, based on the concept of iterative steps, involving an exchange of information (i.e. draft programmes prepared by the respective subsystem levels, their horizontal coordination and vertical confirmation of revision in view of economy-wide criteria);
– the second assumes that the lower subsystem levels are entitled to make final decisions within their respective spheres of activities,

[6] Such questions were tackled by the author in his contribution to the Budapest Conference of the Regional Science Association (K. Porwit "Theoretical and Methodological Questions in the Construction of Comprehensive Models for Regional Planning", RSA Papers, XXII, 1968).

subject to adequate conditions for decentralised decision-making being created by the higher levels (guidelines, indicative information, rules for measurement of performance, incentives etc.).

It may be argued that the first approach gives the subsystems quite an important role, subsystem management being the real source of programmes which result in the economy-wide development pattern. However, subsystems cannot have the final word in determining the outflows and inflows which link them with their environment (i.e. the rest of the economy-wide system). Consequently, suggestions made by the subsystems have to be checked, confirmed or revised within the wider framework of national economic plans.

The second approach is also based on the understanding that the subsystems must be able to coordinate their activities with their own environment (within the economy-wide system). It is assumed, however, that coordination can be implemented by means of indirect instruments, i.e. predetermined indicative information which will enable each subsystem to make a final decision without needing to introduce subsequent stages of confirmation or revision. The question is whether the indicative information supplied to the subsystems will be sufficient to ensure the convergence of decentralised decisions with the desired national pattern.

The solution actually adopted cannot be based on either of these 'pure' concepts but must combine the elements of both. What are the criteria for combining the instruments of the two approaches?

The second approach would be operationally more effective (i.e. less costly and cumbersome) if it were really workable. It can be argued, however, that indirect instruments would not be sufficient to ensure implementation of a desired set of social targets and of the corresponding optimal pattern of resource allocation. Direct inter-level coordination must be concerned, first of all, with problems which are directly related to the implementation of economy-wide goals. The line of demarcation cannot be drawn according to any predetermined institutional criteria. Every subsystem defined by organisational or spatial structural features (i.e. branch or regional subsystem) usually comprises the following types of activities:

– those induced by the environment of the subsystem and oriented to the implementation of exogenous targets,
– those self-induced within the subsystem and oriented to the targets endogenous from the point of view of this subsystem.

These types of activities are mutually interconnected within the subsystem so that they cannot be separated and considered as independent, still smaller, subsystems.

In programming the network of activities for the subsystem, the direct procedure of coordination of the inflows and outflows related to the first type of activities (exogenously oriented) must be ensured. At the same time, the second type of activities (endogenously oriented) can be shaped by decisions made at lower subsystem levels influenced by the following considerations:

(a) the impact of links with exogenously-oriented activities;
(b) the criterion of implementation of endogenous subsystem targets;
(c) the criterion of efficiency, i.e. maximising benefit cost ratios (with adequate pricing rules).[7]
Consequently, considerations (a) and (c) allow decentralised decisions to be made consistent with the system as a whole.

2. MAIN FEATURES OF PLANS COVERING DIFFERENT TIME-HORIZONS

In any planning procedure which leads to decision-making a distinction must be drawn between the following categories of elements:

(i) *autonomous data*, which are determined by the factors outside the scope of a given plan;
(ii) *exogenous variables*, which are predetermined by the planner, as targets to be implemented by means of planned activities;
(iii) *endogenous variables*, which correspond to such activities whose level is set as a result of planning procedures;
(iv) *functional coefficients* and other interrelations which express the way of linking particular activities.

The procedure may be described as follows: within the conditions set by the information on the autonomous data (i) and feasible

---

[7] This criterion is also widely used in procedures related to economy-wide planning systems. However, it is not unique in the sense that any ranking order based on predetermined pricings of costs and benefit can be subject to change due to the consideration of social targets.

variants of functional coefficients (iv), one should determine how to put in motion particular activities, as expressed by the endogenous variables (iii), in order to find the most efficient way to implement the targets (ii).

The contents of each category depend on the scope of the problem to be solved and on the time-horizon it covers. The shorter the time-horizon the more autonomous the elements and the smaller the variety of possible functional coefficients. This will diminish the freedom of choice for setting the exogenous (target) variables and in finding feasible sets of endogenous variables.

With a longer time-horizon the freedom of choice increases, but at the same time, a greater number of elements become uncertain.

Similarly, it must be noted that in solving sectoral, micro-economic problems, we have to deal with a greater number of elements which are externally determined (either as autonomous data or as exogenous variables). However, there is more possibility of specifying particular functional coefficients and of obtaining a more detailed knowledge of constraining factors (e.g. such exogenous data as all factors defining the existing productive capacities). On the other hand if the scope of the problem becomes wider covering the whole economy, the number of external factors decreases, but uncertainty increases in the knowledge of all internal elements.

Within a longer time-horizon it is possible to reshape some elements, which seemed unchangeable in the short-run (e.g. the supply of fixed capital, trained personnel etc.). Certain projects which may effect such changes can be decided upon but it will take some time to implement them. Under medium-term plans such projects can be started. However, not every project can be implemented under these plans; within a medium-term horizon, very often it is only those prepared earlier. These should be based on adequate studies which must indicate where and how to start solving such future problems.

The medium-term plans indicate how to reshape particular aspects of the economy, but the long-term plans should create the conditions to make such a reshaping possible. Without long-term studies (meant to solve future problems) we might be in a better position to smooth actual disproportions than to pursue more distant goals.

3. LONG-TERM PLANNING

Under this heading the following problems deserve particular attention:

(a) country-wide population forecasts, the study of demand and supply of labour with reference to the main skills and professions;
(b) the study of future trends in the pattern of consumption and other aspects of the standard of living of the population;
(c) forecasts and studies related to the expected technological trends including the main directions for research and development activities;
(d) forecasts and studies of external factors affecting the national economy;
(e) the study of the main guidelines provided under the policy for physical planning (i.e. spatial aspects of development).

These problems are dealt with in a way which makes it possible to consider their mutual interrelations. Thus they have a common background which is the detailed studies of macro-economic and structural (intersectoral) development proportions. On the other hand, there are specific studies relating to chosen sectors of the economy (those sectors which need a long-term development policy because development projects need longer gestation periods).

These problems (a) to (e) are priorities under the long-term plan while macro-economic and structural studies play an auxiliary role. The sectoral studies tend to integrate the respective elements of these problems.

Studies of spatial development policy (item e) attempt to do the following:

(i) To analyse and set down lines of development for the main regions of the country in terms of their basic functions, structural features of the regional economy and its growth rate. This includes studies relating to the main resources (population, natural resources, capital, social and physical environment), the possibilities of their optimal utilisation in order to maximise social welfare. Further there is the problem of specifying functions, for the industrial centres, agricultural areas, recreation areas etc.
(ii) To outline the policy for the future development of the network of towns and settlements and their role.

(iii) To formulate policies for such infrastructures as water, the power system, and transport and communications.

Such studies are done with the whole country in view but they are not supposed to deal with every issue nor to go into much detail. Concentrating attention on the major issues, they are meant to provide the backbone for the coordination of spatial (physical) and socio-economic aspects of development. They help to appraise and to coordinate development studies made by particular regions (as seen from the point of view of the regions in question) and also the regional aspects of sectoral development studies made by some branch planning agencies. On the other hand the development studies carried out by the regions and by some branches provide important information for the country-wide studies. Consequently, there is an iterative procedure of consecutive approximations in the application of which various forecasts, ideas, policies and criteria are being matched, revised and reconciled.

It may be said that this iterative procedure gives the character of planning to a system of forecasts and development studies, but that these, carried out separately, are not meant for the purposes of decision-making. They are to indicate the probabilities and possibilities. This is followed by a procedure of appraisals, evaluations and comparative analyses, the contents of which acquire a new sense – that of planning.

For this purpose it becomes necessary to use not only some forecasting techniques but also such techniques as balancing, comparative-cost, and cost-benefit analysis, as well as comprehensive structural analysis and mathematical programming.

Obviously, partial and comprehensive balancing techniques can be applied here in a special sense i.e. not for deterministic, allocative purposes but for purposes of getting a rough idea of probable interdependence among particular studies and forecasts (in relation to problems [a] to [e] above).

Similarly, the use of comparative-cost and cost-benefit analysis for evaluating possible variants of future developments in particular fields, branches and areas must be specially considered. It cannot be based on the system of prices existing at any particular moment but should take into account the approximate estimates of accounting prices as might be affected by changing conditions e.g. relative scarcities of factors of production and changes in production techniques. These conditions will depend partly on various exogenous constraints and partly on the national and regional socio-economic goals.

This leads us to the conclusion that comprehensive programming techniques may be useful in a twofold manner: (i) as the means for obtaining an approximate estimation of accounting prices for the evaluation of partial problems (i.e. problems pertaining to selected sectors of the economy in which the efficiency of feasible solutions may be evaluated on the basis of a more comprehensive and detailed form of such analysis, (ii) as a technique which helps assess the structural proportions of development corresponding to optimal solutions. The reference here is to 'optimal solutions' and not the optimal solution, because we are using aggregated models in which there is a range of possible estimates of particular parameters and also of constraining conditions.

Some of the techniques mentioned above have been used widely, but others are still in the experimental stage. Wide experience has already been gained in the preparation of long-term development plans for specific regions and areas. The elements of economic and physical planning have been integrated into such plans. Extensive studies have been made concerning infrastructural problems, the development of industrial centres, the functions of particular towns etc. Interregional aspects have been studied mainly from the angle of particular problems and also of sectoral development pro-portions. Similarly, there is a long practice of comparative, inter-regional analyses and forecasting of main growth indicators in aggregated terms (value of output, capital, employment, consump-tion of goods and services etc.). There are still problems to be solved in the application of comprehensive programming models which would make possible the explicit integration of particular sectoral problems with interregional proportions.

There is a special network of regional long-term planning centres in Poland and a centre for spatial aspects of the long-term develop-ment of the whole country. These centres are organised as parts of regional planning agencies and the central planning agency respec-tively; they can thus keep in close touch with other planning units (i.e. they are informed about actual issues considered in medium-term plans and are able to exert influence on their form of the latter). It has been realised that the studies of long-term spatial development of the country must be based on adequate research and scientific advice. The problems in question are dealt with by a special committee of the Polish Academy of Science. Further, there is a special advisory board attached to the office of the Chairman of the Planning Commission of the Government. This is composed of prominent scholars, research workers etc. representing various sciences dealing with problems of spatial development planning.

4. MEDIUM-TERM PLANNING

Interregional aspects of planning must be considered in relation to the consecutive stages of constructing the medium-term plan. *In the first stage* the CPA prepares tentative indices of development for the national economy and as a result directive figures are given for the following: the upper limits of investment outlays; the expected value of exports and imports; the expected increase of productivity of labour. The figures are set down for particular organisations supervised directly by the central government (ministries and associations of enterprises) as well as for other organisations supervised by the regional authorities. Some directive figures relating to industrial output are also given. At that same stage all the regions start to prepare the first draft of their development plans. This is based on an outline of development programmes prepared from earlier studies. Thus the regional authorities are already provisionally informed about the development prospects (including locational possibilities) of branches of both kinds of organisation, i.e. those under regional supervision and those directly supervised by the central government. This information is really tentative because all the branches are simultaneously engaged in revising their previous long-term prospects and therefore cannot possibly take into account the centrally determined directive figures for the next five-year period. During the first stage of planning at the regional level attention is concentrated mainly on the problems of population and employment, of infrastructure (housing, communal facilities, transport and communication, power and fuel supply network, social services etc.) The main point is to find out where and to what extent the further development of the region may encounter certain constraints.

This is important because it is necessary to determine the range of outlays which would make it possible to overcome the constraints in order to coordinate the infrastructural and other branch activities. Another aspect of the preparatory studies is the analysis of interregional commodity flows. Such studies lead to interesting conclusions concerning the possible variants of location of new projects in view of the spatial distribution of raw materials output, the markets for fuel products and the labour supply. Again the studies include the problems of spatial interdependence between the location of some major industries (e.g. ship-building, automotive industry etc.) and their numerous suppliers. In many cases regional studies of this kind lead to a more detailed analysis of the present and future role of the region in the national economy. This can be seen in the region's contribution to industrial and agricultural output, national income, employment and investment as well as consumption, social services etc. In short, all these studies may be considered as an important preparatory stage for the next stage in which the RPA will be obliged to prepare more specific draft plans based on directives from the centre and ideas from branch planners.

In the second stage the draft plan is executed by the various sectorial bodies concerned i.e. main enterprises, associations of enterprises, ministries supervising directly some key branches and the regional authorities. This stage is crucial because it is meant to find out and specify the desirable development patterns for each body and consequently to draw up the corresponding programmes for investment and other measures for quantitative and qualitative development. All the bodies are expected to analyse various feasible variants of development patterns (differing with respect to the specification of the output-mix and of the input-mix, to the scale of the future output, to the possibilities of increasing the international specialisation etc.). The variants are appraised using comparative-cost and cost-benefit techniques (the principles of which are uniformly set for this purpose in a manual published by the CPA).

For the following reasons we cannot consider the results of such draft planning as final:

(a) The draft plans of separate organisations are mutually interdependent, thus it is necessary to set in motion the adequate *horizontal* channels of information flows as well as the instruments for horizontal coordination. There are two basic types of such coordinative activities: (i) territorial coordination and (ii) branch-wise coordination. The first enables the RPA to obtain relevant information[8] about all activities undertaken in a region. The RPA

---

[8]   This information is naturally limited to certain relevant elements: such problems as investment, employment, output, housing and social services which a branch has to deal with.

appraises this information for the following two reasons: (a) in order to influence the particular drafts by way of their revision; (b) in order to adapt certain activities directly under the supervision of the regional authorities to the conditions created by other sectoral activities. [9]

(b) The criteria which have been used by certain organisations to select some projects must still be evaluated with due consideration to their impact on the implementation of social targets (both national and regional) and the principle of optimal utilisation of resources. [10] Subsequently it becomes necessary to put into operation *vertical* channels of information and instruments of vertical coordination. Thus the regional authorities utilise the same information they needed for the horizontal coordination, but now they concentrate on the following two aspects: (i) whether the results of all the sectoral activities would make it possible to reach the desired regional targets; (ii) whether it would be possible to increase the efficiency of utilisation of resources and consequently to increase the effects attained with the available resources. The first of these two aspects may give rise to conflicting ideas from the branches concerned. It should be noted here that the regional authorities must act in this case in conformity with the guidelines for regional development which were embodied in the election programme accepted by the constituencies. In order to assess the expected results of all sectoral activities in a region and to decide on how to resolve eventual conflicts the regions prepare comprehensive draft plans (which include a list of basic development indicators), which they submit to the CPA. Simultaneously, the following two other types of plans are prepared by the regions: (i) sectoral draft plans of activities directly supervised by the regional authorities and (ii) investment programmes relating to the so-called 'accompanying' and 'joint' investment projects. These programmes are considered as important measures facilitating a more efficient utilisation of resources. The category of 'accompanying' investment projects includes all projects which create new or fresh investments in

[9] At the level of the branch there are instruments for the horizontal coordination of output, investment, technological solutions etc. by the various organisations. The limited scope of this paper does not allow a more detailed description of this procedure.
[10] This may be explained by the fact that we are not able to determine 'ex ante' a system of prices which would ensure complete correlation between partial cost-benefit criteria and the pattern of targets on the one hand and the optimal utilisation of resources on the other.

transport, communication, power generation and transmission, water supply, housing and all kinds of social services, on the understanding that such investments will be linked with other investment projects (such as industrial plants). There are special regulations governing the manner of financing such 'accompanying' projects but they must all be embodied in one comprehensive programme. The other category of projects (i.e. 'joint' projects) may include all forms of capital formation, which make it possible for a number of separate enterprises to decide to implement a single project to serve their common need.[11] In view of the facilities available regional coordinating bodies have been formed which have the authority to make a final decision on the participation of particular enterprises in any such joint project. Examples are storehouses, garages, repair shops, internal power-stations, internal water supply and waste-water purifying plants, gas generators, all kinds of social services or professional training facilities, data processing centres, administration buildings etc.

In the third stage the central planning authorities gather all the relevant information on the sectoral draft plans and the regional plans. These partial draft plans must be analysed and checked before an over-all plan can be drawn up for approval. The following are the main criteria used for this purpose of analysis and checking:

(a) It is necessary to find out if the partial draft plans are congruent with one another and also feasible considering the available resources. For this purpose balancing techniques relating to output, labour, capital ,foreign exchange, supply and demand are employed.
(b) Those solutions found consistent and feasible must be checked for their conformity with over-all social targets. Naturally, no solutions will be wholly feasible but we must look for the most satisfactory as far as the social targets are concerned. To that effect one could use national indicators which make it possible to appraise a plan.
(c) The solutions suggested in the various partial draft plans must be appraised by relating outlays to their effects, (i.e. costs and benefits). Consequently, a system of national indicators is used to test the efficiency of certain resources (productivity of labour, capital, materials and the output etc.).

[11] This process makes it possible to economise on the use of resources as compared to a situation in which each enterprise engages in new investment projects for its own purposes.

In the third stage it is necessary to revise some sectoral and regional plans. In this way a reconciliation of partial plans with the over-all plan can be approximately effected.

In the fourth stage the draft comprehensive national plan is submitted for approval by the Government and next by Parliament. A detailed discussion of the plan and its various segments, which takes place in the separate Parliamentary Commissions, makes possible scrutiny of the crucial problems, especially those that relate to the ways in which it is proposed to satisfy national and regional targets and to the effectiveness of these suggestions.

5. THE PROBLEM OF CONCENTRATION

Development programmes for all subsystems (regional and branch) must be constructed within the constraints of limited resources, choices must then be made between policies which will:

– allow more ambitious targets to be implemented in certain areas with less attention given to other areas, or
– tend towards a more uniform rate of improvement in meeting all relevant targets.

Targets have a hierarchical structure, with social targets (see section 1.7) at the top followed by other kinds of targets related to outputs and the allocation of resources, forming a network of lower-order targets and means of implementation.

Discussions concerning planning sometimes concentrate on the distribution of second-order targets, i.e. those related to output, investment, employment in particular sectors of economy (industry, agriculture, services etc.). In the earlier stages of economic development, in particular, there is an understandable tendency to consider industrial output and employment as the primordial factors contributing to overall economic development. However, this may lead to policies characterised by deconcentration in a twofold sense: trying to develop simultaneously a too large assortment of products and branches; secondly, scattering new industrial projects over as many localities as possible. Such policies may prove erroneous because of a relatively low efficiency in utilising resources. From a methodological point of view, the error lies in overlooking the rule that second-order targets should be derived from a consideration of social targets, which are the ultimate motives for all activities subject to programming.

In consideration of interregional development proportions, there is no legitimate reason for adopting a policy which would lead to increased differentiation in the living standards of populations in particular regions. On the contrary, the policy adopted in Poland leads to gradual equalisation in that respect. This is a basis for a subsequent question: how to shape the internal development pattern for each region and its sub-regions. The solutions will stress various kinds of activities and the choice of various sets of programmes in terms of location for new utilities, modernization, extension of existing capacities, etc. These choices will depend primarily on efficiency, cost-benefit considerations which in many cases lead to more comprehensive and concentrated programmes with sets of interrelated projects, rather than to the choice of numerous, independent and scattered initiatives.

In this sense, we witness a tendency to concentrate in the process of implementing a given pattern of social targets, whereas this pattern as such does not reflect a principle of concentration, but rather follows the criteria of relative equalisation of opportunities.

13

DAVID M. DUNHAM

THE PROCESSES OF SPATIAL PLANNING IN THE NETHERLANDS

This paper will try to analyse how the processes of spatial planning operate in the Netherlands. The planning machinery will be discussed at each level of government in turn, first laying out its formal structure and then turning to some of the more important informal relations at work and their influence upon the types of policies that can emerge.

1. NATIONAL LEVEL

Responsibility for the initiation and preparation of spatial planning policy in the Netherlands falls to the Minister of Housing and Spatial Planning. He is advised and assisted in this task by the National Physical Planning Agency (R.P.D.) which carries out most of the day-to-day work of policy preparation. Its terms of reference are *inter alia* as follows[1]:

– to assist the minister in the preparation of national policy;
– to carry out surveys and research and to give advice for physical planning purposes to any body that should require it; and
– to generally supervise the proper application of the Physical Planning Law and of the regulations that result from it.

Although the R.P.D. maintains mainly informal contacts with the various government departments, formal inter-departmental discussion in the policy preparation phase is also carried out in the National Physical Planning Committee (N.P.C.) which is a monthly meeting of top civil servants representing the various ministries[2].

[1] Physical Planning Act as revised by the Act of April 20, 1964. This came into operation in August 1965, and will be referred to in future as the 1965 Physical Planning Act.
[2] The director of the R.P.D. is also *ex officio* member to facilitate co-ordination and feedback between bodies.

All ministries are obliged to inform the N.P.C. of any decisions affecting physical planning. The latter's task is as far as possible, therefore, to co-ordinate departmental policies at this level and to prepare issues for ministerial discussion in the Cabinet Committee on Physical Planning. Although legally the N.P.C. acts in an advisory capacity to the Minister,[3] in reality it appears to be the point at which departmental feelings and interests begin to make themselves felt.

The third unit involved is the Physical Planning Advisory Council (P.A.C.), comprising representatives of provincial and municipal government, experts in physical planning such as university dons and other major interest groups such as labour unions or recreational organisations, and which also acts in an advisory role to the minister.[4] This appears to be seen as a channel to promote a more regular exchange of ideas between the government in its day-to-day role of policy preparation and the private sphere, and as a means of stimulating a desirably broader vision than would be likely to emerge within the confines of the civil service alone. The head of the R.P.D. and representatives of various ministries therefore attend these meetings to facilitate such an exchange.

Decision making lies with the minister concerned although the Cabinet Committee on Physical Planning in fact takes responsibility for all major decisions concerning national planning policy. However, as the final authority in each field is vested in the minister concerned this would appear to be on the one hand a matter of joint cabinet responsibility and, on the other, a compromise machinery whereby departmental conflicts are resolved.[5] The execution of national policies lies mainly in the investment programmes and powers of control of the individual ministries.

However, several features seem to limit the effectiveness of national planning. Most prominent in this respect appear to be (i) the fact that the co-ordination between the main departments often appears to be relatively low, which lays more importance upon (ii) the nature of the coordinating machinery, and which has resulted in practice (iii) in the absence of any national spatial plan. These three

[3]   i.e. the Minister of Housing and Spatial Planning.
[4]   There is a further unit, the Socio-Economic Council, representing labour unions, employers and university experts, which, presumably, in advising the cabinet on economic matters also conveys interests in spatial planning.
[5]   It is significant indeed that the Minister-President holds no overall authority in this respect. The coalition structure also means that the British mechanism of 'the cabinet reshuffle' is less readily available.

features are of course extremely interrelated, but they will for the present purposes be discussed apart.

The situation is one in which several ministries have partial responsibilities regarding spatial planning. Thus with, for example, economic and physical planning being the responsibility of different ministries, considerable onus lies upon the question of co-ordination. Indeed the existing arrangement between these departments tends to give the impression of two planning processes largely following their own paths independently of one another. An example of this is the Second Report.[6] This offers a possible physical structure for the year 2000 but suggests no instruments by which the economic mechanisms at work could be steered to achieve this objective, nor does it discuss the financial and political costs involved. Neither does there appear to be a well-defined and consistently applied industrial location policy in the Ministry of Economic Affairs. There would seem, therefore, to be a certain parochialism involved in the outlook of the various departments.

But in such a situation, where in addition no one minister has the responsibility and powers to shape a really effective national policy, the nature of the co-ordinating machinery also becomes very important. The policies of the various departments, in as much as they concern spatial planning, may presumably be co-ordinated in the N.P.C., remain inconsistent or be forwarded for ministerial discussion in the Cabinet Committee where department interests may again be co-ordinated through some form of compromise.[7] Decision making on major issues at Cabinet level is therefore more likely to be based upon political rather than upon technical criteria; the outcome on the other hand is unlikely to be quite the same thing as a clearly defined strategy. The recent rumpus concerning the siting of an additional military training ground would seem to reflect precisely this point. The fact that the alternatives centred largely around a major recreational area or the destruction of a re-afforestation zone illustrates a confusion of objectives that may in some ways be inherent in this type of decision making machinery.

This is emphasised in turn in the third point, the absence of any effective national policy regarding spatial planning. It is already

---

[6] *The Second Report on Physical Planning in the Netherlands*, The Hague 1966.
[7] One can therefore recognise two sub-processes, the first being the intra- and the second the inter-ministry stage, each having its own phase of policy preparation (for example the R.P.D. or Central Planning Bureau on the one hand and the N.P.C. on the other) and policy making (the minister and the Cabinet Committee) phases.

clear that the Second Report does not really meet this need. It remains a hypothesis. It emphasises the seriousness of the problems involved but it seems to look too far ahead and to be too concerned with structure rather than mechanisms to convey any compelling sense of direction, or even at times of its immediate relevance to the day-to-day problems of various government departments. The decision making structure also means at present that to be sure of gaining general agreement policies have often had to be phrased in rather general terms. It would seem significant that the earlier system of establishing a statutory plan was abolished[8] in favour of an indicative proposal which would be more flexible, partly if not mainly because of the difficulties of implementing the kind of plan that could be produced.

On the other side the structure of the planning machinery would seem to have been against the emergence of a really effective plan. This appears really to be the heart of the matter. Indeed it seems quite reasonable to suggest "that on the national planning level all financial, economic and technical means should be concentrated in one ministry".[9] This would simplify the decision making machinery and can be seen as a first requirement for effective planning, but it would not necessarily in itself imply greater co-ordination, closer contact or a more effective flow of information in the plan preparation phase. It may only produce an unwieldy structure. What it would also have to effect, and which seems unlikely to emerge within the framework of the existing structure, is a change of attitude on the part of the departments involved and greater co-ordination in the execution of their policies.

A final point to be raised in this section concerns political and institutional inputs into the system. Predominant in this respect would appear to be the political interests of the various departments. On the other hand, as also noted above, public attention is more concerned with proposals and occasional reports than with the machinery of planning. Participation tends consequently to be mainly a reaction to the ideas conveyed by them. There does not appear to have been the type of publicity regarding the machinery of planning that the series of Royal Commissions has aroused in Britain and which, though focused at lower levels, has almost certainly had its repercussions upon thinking about national

---

8   Post-dated by the 1965 Physical Planning Act.
9   W. Steigenga, "Recent Planning Problems in the Netherlands", in *Regional Studies*, Vol. II, 1968, p. 106.

structures. The political input in this particular direction would appear, therefore, to be less well developed.[10] However, it would now seem in place at this point to take discussion down to the lower levels where the effectiveness of national policy is more clearly to be seen.

2. PROVINCIAL LEVEL

In outline the organisational structure of provincial planning closely mirrors that at national level. Three main units are again involved. The day-to-day work of plan preparation is carried out by the Provincial Physical Planning Service (P.P.D.). This is a government unit responsible in turn to the Provincial Council which is the decision making body at this level.[11] The latter is also, however, advised by a Physical Planning Committee (P.P.C.) on which various organisations within the province are represented, and which provides the formal political and institutional input of interest groups.

Co-ordination with national thinking is in addition maintained through an Inspector of Physical Planning who represents the R.P.D. at the provincial level.[12] This inspector acts in an advisory capacity and, to facilitate this liaison role between provincial and national interests, is also *ex officio* member of the P.P.C. Concerning co-ordination downwards, the province is also required to consult the municipalities that are likely to be affected by any proposal in order to promote the maximum possible co-ordination with these local authorities. Draft and adopted plans are also placed on show at both provincial and municipal level, and objections can be registered with the Provincial Council, or, ultimately, with representatives of the Crown.[13]

Several other bodies are also, if less directly, involved in planning at the provincial level. With the notable exception of the Ministry

---

10 The different political context must also be borne in mind. The type of ministry proposed would also to be effective imply the creation of a post that wielded very considerable political power.

11 Provincial governments are empowered under the Physical Planning Act to prepare plans indicating the future development of all or part of their territory in broad outline, and may be obliged by the Crown to do so.

12 If national policies are seen to be violated the Minister can give directives to the provincial government obliging it to bring its policies into line.

13 It is noteworthy that the maximum time period is legally specified for each stage.

of Economic Affairs the majority of government departments have provincial offices. There are also the Economic-Technological Institutes (E.T.I.) and Institutes for Social Planning (S.M.O.) which are semi-private bodies subsidised by the various levels of government and performing a mainly consultative function. To facilitate co-ordination between these units they are also represented on the P.P.C.[14] The implementation of plans at this level lies in turn with either the investment programmes of the various branches of provincial government or through the approval of municipal plans.

On paper the structural and legal provisions for planning at provincial level appear to be both attractive and rather well designed. But in reality this planning tends in many cases to play a less effective role. The critical issue would seem in large part to lie in its ability to control the process of suburbanisation, and in this it would seem mainly to have failed.[15] It appears in practice to have insufficient binding power upon many of the local units to be really effective. The reasons for this, however, seem rather complex. Nor does the situation seem to be quite the same in each province.

A main feature in this respect appears to lie in the nature of provincial plans. Problems often seem to emerge from the fact that a satisfactory balance may not always be achieved between the elaboration of national proposals and the co-ordination of local plans. It has been argued that the kind of long-term structural proposals that have been produced at national level have at times been interpreted rather rigidly by the P.P.D. This has meant that, even though it has in many respects been much closer to the economic pressures of the immediate situation, its plans have often still tended to be 'physical' in a rather static and restrictive sense. There is indeed little evidence of any real economic planning being carried out within the provincial government.[16] In part this appears to have been the origin, firstly, of certain conflicts between provincial and local planners in that the latter, and particularly the

[14] The representation of the S.M.O. often appears to be less automatic than in the case of the E.T.I., however.

[15] See Steigenga, *op. cit.* 1968, p. 108 where he points out that while the population of the urban agglomerations increased by only 5 percent from 1960-66, in the area outside it rose by 11 percent.

[16] It is significant in this respect that its financial resources appear to be relatively small. In some of the depressed areas one can see an active 'economic policy' at provincial level. Their interpretation of economic planning is the important point, however. It has tended to be indicative and subsidiary to the physical planning function. The P.P.D. does not offer a real economic alternative to the requests of the municipalities.

larger units, cannot avoid these economic pressures in the same way, and, secondly, of a lack of confidence in some quarters of municipal government in the types of plans being produced at the provincial level.

It would seem fairly clear that in municipalities such as, for example, that of Rotterdam, economic needs will tend to be more clearly felt and more readily taken into account by planners than elsewhere. It is perhaps significant in this respect that while the P.P.D. for South Holland is situated in The Hague the E.T.I. is in fact in Rotterdam. However, the situation tends to be further compounded by the fact that the P.P.D. is in some cases not as well equipped technically and scientifically for the tasks of plan preparation as some of these larger municipalities.

When it comes to the political process of decision making, however, the P.P.D. may not necessarily be any better placed. On the one hand the larger municipal bodies are often in a position to present better arguments for expansion than the P.P.D. can for their containment. There also appears to be evidence, on the other hand, that Provincial Councils may well be keenly aware of their relationships with these municipalities if, as is likely, the latter comprise a major political force within their province. There is a danger, therefore, that the provincial planners are caught, technically, between national theories and local arguments and, politically, between the Provincial Council and the larger municipalities without having the instruments and powers to be really effective.

It should be noted that although the minority of municipalities to which this situation really applies are exceptional in that they generally perform outspoken national functions, at the same time they comprise the very centres that are having the maximum influence upon the spatial structure of the country and particularly in this upon the process of suburbanisation. It could be argued indeed that it is not really of so much consequence that the system works better in other cases.

Co-ordination with local authority units does not always appear to be as effective as might be desired, therefore. This is quite significant for the present discussion in that the municipalities necessarily play an important role in the implementation of spatial policies. It is interesting to note in comparison that the provincial governments do not in many cases appear able to promote the same degree of co-ordination with local and national departments as could the British regional boards. The municipalities are not, for example, individually represented at provincial level, nor are they always consulted in any great detail in the course of plan preparation.[17] Nor does it seem that the Agglomeration Boards in working out a co-operative policy have always put great emphasis upon working closely with the P.P.D.[18] There does, however, seem evidence that the latter plays a more positive role in the more depressed areas where there appears to be more general co-operation in efforts to upgrade the region as a whole.

The situation is doubtlessly compounded in part by the low level of publicity that seems to be associated with provincial planning. The P.P.D. does not in general undertake any major role in this direction itself. In South Holland, for example, this rests with a public relations unit which performs the task for provincial government as a whole. The general outcome of this rather complex situation is that interest tends to be focused again not on the machinery of planning but on its results – upon the plans and proposals, and often in as much as these might impinge upon other interests. This means in fact that interest group inputs tend to lie outside the plan preparation phase, to be a reaction to rather than participation in it, and that a provincial plan can at times be seen as much as a starting point for interested discussion and perhaps pressure as a technical document. There is evidence, however, that the nature of these objections is beginning to change. Whereas they have centred largely in the past upon the violation of property rights they appear now to be beginning to take on a somewhat broader view of an area's prospects.

But the whole role of the provinces with regard to the planning process appears to be increasingly questioned in some quarters. It is not entirely undisputed that they offer "for the most part reasonably appropriate units for regional planning purposes".[19] In theory they may: but they can not really be assessed in isolation. Indeed their appropriateness would appear to be undergoing a certain

---

[17] It has been suggested from several quarters that the legal obligation to consult municipalities concerned is sometimes met when it is largely too late for the latter's opinions to have any real influence upon plan preparation.

[18] These Agglomeration Boards reflect a trend towards greater co-operation between municipalities. The idea has emerged of creating new units, not imposed from above but growing spontaneously from the needs of the municipalities themselves. They have been seen in some quarters as perhaps in time the natural successors of the present form of provincial government. This may be stating the case too ambitiously, but they do seem to be pointing the way to possibilities of more effective spatial planning.

[19] J. W. Burke, *Greenheart Metropolis*, London 1966, p. 154.

reappraisal in the light of the considerable growth of Agglomeration Boards, which will be discussed in the next section. Indeed the city-regions which the latter tend to comprise would in many ways seem eminently suited to the Dutch urban context as local planning units. Yet certainly they also tend to complicate the structural arrangement and to confuse the issue of provincial responsibilities. Would it be necessary to have a province to co-ordinate at the very most half a dozen agglomeration units? Suggestions have consequently been raised, and would seem far from ungrounded, that either the latter should ultimately replace the province or that the provinces should become larger and fewer in number, agglomeration units becoming the bodies responsible for structural planning and the municipalities for local affairs.

The latter suggestion would seem particularly interesting from the point of view of the machinery of spatial planning, and perhaps in several ways to be a politically more acceptable solution. It has the attraction, firstly, that two or three provincial units might institutionalise machinery to deal with distinct problem areas, namely the north and north-east, south and south-east and west of the country, and to lessen the periodic importance of their economic fortunes in the attention they receive. In such a context they might be able to play a very positive co-ordinative role. Secondly, as such they might also prove more representative of local interests and, thirdly, might also facilitate a greater possibility of spatial, as against physical or economic planning. The extent to which this could be realised, however, would seem to rely largely upon the climate of Dutch thinking becoming focused much more clearly upon the machinery of planning and to become politically more forceful. The effectiveness of these various units would in all probability depend strongly again upon the specific definition of their role, the powers at their disposal and the way in which the process evolves, in that the latter will tend to strongly influence the attitude of the various parties concerned.

3. MUNICIPAL LEVEL

The municipality presents in several ways the most interesting level of the planning process in the Netherlands precisely because it tends to be much nearer to the political heartbeat of every-day affairs. Moreover, in the manner in which it reflects these affairs it also differs quite noticeably from, for example, the local authority unit in Britain.

The day-to-day work of plan preparation is carried out either in the physical planning department of the municipal government, or, if the latter is too small to support such a unit, by a consultant bureau. This phase can involve the preparation of both allocation and structural plans.[20] The municipality is in fact legally obliged to prepare an allocation plan which, once adopted, comprises the major instrument of development control and is legally binding upon the general public. Preparation of the longer-term structural plan, indicating broad lines of expected development within the municipality or, if formulated in co-operation, within the area of a number of contiguous municipalities, is in contrast neither compulsory nor legally binding.[21] The first seems, therefore, to be mainly a legal and the latter much more of a co-ordinating instrument of planning.

In terms of procedure, the planning process at this level appears to work largely as follows. Draft plans are initially deposited for public view in the town hall for one month during which time objections may be raised and registered with the municipal council. In reality the extent to which this publicity goes would seem to vary considerably from the bare legal requirements to a substantial operation. However, when objections have been heard and the municipal council has made its decisions[22] the adopted plan is again deposited for view for a similar period and forwarded for approval to the provincial council[23] and, in the case of structural plans, to the inspector for physical planning. Objections to the allocation plan can then if unmet be carried to the provincial council. The municipality can also register any objection with the latter's decisions with representatives of the Crown. Applications regarding any development are then assessed by the town planning department on the basis of the allocation plan through the issue of construction permits.

[20] See the 1965 Physical Planning Act, Chapter IV. The municipality is obliged to review both at least once every ten years. It must also inform the provincial government of its intention to review an allocation plan.
[21] In cases of default, where a municipality does not respond to its obligations to prepare or revise a plan, this right falls to the Provincial Council at the municipality's expense.
[22] This is specified again as within a three month period.
[23] A six month period is again specified during which the provincial council is bound to inform any other bodies, such as the Monuments Council, if their interests appear to be involved.

One of the main attractions of planning at this level is that plan preparation, policy making and execution lie clearly within the one unit, although subject of course to the requirements of consistency with national and provincial policy.[24] Nor in general do they appear to stand in the same paternalistic relation with the higher authority that has often been the case in Britain. It seems indeed that the municipality has often had considerably more say in planning local affairs than many of its British counterparts and that, providing it does not openly violate provincial policy, it has also in consequence had greater latitude regarding the form and content of its plans. In being more clearly one process, and having at the same time preserved a certain independence, the municipality would seem to have the advantage of facilitating simpler mechanisms of co-ordination and feedback than is presently available at the other levels of planning. It would also seem in a better position to maintain an overall view of, and to be more in touch with what is in fact happening within its boundaries.

In reality the burgomaster system also appears to have played an important role in spatial planning through the lead that it gives. Indeed it would seem that the vitality and initiative of a forceful burgomaster can have a significant influence upon the prospects of a municipality. For example, as no local government unit can finance all the investments made in its area it has to rely in general upon direct financing from the national and provincial levels and, more indirectly, via the investment decisions of the various ministries.[25] But, on the one hand, these decisions do not always seem to be spatially specified while, on the other, they do not always appear to contain formal guidelines regarding the ranking of priorities. Indeed, there is even competition among municipalities for these funds, and in this the efforts of a forceful burgomaster can be quite rewarding. His abilities can also play a similar role in, for example, winning a modification of housing allocations, which is a somewhat different case, and may at times represent the difference between semi-resignment to the policy of higher levels and a

---

[24] There appears to be some evidence to suggest, however, that co-ordination in this respect could more frequently be interpreted as alignment with published plans rather than as extensive discussion. Directives can in fact be issued by the higher levels to oblige compliance.

[25] There is evidence that the whole question of financial relations between national and local levels is in need of review. The following example is a case in point. The Bank voor Nederlandse Gemeenten also plays a particularly important role in terms of municipal finances.

forceful representation for review of the municipality's case.

Yet at a certain point this system tends, as stressed in section 2, to have if anything a negative influence upon the effectiveness of spatial planning. Several points would seem relevant in this respect. Firstly, while national 'policy' has tended to be one of containment, the larger municipalities invariably view constraints on their growth with certain misgivings: it would seem true that "none of the three great cities can quite shake off the notion that limitation is more wisely and appropriately applied to the other two than to itself".[26] Their persistence in this respect is quite significant because national ideas can only really be effected through a rigorous control at provincial and local level.[27] Secondly, it can be argued that national ideas – as illustrated for example in the Second Report – have paid relatively little attention to the types of specifically urban problems that these municipalities are having to face, despite their major role in shaping the spatial structure of the nation. While the economic importance of Rotterdam is stimulated, and while it contains the economic facilities, employment and prospects which it does, it might in fact be unrealistic to expect its development to be contained by measures of physical planning control. Problems at this level may well, therefore, be part of a more general malaise.

Among the majority of municipalities one of the principal problems would appear to be their size.[28] Many local government units are too small to support their own planning office and look to consultant bureaus for their planning work. In this a basic problem seems to lie in the adequacy of the brief. Indeed it seems that this may frequently reflect the personal views of the burgomaster or aldermen who may by no means be fully aware of the issues involved and that, although consultants may listen to other interests and may give broader advice, they tend frequently to fulfil this brief to the letter. At the decision making stage there often follows then an inability to evaluate the content of these policy and planning proposals in any technical sense. Although it seems that the standards of the consultants tend to be fairly good, in terms of the planning process involved, there often appears to be too ready an acceptance of their proposals.

[26]   Burke, *op. cit.* 1966, p. 154.
[27]   It is tempting to ask how many Zoetermeers are likely to prove unavoidable with the present policies and machinery of planning.
[28]   The picture is basically one of a few dominant urban municipalities containing a very significant part of the total population and surrounded by the remainder which tend to be extremely small and considerably weaker.

It can be argued that within the existing structure the consultants perform an important nursing function and in many cases they have doubtlessly stimulated thinking on wider implications and longer-term repercussions than had previously existed. But the crux of the matter is that the structure is not always very efficient. Many municipalities are much too small to be effective planning units, whoever draws up the plans. The growth in co-operative efforts and the formation of agglomeration boards discussed in section 2 is indeed largely a consequence of this and can be viewed as a major effort towards increased co-ordination and effectiveness.

Several points would seem warranted on this, however. Firstly, co-operation can at the moment only be established with the full consensus of those involved, which means that it can only as yet be seen as a partial solution. For the near future one cannot foresee such a unit evolving easily for The Hague, Rijswijk and Voorburg for example, despite the obvious interrelation as part of the urban centre. Secondly, this co-operation would seem to work best where the peripheral municipalities are reasonably strong although this tends to be the exception. The danger seems to be that for too many politicians in the smaller municipalities the interests of the agglomeration are to be identified with those of the big town.[29] Thus although co-operation would seem in many ways to be more easily established where there is one strong central municipality and a relatively weak periphery, there appears to be evidence that this situation of dominance may also be one reason for its partial breakdown.[30] It can also be noted, thirdly, that even within such a structure municipalities tend to hold very tightly to their own interests and that in practice it is often very difficult, given the limited legal nature of the co-operation, to get them to take a broader view. It seems, for example, to have been consistently easier to gain co-operation on topics such as recreational areas or refuse disposal that do not directly influence a municipality's position, than in questions of growth and development which do. Thus one of the great attractions of these agglomeration boards, that it would facilitate development planning rather than just control, may not always be as easily accomplished as is sometimes implied. Finally, within the present structure it seems that while structure plans may be prepared for an agglomeration, the allo-

---

[29] In fact this is not always far from the truth as in terms of their problems the big towns need this co-operation more.

[30] The Rijnmond example appears in part to be such a case.

cation plan which is the binding one remains the responsibility of the municipality. The real decision making and implementation still remain with the latter. It is therefore one thing to prepare a structure plan in common and quite another to implement it, especially when questions of substantial financing become involved. However, it may be more meaningful to view these groupings more as an indication of future directions rather than as a unit that can really be effective within the present structure. Nevertheless it is equally apparent that much will rest upon the thinking that takes place as to whether or not they become anything more than ineffective provinces within better defined boundaries.

Finally in this section comment seems warranted regarding the situation within municipal government itself. It is evident firstly that, while there are also considerable planning units in some of the larger municipalities, in many cases the amount and types of information and personnel available for plan preparation are scarcely adequate for the task at hand. This would seem to be quite important due to the fact that the flow of technical information from national to local level does not always seem to be so well developed, and that a clear lead is not always given regarding the major problems faced at municipal level.[31] Secondly it would seem that with an elected alderman representing, for example, the interests of the town planning department at council level there is a danger that he will prefer a view that corresponds more with his term of office than with long-term strategies. There appears at times to be a danger of continuity being lost between plan preparation and policy making over the long-term.

4. CONCLUSIONS

Thus, although the machinery for spatial planning in the Netherlands may seem on paper to be rather well designed, it turns out in practice to be less efficient. Planning at the national level clearly lacks effective horizontal co-ordination between ministeries. The provinces are inadequate units; they are ill-defined for present needs, they are financially and politically rather weak, and are in consequence squeezed by both national and local interests. At local

---

[31] Indeed it can be argued that many of the urban problems that municipalities have to face really need a national and not local approach if they are to be solved effectively.

level, despite the vitality of many municipalities which is attractive at first sight, the fact that they associate their growth potential not so much with national policy as with 'getting a good burgomaster' suggests that the system is equally suspect at this point. In the light of this situation the growth of Agglomeration Boards can be seen as a significant reaction, and one that poses considerable interest for the future.

Finally, as a more general conclusion, it should be clear that formal relations do not necessarily pose a very complete picture of the workings of an administrative structure at least for planning purposes. It is perhaps indicative of the direction and content of the general approach to administration for regional planning that a systematic study of required informal communication has not yet been attempted.

CONCLUSIONS
AND
APPENDICES

CONCLUSIONS

The conclusions presented in this section cannot, of course, entirely reflect the debate, or even degree of agreement that was reached during four weeks of discussions. With participants coming from such different backgrounds disagreement was perhaps to be expected rather than agreement. If this is the case, that is reason enough to concentrate on the latter as of more significance and as more important for furthering the field. The points of coincidence in opinion that could be registered will be given in the order of sections 2 to 5 after which we will confront them with the lessons that can be drawn from the papers of the first section. During discussion of the papers of the second section and also in the written comments of Lambooy,[1] it was argued that growth poles should be viewed not only as economic but also as political centres, as 'power poles'. It was felt, however, that this statement might well be qualified for certain countries – mention was made of West Africa where because of the superimposition of a new system of cities over traditional ones a great deal of political power could still be formed in what, in terms of the new system, are generally considered to be rural areas. Nevertheless, this power seems to be becoming less and less important.

This argument plays a crucial role in literature on centre-periphery models and domination theory. It is an approach that has also started to develop its own methods of analysis and regional planning strategies, and these were considered a particularly useful addition to the practitioner's planning equipment. Recognising, however, that this approach contains a certain bias, a warning was given that certain important problems may not be revealed in using it for analysing a particular region. This was expecially pointed out

---

[1] J. G. Lambooy, Comments on the paper presented by P. van Loon. Seminar on Regionalisation of National Policies, ISS, The Hague, March 1970 (mimeo) p. 1.

by sociologists, who felt that more elaboration of the socio-political implications and of the implied processes of diffusion was warranted. Discussion leading to these conclusions also shed light on the issue of recognition of the regional development problem, as it considered the urge for decentralisation as expressed by many backward regions to be one of the political expressions of emerging growth poles in these regions. Especially in young countries, but but also in 'old' and established ones, decentralisation is feared by many national politicians as a disintegrating force and this fear may often lead them to neglect the special problems of specific regions. However, while the experience with regional planning gained in other countries ought to make clear that these fears are in general better suppressed, the introduction of relevant subjects in university curricula was also accepted as a step forward towards recognition. In this respect, Shibli's paper is quite clear when he discusses the attitude taken by a number of economists in Pakistan's Planning Commission.

In fact, it was argued that the issue of decentralisation need not stand in the way of successful regional planning. It was stressed on the contrary that the way in which participation processes were organised was extremely important. Here a distinction has to be made. Participation can be understood to mean (i) the increased involvement of those who are already a part of the national system in the processes of plan preparation and implementation and (ii) the integration of large parts of the population into the system, an issue considered particularly important and topical at present in the Latin American context. The latter type requires changes in decision-making structures and investment patterns that are often regarded as being too revolutionary. The promotion of the former type would not only require leaders that are trusted by the local population and the creation of adequate institutions, it would also need a change in attitude on the part of the planners. As Kalk[2] said in reference to France: "One wonders who are the men behind and inside this smoothly running machine of a centralised administration and of system-immanent procedures of decision-making, where citizens and their representatives have hardly any possibility of participation, and where – even worse – the concept of 'participation' has already been embedded in the main stream of (post-) gaullist technocracy".

[2] E. Kalk: "Technocracy's children", comments on Pierre Viot's paper, *Ibid*, p. 1.

The technocrat's approach to participation would not lead to effective participation. Instead, the planner should be willing to make people aware of the issues involved in formulating the plan at as early a stage as possible.

Two lines of arguments flow from this point: one is concerned with bringing about coincidence between the objectives as expressed by individual regions and as put forward by the national government and the other related to the question as to whether alternative comprehensive plans could or even should be attempted.

Regarding the latter point it was argued that the concept of planning should be understood to stretch from the first outlines of a plan to its implementation. Thus planning occurs not only in preparing alternatives in the earliest stages but also in the phase of implementation, when new conditions prevail and new choices are open. Although this is easily recognised, planning machineries throughout the world seem to be geared to producing one plan at a time. We are therefore faced with this question as to whether the preparation of alternative comprehensive plans is at all possible or even desirable.

Three criteria were considered important in assessing whether several variants could in fact be produced: (i) the level at which the plan is made; (ii) the time horizon of the plan; and (iii) the phase which the plan has reached. It was pointed out that these criteria considerably determine the scope and degree of detail of a plan, in the sense that alternatives are more easily presented for undetailed plans which in turn are more meaningful the higher the decision-making level, the farther the time horizon and the earlier the planning phase. It was further argued that decisions on the basic choices that are available among the alternatives of such undetailed plans in fact largely determine the subsequent development of alternatives for the more detailed versions. In fact, the scope for meaningful and essential alternatives was taken to decrease continuously as the planning process progresses. It was stressed, therefore, that in order to enable optimal participation it is essential to study more systematically what kinds of decisions have to be made in each of the phases of the planning process and to show how these decisions are interrelated.

It will then be possible to acquire more insight into why and how the ranges of alternatives are decreased.

This issue is intimately connected with the problem of the technique used in preparing plans. It was agreed that on the whole the various techniques that have been developed so far are most suited to the problems of short term or medium term planning and that important mistakes can be made in applying them mechanically to problems of long term planning. The latter was considered a necessity for solving the problems of interregional and intraregional planning, but the available techniques were not considered adequate. Although futurologists of a constructive rather than visionary vein were accepted as performing a useful function by providing thought on the crucial issues to be solved in order to achieve desirable long term development, more technically-oriented long term planners were also needed. They would have to perform the function of drawing attention to the consequences of imminent decisions for long term development and of providing alternatives that would optimise a country's development path.

Within the complicated network of relations between magnitudes now and in the future and in different phases of the planning process an additional complication is presented with the problem of making national and regional development objectives mutually reinforcing. Concerning this issue, it was emphasised that national authorities would meet with more cooperation and success in planning and implementing certain policies if more notice were taken of the objectives expressed by the various regions. Deconcentration – eventually perhaps followed by decentralisation – of central government authority was considered one of the most important means for solving this problem as it would also allow national decision-makers to be better informed about a region's resources as well as its constraints. In addition, such a deconcentration could play a crucial role in bringing about the much needed solution to the problem of horizontal co-ordination, especially in the phase of implementation.

It was pointed out, however, that problems of horizontal and vertical co-ordination could be best studied in connection with the issue as to the levels at which decisions have to be made.

This advice was based on the consideration that a lack of co-ordination often originates in ill-defined responsibilities and misplaced feelings of self-importance.

During the seminar emphasis was laid continuously on the need for information. This should not only consist of statistical information, concerning the past or presently available resources, and the type of information on preferences that would come available through participation processes as mentioned above, but also of scientific research information that would serve as inputs for the long term planners and of purely planistic information resulting from simulation procedures. Whereas this information was considered as having to flow to planners through formal channels of communication which as such should be made a part of the planning machinery, it was stressed that the effectiveness of informal communication could not be disregarded. Hafid[3] quotes in this connection the case of Indonesia where the information flowing through civil formal channels of communication is largely disregarded at the provincial level in favour of that which flows through military (informal) channels.

Although this is an extreme example, informal communication between decision-makers and parts of the administration as well as among the latter were taken as important causes for improving or hampering the planning process.

It was considered unfortunate that particularly sociologists and public administration specialists, but also others, had devoted too little attention to systematic study of the importance of informal communication for the planning process and its effectiveness.

As these conclusions show, there is considerable scope for debating the question of emphasis as regards the desired content and approach in education for regional planners. This was, of course, in the back of the minds of the participants in the seminar when they agreed that this education should be interdisciplinary in character. It was pointed out, however, that there is a danger that this type of training tends to emphasise the biases of the various disciplines rather than to show in what way they contribute to the solution of regional planning problems and where the one discipline complements or overlaps the other. In fact it was said that this has resulted in some cases in a return to a single disciplinary approach. Whether this step backwards has been made or not, most training programmes are felt to be determined more by conditions on the supply side of the market than on the demand side. This situation is explained as follows:

Firstly, although a large number of courses have sprung up in recent years, shortages of facilities and trained personnel and often the type of university structure within which these courses have had to be organised, have meant that the various disciplines and approaches could not always be sufficiently integrated.

3 A Hafid, 'Some Development Planning Problems in Indonesia', *Ibid* (mimeographed).

Secondly, these courses have generally accepted certain traditional assumptions as to what regional planning is really about. This in turn, is reinforced by the considerable time lag between the moment new information is conceived and the moment it is fully incorporated in university curricula. But it is often during this period of delay that the information, even in its raw form, would be most useful for those doing the teaching. It was agreed that some of the best material and most important ideas are coming out of practice and that any sensible approach that is worked out should be made available to others almost immediately. Indeed it was thought that a closer interaction between training and practice was becoming an essential requirement for strengthening education and research, and in turn for strengthening regional planning in the developing countries.

A number of these failings are of course characteristic of the 'newness' of regional planning and reflect the general need for more, better trained personnel. It has to be hoped that these bottlenecks can rather quickly be overcome. They point to the fact that, under the growing pressure to train more men, the content and at times the whole orientation of teaching courses is often inadequate and that there is a need to continually re-assess and update this content and to incorporate new ideas and new approaches into our training programmes.

The type of institutional network that is required in order to train regional planners at the required level and in the necessary numbers was inevitably a very central point in the discussions. This issue, raised particularly by the paper of Perloff, came to focus largely upon the contention that in order to make the most of the existing and rather limited facilities training programmes should be organised systematically on a world-wide scale, that contact and co-ordination should be built up in an effective manner and that where possible specialisation should be encouraged. It was argued that there was a case for a world-wide network of institutions with various complementary responsibilities with regard to regional planning education. Three levels of responsibility were distinguished:

1. A responsibility at the international level. This responsibility would have three aspects: administrative-financial, research and teaching. The first would be carried by United Nations, the second by UNRISD while the third would lie with a specialised training institute. The financial-administrative responsibility would primarily imply that UN would see that the programme runs well and that financial resources are made available. The UNRISD responsibility would primarily relate to research into the needs for various types of training in regional planning, while the training institute responsibility would be to provide broad training in particular for teachers.

2. Secondly there should be multi-national bodies having regional responsibility, which would both organise their own courses and undertake the responsibility of helping national training and research programmes within their region. It was suggested that all the U.N. regional commissions might undertake this task in collaboration with the centres already underway in Japan, Israel and Pakistan.

3. Finally, there should also be a series of national centres undertaking responsibilities for teaching and research within the specific framework of needs of individual countries.

Once such an international system of regional planning education was established with close lines of communication between its elements, it could start to organise itself in terms of various kinds of specialisation so as to relieve elements from internal pressures.

In addition, such a system would more easily establish adequate channels of communication with the practitioner. The first step in bringing about such a system would be the gathering of relevant information.

Even without such a system, however, education in regional planning could be improved by devoting more attention to the problems of the non-metropolitan region. Other important improvements were expected to come from research in (i) capital theory, which would enable the regional planner to better understand the depreciation of structures consisting of differently aged elements so that decisions with regard to different types of capital structures for one particular location could be made on more thorough grounds than is done to date; (ii) the sociology of regional development, so that more could be said about social planning at the regional level, especially in terms of changes in social structure and their relation to changes in economic structure; and (iii) the way in which the planning process in the widest sense of the word actually works; too much of what is known (and unknown) about this is left out from the training programmes, pushing the young planner as it were unprepared into the wilderness of organisations and authorities about which he may just know their legal status and responsibilities but not what makes them work as they do.

APPENDIX A

A DESCRIPTION OF THE TWELVE-MONTH POST-GRADUATE COURSE IN COMPREHENSIVE REGIONAL DEVELOPMENT PLANNING REHOVOT, ISRAEL (1970)

1. BACKGROUND

The research and training programme on regional development originated in a recommendation made by the United Nations Social Commission to the thirty-ninth session of the Economic and Social Council. Its purpose was to initiate a new United Nations programme to assist countries facing problems of excessive migration from rural areas to overcrowded cities, with concomitant unemployment and other social problems. The Council, noting the common aspiration of developing countries "to modernise their economies through industrialization and agricultural improvement as a basis for raising the standard of living of their populations", and recognising "that regional development and an appropriate distribution of population within the country are essential factors in achieving such modernization and social development", requested the Secretary-General to "prepare a draft programme of research and training on regional development based on current regional development activities in different parts of the world". The Secretary-General was further asked to select, after consultation with the host-Governments concerned, a reasonable number of development regions best suited for the proposed research and training and reflecting different stages of development.

In his report to the seventeenth session of the Social Committee the Secretary-General outlined the general framework of the programme and stated that formulation of a concrete programme would have to be preceded by short visits of Preparatory Teams to the different development regions.

The preparatory teams began their visits to the proposed regions in October 1966. Their specific aim was to ascertain whether in the countries and regions so far selected for study there existed conditions for a successful long-term programme in which all levels of government concerned and the existing research and training bodies were ready to participate. Development regions in Asia, Africa, Latin America and the Middle East were visited by preparatory teams. Among them was the Lakhish region in Israel. On the basis of this visit in May 1967, the preparatory team found that the development of this region encompassed all the aspects of direct relevance to the programme: comprehensive planning for the agricultural sector; a hierarchical pattern of rural settlement; the location of new towns as growth points; the establishment of industries including agricultural processing industries; and the construction of a new port as an outlet for the produce of the region. This, as well as the already existing facilities available for high-level training and research at the Settlement Study Centre in Rehovot and the intensive work that Israeli institutions have accomplished in formulating regional development plans for some of the developing countries made this Centre ideal for inclusion in the United Nations research and training programme in regional development.

In accordance with this decision, the first in a series of twelve month courses was opened May 5, 1969 with 21 participants from Asian, African, and Latin American countries.

Israel, herself, offers a unique environment for such a course, being in many senses a social science laboratory. Her population has more than trebled during the past 20 years by mass immigration from both eastern and western countries, with widely divergent socio-economic backgrounds. The urgent problems thus raised have been met at all levels of planning and implementation by application of varied methods and techniques. The success and failure of these measures offer the student rich material for study and evaluation. As a small country facing major problems, Israel's specific experience can indicate approaches to related problems and issues in other developing countries.

2. AIMS

The purpose of the course is to train professional personnel in integrative skills in order that they can relate their own specialities to other needs and problems in the region to be developed. This will require knowledge of associated fields of development, experience in team approach to regional analysis and planning skills in implementing integrated development programmes.

3. DESCRIPTION OF THE COURSE

The course in Comprehensive Regional Development Planning at the Settlement Study Centre is designed mainly for civil servants with an academic education who are engaged, or about to be engaged, in development activities. Priority is given to candidates who have already had some field experience in development planning and implementation, particularly in the developing countries. The course will provide participants with an opportunity to widen the scope of their theoretical knowledge through a systematic study of the principles and methods of regional development planning. Emphasis will be put on problems of some developing countries in order to make the studies in the course useful for practical purposes. It is expected that participants returning to their countries will be engaged in actual planning work.

The Curriculum of the course was prepared by the Settlement Study Centre staff, headed by Prof. S. Hurwitz, former Dean of the Faculty of Agriculture of the Hebrew University. It covers the following subjects:

Introductory Course	270	hours
Management	98	,,
Economics	138	,,
Cooperative Organization in Developing Countries	80	,,
Sociology of Development	85	,,
Agriculture	90	,,
Physical Planning and Development	108	,,
Comprehensive Regional Planning, and	205	,,
A Case Study	90	,,
Total	1,164	hours

NOTE: The students will be required to devote 200 additional hours to the preparation of a Case Study under the guidance of the lecturers and project instructors This will involve both classroom and field work.

The course is of twelve months duration and is divided into two sections.

I. An *Introductory Course* of 9 weeks from May 18, 1970 to July 18, 1970 in the subjects Sociology, Economics, Agriculture, Mathematics and Statistics. The introductory course will provide all participants with the terminology and basic techniques of the disciplines relevant to comprehensive planning, so as to prepare them adequately for the major course and a deeper understanding of one another's specialisations.

Vacation July 19, 1970 – July 26, 1970.

II. The *Major Course* will be divided into three trimesters and will include the main body of the classroom studies as well as preparation of the case studies.

First Trimester: July 27, 1970 – October 14, 1970.
Vacation: October 15, 1970 – October 25, 1970.
Second Trimester: October 26, 1970 – December 23, 1970.
Vacation: December 24, 1970 – January 3, 1971.
Third Trimester: January 4, 1971 – April 15, 1971.

During the third trimester of 15 weeks students will form inter-disciplinary work teams, each assigned with the planning of a certain regional development project. Each student will be given a particular aspect of the project for individual study and the team will submit the joint report on its case study. The projects will be carried out under the guidance of staff members of the Centre, with the assistance of experts from outside, both from Israel and from other countries.

A DESCRIPTION OF THE RESEARCH AND TRAINING PROGRAMME IN REGIONAL DEVELOPMENT CHUBU CENTRE, NAGOYA, JAPAN
(preliminary outline)

This information describes the training programme in regional development jointly sponsored by the Government of Japan and the United Nations at the Chubu Centre for the United Nations Research and Training Programme in Regional Development, Nagoya, Japan. Sixteen training grants are available to qualified persons mainly from the ECAFE region for the 1971 programme which will be conducted in Nagoya from January through May, 1971.

1. PURPOSES OF THE PROGRAMME

The Research and Training Programme in Regional Development is intended to give training to groups of qualified candidates from mainly the Asia and Far East Region on the methods of comprehensive planning for regional development. The programme seeks to attract persons with backgrounds in the social sciences, architecture and engineering, and public administration.

The curriculum provides an introduction to national planning, regional planning, and local development. It will deal with highly urbanized, semideveloped, and rural areas. It will stress the contributions which economists, social scientists, engineers, public administrators, and the other professions, must make jointly to the preparation of a successful development programme.

It will deal with both the preparation of programmes and plans, and their implementation. However, in view of the limitation of a programme that runs for only a few months, the objectives pursued in the course are kept within moderate bounds. Essentially, these objectives are to convey the significance for specialist planners of what is meant by comprehensive regional development planning.

Included in this attempt is recognition of the newly evolving techniques of analysis appropriate to the solution of planning problems in the developing countries of Southeast Asia. The training programme will be performed mainly in two ways. The first is by demonstration through lectures, discussions, reading and displays all designed to communicate to specialists from specific disciplines what the other can contribute to the process. The second method is to incorporate the invited participants in the functional work of the Centre as its members seek solutions to the problems of regional development in Japan and overseas. To the extent possible the core of the training programme consists of what might be termed in-service training or internship. In those circumstances when the work of the Centre does not provide such opportunity the in-service training is simulated by projects that are concerned with real problems for which study materials and data have been prepared. The emphasis will be placed on the pursuit of effective results obtainable through a participatory training. In the participatory training, not only do the participants discover the operational meaning of comprehensive regional development by observing and contributing to the process, but they learn the application of techniques. This discovery of techniques appropriate to regional analysis is made in the most meaningful way, not as abstract models of procedure but rather as the imperfect but most useful way of resolving problems. This approach will also enable a competent practitioner to realize the limitations of such procedures. By alternating between the reception of formal instruction with the application of suggested procedures to projects the participant has the opportunity to substantially enhance his capabilities.

The programme is not designed simply as a one-way street of improvement of professional abilities for the persons attending the training course at the Centre. Because comprehensive regional development planning is far from a mature body of science each participant can be expected to contribute to understanding of the nature and problems of that study area. Beginning with the preparation of a paper to be used in the selection of candidates from countries joining the programme, each of the participants can contribute from his experience, his training, and from his field of special competence.

2. TENTATIVE PROGRAMME

International Comparative Studies
(i) *International Seminar* – to provide opportunities for all involved in the programme to know each other; exposure to problems, needs of respective countries or regions as well as background and personalities of the group members.
(ii) *Introduction to Japan* – to provide background information required for subsequent developmental studies. Socio-cultural, historical and political characteristics of the country.

Comprehensive Regional Development: Overall Orientation
Policy and over-all design strategy in launching planning steps.
Case study: Implication of National and Regional Plans in Japan to ECAFE Region Countries.

Field Trip – A
First-hand opportunity of exposure to real developmental scene in Aichi, the most rapidly growing part in Chubu. The projects to be visited during the tour will be closely related to the subsequent project study work.

Identification of Problems
Identification of research needs and basic data requirements
Feasibility, design and performance of research
Analysis of obtained data
Utilization of research findings
Case study: statistics of Japan and other ECAFE countries, a social survey demonstration.
(Collaboration of UN Statistical Institute is expected.)

Project Work
Four to five research projects will be chosen as themes of project study group work from among the on-going research efforts launched by the agencies concerned as well as by the Chubu Centre. Participants will be organized into four to five study teams. The Project Work will proceed side by side with the lectures and discussions designed for all participants, as shown in the tentative programme.

Field Trip – B (Tokyo) is designed to visualize Tokyo where huge developmental efforts are being launched at National level by Governmental, semi-Governmental and private bodies.

Sectoral Approaches, as indicated in the programme, consist of the four major central fields in comprehensive regional development planning.

(1) *Social Planning* will deal with the functional tools and their application to social planning goals, i.e. those in terms of education, health, nutrition, participation and community development, etc. Case study: A typical example of depressed regions in newly developing countries.

(2) *Economic Planning* will introduce modern theories and skills being developed in relation to development work, model approaches. Their effectiveness and limitations will be examined through the case study analysis.

Case study: Topic will be chosen out of:

New Comprehensive National Development Plan of Japan.

One relevant case from among ECAFE Regions.

Ise Bay Industrial Complex development, etc.

(3) *Physical Planning* will touch upon living examples in terms of metropolitan land use, housing, transport and over-all social infrastructures.

The case study will deal among others with feasibility studies on attaining alternative levels of environmental goals.

(4) *Planning, Administration and Finance* is the focal tool for plan implementation. Significant examples in the world will be introduced for comparative analysis. The case study is designed to identify implications of the Japanese system for other Asian countries.

(5) *Formulation of Plans* is intended to find out logical processes of synthesis from sectoral judgements towards a comprehensive decisionmaking. Newly emerging techniques in this connection, such as systems analysis or programming, budgeting etc. will be introduced as prospective tools for such decision-making process. Their effectiveness and limitation will be identified through the case study, which will examine development plans in the Chubu Region at regional, prefectural and municipal levels through application of relevant methods.

A DESCRIPTION OF THE NINE-MONTH POST-GRADUATE COURSE IN REGIONAL DEVELOPMENT PLANNING, THE INSTITUTE OF SOCIAL STUDIES, THE HAGUE
(as of August 1970)

1. BACKGROUND

The activities of the Institute of Social Studies in the field of regional planning date back to 1959 when a first symposium on Regional Planning was organised. This occurred at a time when the problems of regional development and planning had scarcely attracted the attention of the social sciences, and remained the concern mainly of physical planners involved in problems of town and country planning. The idea of scale-enlargement had not penetrated and the problems of metropolitan areas were taken to be the most pressing. The proceedings of the Symposium bear witness to the understanding that the problems of regional planning are neither confined solely to these areas nor to physical planning, and one of its major conclusions was that they required a comprehensive planning procedure. Given the Institute's preoccupation with the problems of the developing countries and accepting the recommendation of the Symposium that training in comprehensive planning would be an important contribution to solving these problems, the Institute of Social Studies decided to prepare a course in this subject. This four-month course was offered every year from 1960 to 1966 and was intended for high-ranking planners.

During this period, however, a somewhat broader view of the role of regional planning emerged both in practice and in the social sciences, and in 1967 the Institute decided to interrupt its Comprehensive Planning Course. In the same year it organised a workshop in regional development planning and undertook preparation of a nine-month course in this field which was first offered in 1968.

2. THE AIMS AND STRUCTURE OF THE PRESENT COURSE

The Diploma Course in Regional Development Planning is designed to provide both civil servants and those who arc undertaking the training of regional planners in their own country with the opportunity to gain a broader insight into the problems of regional development and into the methods and techniques related to regional development planning. It is primarily intended for those who are currently engaged in regional planning activities or who are teaching in this field. The focus of the course is upon the theory, strategies and methodology of regional planning in the developing countries.

The course comprises three terms which are organised as follows:

First term: A series of seminars on theoretical approaches to regional development and planning and on their applicability in the developing countries. Participants are also required to work with some of the methodological implications of these ideas in a parallel series of workshops.

Second term: Lectures and tutorials dealing with the methodology, strategies and, in more detail, with specific techniques of regional analysis and planning. Through the combination of required and optional courses participants have an opportunity to mould this part of the programme to their own needs and interests but having determined their programme, attendance will be made compulsory. An excursion of two weeks to a regional development programme abroad closes this term.

Third term: A detailed case study. This will have been introduced during the earlier parts of the Course, providing a common source of data for the workshops and technical discussion. Working knowledge of the case area obtained in this way will facilitate a practical and more detailed examination of the strategies and methodology of regional planning during the case study. Participants are also required to write a research paper on a specialised topic of their own choosing.

Successful participants are awarded the Diploma in Regional Development Planning as laid down by the regulations of the Institute.

3. CONTENTS OF THE COURSE

First term: For each seminar in this series a paper will be prepared by a staff-member who will be required to summarise and to criticise the body of theoretical knowledge that is relevant to his topic and to assess its applicability to the problems of the developing countries. The preparation of these papers comprises an integral part of the Institute's Research Programme in Regional Development Planning and it is intended that they stimulate thinking into new directions.

The topics of these seminars are as follows:

Seminar 1: *National and Regional Structure* – Centre-periphery relations; socio-economic factors; political administrative structure; inter- and intraregional growth theory.

Seminar 2: *The Distribution of Centres* – Theories of location; the evolution of settlement patterns; central place theory.

Seminar 3: *The Regional Centre* – The socio-economic significance of the city: the city as an information, innovative and cultural centre; the city as a problem area; city-regional relations.

Seminar 4: *Rural-Urban Integration* – The diffusion of information and technology; their influence upon rural-urban relations; their effects upon the peasant community and its activities.

Seminar 5: *Planning Theory for Regional Planning* – Planning as a method and as a process: the theory of planning; regional planning in a national framework; the decision making process; administrative considerations in regional planning.

During this term the workshops on Regionalisation will also be held.

Second Term: Required and Optional Subjects by Specialisation.

Subjects	Class hours	Economic Planning	Physical Planning	Rural Planning	Social Planning	Administration
A. *Methods of Analysis*						
1. Natural Resource Analysis	8	R	R	O	—	—
2. Demography	8	O	O	—	R	O
3. Human Resource Analysis	6	O	O	—	R	R
4. Techniques of Economic Analysis						
4a. Input-Output Analysis	8	R*	—	—	—	—
4b. Regional Accounting & Flow of Funds	8	R	—	—	—	—
5. Techniques of Spatial Analysis						
5a. Location Analysis	8	O	R	R	O	O
5b. Factor Analysis	10	O*	O*	O*	O*	—
B. *Regional Planning Strategies*						
6. Regional Planning Strategies	8	R	R	R	R	R
C. *Planning Techniques*						
7. Inter- and intra Regional Economic Models	10	R*	—	—	—	—
8. Linear Programming	12	O*	O*	O*	—	—
9. Agricultural Planning	10	O	—	R	O	O
10. Transportation Planning	10	O	R	O	—	—
11. Community Development	30	—	—	R	R	R
12. Education and Manpower Planning	10	O	O	—	O	—
13. Housing	8	—	R	O	R	O
14. Co-operatives	8	—	—	R	O	O
15. Environmental Planning	6	—	R	O	O	O
D. *Plan Implementation*						
16. Procedures in Plan Implementation	10	R	R	R	R	R
17. Project Preparation and Evaluation						
17a. Cost-Benefit Analysis	6	R	—	O	O	O
17b. Problems of Spatial Consistency	6	—	R	—	—	O
18. Industrial Estates	6	O	O	—	—	O
19. Programme Budgeting	6	R	—	—	—	R
20. Local Government and Administrative Reform	8	—	—	—	O	R

R = Required class-hours. *mathematical background required.
O = Optional class-hours
– Class-hours last 75 minutes.
– The number of class-hours to be taken has to amount to 100.
– Options will only be realised when more than two persons apply.
– Combinations of options may be obligatory to avoid overlapping cq. a lack of needed knowledge.
This term programme is subject to change according to staff availability.

Third term: During this term a case study of Northwest Argentina will be an exercise in the use of planning techniques in a methodological context and in team work.